FRENCH

A ROUGH GUIDE DICTIONARY PHRASEBOOK

Compiled by

LEXUS

Credits

Compiled by Lexus with Nadine Mongeard Morandi
Lexus Series Editor: Sally Davies
Rough Guides Phrase Book Editor: Jonathan Buckley
Rough Guides Series Editor: Mark Ellingham

First edition published in 1995 by Rough Guides Ltd, 62–70 Shorts Gardens, London WC2H 9AB.
Reprinted 1995 and 1996.
Revised in 1999.

Distributed by the Penguin Group.

Penguin Books Ltd, 27 Wrights Lane, London W8 5TZ
Penguin Books USA Inc., 375 Hudson Street, New York 10014, USA
Penguin Books Australia Ltd, 487 Maroondah Highway, PO Box 257, Ringwood, Victoria 3134, Australia
Penguin Books Canada Ltd, Alcorn Avenue, Toronto, Ontario, Canada M4V 1E4
Penguin Book (NZ) Ltd, 182–190 Wairau Road, Auckland 10, New Zealand

Typeset in Bembo and Helvetica to an original design by Henry Iles.
Printed in Spain by Graphy Cems.

256pp.

British Library Cataloguing in Publication Data
A catalogue for this book is available from the British Library.

ISBN 1-85828-576-3

Help us get it right

Lexus and Rough Guides have made great efforts to be accurate and informative in this Rough Guide French phrasebook. However, if you feel we have overlooked a useful word or phrase, or have any other comments to make about the book, please let us know. All contributors will be acknowledged and the best letters will be rewarded with a free Rough Guide phrasebook of your choice. Please write to 'French Phrasebook Update', at either Shorts Gardens (London) or Hudson Street (New York) – for full addresses see opposite. Alternatively you can email us at mail@roughguides.co.uk

Online information about Rough Guides can be found at our Web site www.roughguides.com

CONTENTS

Introduction

The Rough Guide French dictionary phrasebook is a highly practical introduction to the contemporary language. Laid out in clear A-Z style, it uses key-word referencing to lead you straight to the words and phrases you want – so if you need to book a room, just look up 'room'. The Rough Guide gets straight to the point in every situation, in bars and shops, on trains and buses, and in hotels and banks.

The main part of the Rough Guide is a double dictionary: English-French then French-English. Before that, there's a page explaining the pronunciation system we've used, then a section called The Basics, which sets out the fundamental rules of the language, with plenty of practical examples. You'll also find here other essentials like numbers, dates and telling the time.

Forming the heart of the guide, the English-French section gives easy-to-use transliterations of the French words wherever pronunciation might be a problem, and to get you involved quickly in two-way communication, the Rough Guide includes dialogues featuring typical responses on key topics – such as renting a car and asking directions. Feature boxes fill you in on cultural pitfalls as well as the simple mechanics of how to make a phone call, what to do in an emergency, where to change money, and more. Throughout this section, cross-references enable you to pinpoint key facts and phrases, while asterisked words indicate where further information can be found in the Basics.

In the French-English dictionary, we've given not just the phrases you're likely to hear, but also all the signs, labels, instructions and other basic words you might come across in print or in public places.

Finally the Rough Guide rounds off with an extensive Menu Reader, giving a run-down of food and drink terms that you'll find indispensable whether you're eating out, stopping for a quick drink, or browsing through a local food market.

bon voyage!
have a good trip!

Basics

Pronunciation

In this phrasebook, the French has been written in a system of imitated pronunciation so that it can be read as though it were English. Bear in mind the notes on pronunciation given below:

AN	a French nasal sound; say the English word 'tan' clipping off the final 'n' and you are close
ay	as in m**ay**
e	as in g**e**t
g	always hard as in **g**oat
ī	as the 'i' sound in m**i**ght
j	like the 's' sound in plea**s**ure
ñ	like the final sound in 'lasa**gn**e'
ON	a French nasal sound; say the English word 'on' through your nose and cutting off the final 'n'
ꝏ	like the 'ew' in f**ew** but without any 'y' sound
r	comes from the back of the throat
uh	like the 'e' in butt**er** but a little longer
y	as in **y**es

The French often run together or elide a word ending with a consonant and a following word that starts with a vowel. This has been shown in the pronunciation as, for example: 'do you have ...?' **est-ce que vous avez ...?** [eskuh voo zavay]. The 'z' at the beginning of 'zavay' has been run on from the preceding word.

Abbreviations

adj	adjective	**m**	masculine
f	feminine	**mpl**	masculine plural
fpl	feminine plural	**sing**	singular

Notes

In the English-French section, when two forms of the verb are given in phrases such as 'can you ...?' **est-ce que tu peux/vous pouvez ... ?**, the first is the familiar form and the second the polite form (see entry for **you**).

An asterisk (*) next to a word means that you should refer to the Basics section for further information.

Nouns

All French nouns have one of two genders – masculine
(**un** / **le**) or feminine (**une** / **la**).

Plural Nouns

The most common way of forming the plural of a noun –
of saying, for example, 'the passports' instead of 'the passport'
– is by adding an **-s** to the singular:

le passeport	**les passeports**
luh pass-por	lay pass-por
the passport	the passports
le magasin	**les magasins**
luh magazAN	lay magazAN
the shop	the shops

This **-s** is not normally pronounced in French.

To make the plural of words ending in **-au** or **-eu** you add
an **-x**:

un bureau	**leurs bureaux**
AN bOOro	lurr bOOro
an office	their offices
le lieu	**les lieux**
luh l-yuh	lay l-yuh
the place	the places

This **-x** is not normally pronounced in French.

To make the plural of words ending in **-al** change **-al** to **-aux**:

un cheval	**deux chevaux**
AN shuhval	duh shuhvo
a horse	two horses

One important irregular plural:

mon oeil	**mes yeux**
mON uh-ee	may z-yuh
my eye	my eyes

Articles

The words for articles ('the' and 'a') in French vary according to three elements:

the gender of the noun
the first letter of the noun
whether the noun is singular or plural

Singular Articles

The equivalents for saying 'the' are:

le luh	for masculine singular nouns
la	for feminine singular nouns

In front of a noun beginning with a vowel (or an 'h' that is not pronounced) **le** and **la** change to **l'**.

le marché	**la gare**
luh marshay	la gar
the market	the station
l'homme	**l'actrice**
lom	laktreess
the man	the actress

The equivalents for saying 'a' are:

un AN	for all masculine nouns
une ∞n	for all feminine nouns

un marché	**une gare**
AN marshay	∞n gar
a market	a station

Plural Articles

les lay for both masculine and feminine nouns

<table>
<tr><td>les marchés</td><td>les gares</td></tr>
<tr><td>lay marshay</td><td>lay gar</td></tr>
<tr><td>the markets</td><td>the stations</td></tr>
<tr><td>les hommes</td><td>les actrices</td></tr>
<tr><td>lay zom</td><td>lay zaktreess</td></tr>
<tr><td>the men</td><td>the actresses</td></tr>
</table>

The plural form of the indefinite article, translated in English as 'some', or often omitted, is **des** day:

<table>
<tr><td>des marchés</td><td>des gares</td></tr>
<tr><td>day marshay</td><td>day gar</td></tr>
<tr><td>(some) markets</td><td>(some) stations</td></tr>
</table>

Prepositions

When used with the prepositions **de** and **à**, the definite article may change its form:

If you are using **le / les** with **de** (of; from) make the following changes:

de + le	**= du**	doo
de + les	**= des**	day

With **à** (to; at) make these changes:

à + le	**= au**	o
à + les	**= aux**	o

le nom du supermarché
luh noN doo soopairmarshay
the name of the supermarket

il vient des Etats-Unis
eel v-yAN day zaytazoonee
he comes from the United States

au supermarché	**aux Etats-Unis**
o sOOpairmarshay	o zaytazOOnee
at the supermarket	to the United States

If you are using **la** or **l'** the preposition does not change.

à la plage	**à l'hôtel**
a la plahj	a lotel
at the beach	at the hotel

Adjectives and Adverbs

In French, adjectives have to 'agree' with the noun they are used with. This means that if a noun is feminine, then an adjective used with it must be in the feminine form too. If a noun is plural, then an adjective used with it must be in the plural form too, masculine or feminine. In the English into French section of this book, all adjectives are translated by the masculine form – the form used with nouns preceded by **un** or **le**.

For most adjectives, the feminine form is made by adding **-e**. The plural is formed in two ways: for those with masculine nouns, by adding **-s**; and for those with feminine nouns, by adding **-es**. Plurals for adjectives ending in **-au** are usually formed by adding **-x**, although the **-s** or **-x** is not pronounced.

Important exceptions are shown in the English into French section.

un journal allemand	**une famille allemande**
AN joornal almON	OOn famee almONd
a German newspaper	a German family
des journaux américains	**deux familles écossaises**
day joorno zamaayreekAN	duh famee zaykossez
American newspapers	two Scottish families

Most adjectives in French, as in these examples, are placed after the noun, not in front of it as in English.

Some common adjectives, however, are put in front of nouns:

beau	bo	beautiful	**nouveau**	noovo	new
long	lON	long	**grand**	grON	big
bon	bON	good	**petit**	puhtee	little
joli	jolee	pretty	**jeune**	jurn	young
mauvais	movay	bad	**vieux**	vyuh	old
gentil	jONtee	nice			

Comparatives

To say that something is, for example, more expensive or faster than something else, you use the comparative form of the adjective (or adverb). In French these are all formed by using the word plus in front of the adjective or adverb:

grand grON big	**plus grand** ploo grON bigger
intéressant ANtayressON interesting	**plus intéressant** ploo zANtayressON more interesting

je voudrais une plus grande chambre
juh voodray zoon ploo grONd shONbr
I'd like a bigger room

c'est plus intéressant que le château
say ploo zANtayressON kuh luh shato
it's more interesting than the castle

cette plage est plus calme que l'autre
set plahj ay ploo kalm kuh lohtr
this beach is quieter than the other one

pouvez-vous parler plus clairement, s'il vous plaît?
poovay-voo parlay plOO klairmON seel voo play
could you speak more clearly please?

'As ... as' is translated as follows:

ce restaurant est aussi cher que l'autre
suh restorON ay tohsee shair kuh lohtr
this restaurant is as expensive as the other one

ce n'était pas aussi cher que je croyais
suh naytay pa zohsee shair kuh juh krwy-ay
it wasn't as expensive as I thought

aussi lentement que possible
ohsee lONtuhmON kuh posseebl
as slowly as possible

Superlatives

To say that something is, for example, the most expensive or the fastest, you use the superlative form of the adjective (or adverb). This is formed by using the words **le plus** in front of the adjective for a masculine singular noun; **la plus** for a feminine singular noun; and **les plus** for a plural noun (see **Adjectives**):

grand grON big	**le plus grand** luh plOO grON biggest
intéressant ANtayressON interesting	**le plus intéressant** luh plOO zANtayressON most interesting

le plus grand hôtel de la ville
luh plOO grON otel duh la veel
the biggest hotel in town

où est la poste la plus proche?
oo ay la posst la plOO prosh
where is the nearest post office?

le barman parle le plus clairement
luh barman parl luh plOO klairmON
the barman speaks the most clearly

Some forms are irregular:

bon	bON	good
meilleur	may-yurr	better
le meilleur	luh may-yurr	best
mauvais	mo-vay	bad
pire	peer	worse
le pire	luh peer	worst

Adverbs

Adverbs are formed by adding **-ment** to the feminine form of the adjective if it ends in a consonant, and to the masculine form if it ends in a vowel:

vrai / vraie	**vraiment**	**final / finale**	**finalement**
vray	vraymON	feenal	feenalmON
real	really	final	finally

Adjectives which end in **-ent** and **-ant** change to **-emment** and **-amment**:

évident	**évidemment**	**constant**	**constamment**
ayveedON	ayveedamON	kONstON	kONstamON
obvious	obviously	constant	constantly

But not:

lent	**lentement**
lON	lONtuhmON
slow	slowly

Some forms are irregular:

bon	**bien**	**mauvais**	**mal**	**meilleur**	**mieux**
bON	b-yAN	movay	mal	may-yurr	m-yuh
good	well	bad	badly	better	better

Possessive Adjectives

If you want to say that something is 'your car' or 'his car' or 'her car' etc, then you use the following words in French. Notice that there are three forms: one for masculine words (given with **le** in the phrase book); one for feminine words (given with **la**); and one for plural words.

	masculine		feminine		plural	
my	**mon**	mON	**ma**	ma	**mes**	may
your	**ton**	tON	**ta**	ta	**tes**	tay
his / its	**son**	sON	**sa**	sa	**ses**	say
her / its	**son**	sON	**sa**	sa	**ses**	say
our	**notre**	notr	**notre**	notr	**nos**	no
your	**votre**	votr	**votre**	votr	**vos**	vo
their	**leur**	lurr	**leur**	lurr	**leurs**	lurr

Some points to note:

The forms **ton / ta / tes** are used for people you are speaking to as **tu**. The forms **votre / vos** are used for people you are speaking to as **vous** (see **Pronouns**).

Whether you use **son / sa** or **mon / ma** depends on the gender of the thing / person 'possessed'. So for example:

> **ma chambre**
> ma shONbr
> my room

can be said by both a man and a woman. Likewise:

> **sa chambre**
> sa shONbr

can mean either 'his room' or 'her room'.

If this is confusing you can say:

sa chambre à lui	**sa chambre à elle**
sa shONbr a lwee	sa shONbr a el
his room	her room

Ma / ta / sa change to **mon / ton / son** in front of a vowel:

mon épouse
mON aypooz
my wife

Pronouns

Subject Pronouns

If you are using a pronoun as the subject of a verb, saying 'he is' or 'we are' or 'can you?' etc, the words are:

je	juh	I	**nous**	noo	we
tu	too	you	**vous**	voo	you
il	eel	he / it	**ils**	eel	they
elle	el	she / it	**elles**	el	they

Points to note:

YOU: **tu** is used when speaking to someone who is a friend, or to someone of your own general age group with whom you want to establish a friendly atmosphere. **Vous** is used when speaking to several friends (ie it is the plural of **tu**) or when speaking to someone you don't know. In the vast majority of cases, as a foreigner in France you will use the **vous** form. Certainly, if you are in any doubt as to which form to use, choose the **vous** form.

IT: if you are using 'it' to refer to something like 'the car', 'the train' etc (as opposed to saying 'it is cold today' etc), you should use either **il** or **elle** depending on the gender of the thing you are talking about (see **Articles**). For example, **la voiture** (the car) is **elle** (it) and **le train** (the train) is **il** (it).

Direct Object Pronouns

If you are using the pronoun as an object, saying 'Peter knows him' or 'Mary saw them' etc, you must use the following object pronouns, which will normally precede the verb:

me	muh	me	**nous**	noo	us
te	tuh	you	**vous**	voo	you
le	luh	him / it	**les**	lay	them
la	la	her / it			

je le vois
juh luh vwa
I see him

il les a achetés
eel lay za ashtay
he bought them

vous me comprenez?
voo muh KONpruhnay
do you understand me?

Indirect Object Pronouns

If you are using a pronoun to say, for example, you sent something to her or that you spoke to him, then you must use the following indirect object pronouns:

me	muh	to me	**nous**	noo	to us
te	tuh	to you	**vous**	voo	to you
lui	lwee	to him / her / it	**leur**	lurr	to them

je lui ai écrit
juh lwee ay aykree
I wrote to him

je le lui ai expliqué
juh luh lwee ay expleekay
I explained it to him

Emphatic Pronouns

If you are using a pronoun to say 'it's me', 'with her', 'for them' etc, then you must use the following emphatic pronouns:

moi	mwa	me	**nous**	noo	us
toi	twa	you	**vous**	voo	you
lui	lwee	him	**eux**	uh	them
elle	el	her	**elles**	el	them

c'est eux
set uh
it's them

venez avec moi
vuhnay avek mwa
come with me

ces cafés sont pour nous
say kafay SON poor noo
those coffees are for us

A useful word for 'it' or 'that' to refer to a specific thing, or a more general situation, is **ça** sa:

donne-moi ça!
don mwa sa
give it / that to me!

tu as vu ça?
too a voo sa
did you see that?

Reflexive Pronouns

These are used with reflexive verbs like **se laver** (to get washed, to wash oneself), where the subject and the object are the same.

me	muh	myself
te	tuh	yourself
se	suh	himself / herself / itself
nous	noo	ourselves
vous	voo	yourself / yourselves
se	suh	themselves

There are many more verbs used reflexively in French than in English. Some examples are:

je m'appelle Anna
juh mapel anna
I am called Anna

nous nous levons toujours de bonne heure
noo noo luhvON toojoor duh bon urr
we always get up early

ils se sont bien amusés
eel suh sON b-yAN amOOzay
they enjoyed themselves very much

Possessive Pronouns

If you want to say that something is yours or his or hers etc, then you use the following possessive pronouns. Notice that there are four forms: masculine singular and plural, and feminine singular and plural:

	m sing	mpl	
mine	**le mien**	**les miens**	luh / lay m-yAN
yours	**le tien**	**les tiens**	luh / lay t-yAN
his / its	**le sien**	**les siens**	luh / lay s-yAN
hers / its	**le sien**	**les siens**	luh / lay s-yAN
ours	**le nôtre**	**les nôtres**	luh / lay nohtr
yours	**le vôtre**	**les vôtres**	luh / lay vohtr
theirs	**le leur**	**les leurs**	luh / lay lurr

	f sing	fpl	
mine	**la mienne**	**les miennes**	luh / lay m-yen
yours	**la tienne**	**les tiennes**	luh / lay t-yen
his / its	**la sienne**	**les siennes**	luh / lay s-yen
hers / its	**la sienne**	**les siennes**	luh / lay s-yen
ours	**la nôtre**	**les nôtres**	luh / lay nohtr
yours	**la vôtre**	**les vôtres**	luh / lay vohtr
theirs	**la leur**	**les leurs**	luh / lay lurr

Again, the use of '**le sien / la sienne**' and '**le mien / la mienne**' etc will depend on the gender of the thing(s) possessed:

cette voiture n'est pas la nôtre
set vwatOOr nay pa la nohtr
this car isn't ours

cette valise est la mienne, la tienne est là-bas
set valeez ay la m-yen, la t-yen ay la-ba
this suitcase is mine, yours is over there

After the verb **être** (to be), the possessive pronouns can be replaced by **à** + the appropriate emphatic pronoun (see **Pronouns**).

ce sac est à moi
suh sak ay ta mwa
this bag is mine

est-ce que cet appareil photo est à vous?
eskuh set aparay foto ay ta voo
is this camera yours?

Verbs

There are three main verb types, recognizable by their endings: **-er**, **-ir**, and **-re**.

Present Tense

The present tense of a verb corresponds to 'you are doing' or 'you do' or 'something happens' etc. To form the present tense for the three main types of verb, remove the endings and conjugate as follows:

donner (to give)

je donne [juh don]	I give
tu donnes [too don]	you give
il / elle donne [eel / el don]	he / she gives
nous donnons [noo donON]	we give
vous donnez [voo donay]	you give
ils / elles donnent [eel / el don]	they give

finir (to finish)

je finis [juh feenee]	I finish
tu finis [too feenee]	you finish
il / elle finit [eel / el feenee]	he / she finishes
nous finissons [noo feeneessON]	we finish
vous finissez [voo feeneessay]	you finish
ils / elles finissent [eel / el feeneess]	they finish

attendre (to wait)

j'attends [jatON]	I wait
tu attends [too atON]	you wait
il / elle attend [eel / el atON]	he / she waits
nous attendons [noo zatONdON]	we wait
vous attendez [voo zatONday]	you wait
ils / elles attendent [eel / el zatONd]	they wait

Remember that this tense also covers English forms like 'I am doing':

je lui parle
juh lwee parl
I talk to him OR I'm talking to him

Some common verbs have irregular forms in the present tense:

aller (to go)

je vais	juh vay
tu vas	too va
il / elle va	eel / el va
nous allons	noo zalON
vous allez	voo zalay
ils / elles vont	eel / el vON

boire (to drink)

je bois	bwa
tu bois	bwa
il / elle boit	bwa
nous buvons	boovON
vous buvez	boovay
ils / elles boivent	bwav

devoir (to have to, must)

je dois	dwa
tu dois	dwa
il / elle doit	dwa
nous devons	duhvON
vous devez	duhvay
ils / elles doivent	dwav

dire (to say)

je dis	dee
tu dis	dee
il / elle dit	dee
nous disons	deezON
vous dites	deet
ils / elles disent	deez

faire (to do, to make)

je fais	fay
tu fais	fay
il / elle fait	fay
nous faisons	fuhzON
vous faites	fet
ils / elles font	fON

partir (to leave, to go away)

je pars	par
tu pars	par
il / elle part	par
nous partons	partON
vous partez	partay
ils / elles partent	part

pouvoir (to be able to)

je peux	juh puh
tu peux	too puh
il / elle peut	eel / el puh
nous pouvons	noo poovON
vous pouvez	voo poovay
ils / elles peuvent	eel / el puhv

savoir (to know)

je sais	say
tu sais	say
il / elle sait	say
nous savons	savON
vous savez	savay
ils / elles savent	sav

sortir (to go out)

je sors	sor
tu sors	sor
il / elle sort	sor
nous sortons	sortON
vous sortez	sortay
ils / elles sortent	sort

venir (to come)

je viens	juh v-yAN
tu viens	too v-yAN
il / elle vient	eel / el v-yAN
nous venons	noo vuhnON
vous venez	voo vuhnay
ils / elles viennent	eel / el v-yen

vouloir (to want)

je veux	juh vuh
tu veux	tOO vuh
il / elle veut	eel / el vuh
nous voulons	noo voolON
vous voulez	voo voolay
ils / elles veulent	eel / el vurl

See also **Past Tenses** for **avoir** (to have) and **être** (to be).

Past Tenses:
Perfect Tense

To put something into the perfect tense – to say that 'you have done' or 'did do' something – you use the present tense of the verb avoir plus the past participle of the verb:

avoir (to have)

j'ai	jay
tu as	tOO a
il / elle a	eel / el a
nous avons	noo zavON
vous avez	voo zavay
ils / elles ont	eel / el zON

A basic rule for forming the past participle is: for verbs ending in **-er**, change **-er** to **-é** (pronunciation the same: ay); for verbs ending in **-ir**, change **-ir** to **-i**; for verbs ending in **-re**, change **-re** to **-u**.

où est-ce que vous avez mangé hier soir?
oo eskuh voo zavay mONjay yair swahr
where did you eat last night?

nous avons visité la cathédrale cet après-midi
noo zavON veezeetay la kataydral set apray-meedee
we visited the cathedral this afternoon

vous avez fini de manger?	**je l'ai attendu toute la journée**
voo zavay feenee duh mONjay	juh lay atONdoo toot la joornay
have you finished eating?	I waited for him all day

For some verbs the perfect tense is formed using **être** instead of **avoir**.

être (literal sense: to be)

je suis	juh swee
tu es	too ay
il / elle est	eel / el ay
nous sommes	noo som
vous êtes	voo zet
ils / elles sont	eel / el sON

The most common and useful of these are:

aller	to go	**je suis allé**	juh swee alay
arriver	to arrive	**arrivé**	areevay
descendre	to go / come down	**descendu**	duhsONdoo
entrer	to go / come in	**entré**	ONtray
monter	to go / come up	**monté**	mONtay
naître	to be born	**né**	nay
partir	to leave / go away	**parti**	partee
passer	to pass	**passé**	passay
rentrer	to go / come back	**rentré**	rONtray
rester	to stay	**resté**	restay
retourner	to return	**retourné**	ruhtoornay
revenir	to come back	**revenu**	ruhvuhnoo
sortir	to go / come out	**sorti**	sortee
tomber	to fall	**tombé**	tONbay
venir	to come	**venu**	vuhnoo

il est parti	**nous sommes revenus samedi dernier**
eel ay partee	noo som ruhvuhnoo samdee dairn-yay
he has left	we came back last Saturday

elle est restée deux semaines
el ay restay duh suhmen
she stayed for two weeks

je suis rentré très tard hier soir
juh swee rONtray tray tar yair swahr
I got home very late last night

The following verbs have irregular past participles:

avoir	to have	**eu**	ꝏ
comprendre	to understand	**compris**	kONpree
connaître	to know (person, place)	**connu**	konꝏ
croire	to believe	**cru**	krꝏ
devoir	to have to	**dû**	dꝏ
dire	to say	**dit**	dee
disparaître	to disappear	**disparu**	deesparꝏ
être	to be	**été**	aytay
mourir*	to die	**mort**	mor
naître*	to be born	**né**	nay
offrir	to offer	**offert**	ofair
ouvrir	to open	**ouvert**	oovair
permettre	to allow	**permis**	pairmee
plaire	to please	**plu**	plꝏ
pouvoir	to be able to	**pu**	pꝏ
prendre	to take	**pris**	pree
recevoir	to receive	**reçu**	ruhsꝏ
s'asseoir*	to sit down	**assis**	assee
savoir	to know	**su**	sꝏ
venir*	to come	**venu**	vuhnꝏ
voir	to see	**vu**	vꝏ
vouloir	to want	**voulu**	voolꝏ

* conjugated with **être**

Imperfect Tense

This is used to describe an action in the past which was

repeated, habitual, or often taking place over a period of time. To put something into the imperfect tense – to say that you 'were doing', 'used to do', or 'did do' something – change the verb endings as follows:

donner (to give)

I was giving, I used to give, I gave etc

je donnais	juh donay
tu donnais	too donay
il / elle donnait	eel / el donay
nous donnions	noo donee-ON
vous donniez	voo donee-ay
ils / elles donnaient	eel / el donay

finir (to finish)

I was finishing, I used to finish, I finished etc

je finissais	juh feeneessay
tu finissais	too feeneessay
il / elle finissait	eel / el feeneessay
nous finissions	noo feeneessee-ON
vous finissiez	voo feeneessee-ay
ils / elles finnissaient	eel / el feeneessay

attendre (to wait)

I was waiting, I used to wait, I waited etc

j'attendais	jatONday
tu attendais	too atONday
il / elle attendait	eel / el atONday
nous attendions	noo zatONdee-ON
vous attendiez	voo zatONdee-ay
ils / elles attendaient	eel / el zatONday

Three common verbs have irregular imperfect tenses:

être (to be)

j'étais	jaytay	I was
tu étais	too aytay	you were
il / elle était	eel / el aytay	he / she / it was
nous étions	noo zaytee-ON	we were
vous étiez	voo zaytee-ay	you were
ils / elles étaient	eel / el zaytay	they were

avoir (to have)

j'avais	javay	I had
tu avais	too avay	you had
il / elle avait	eel / el avay	he / she / it had
nous avions	noo zavee-ON	we had
vous aviez	voo zavee-ay	you had
ils / elles avaient	eel / el zavay	they had

faire (to do, to make)

je faisais	juh fuhzay	I did
tu faisais	too fuhzay	you did
il / elle faisait	eel / el fuhzay	he / she / it / did
nous faisions	noo fuhzee-ON	we did
vous faisiez	voo fuhzee-ay	you did
ils / elles faisaient	eel / el fuhzay	they did

Future Tense

To talk about what is going to happen in the future both French and English very often use the present tense (see **Present**), for example:

nous allons à la plage demain
noo zalON a la plahj duhmAN
we're going to the beach tomorrow

il rentre bientôt à Londres
eel rONtr b-yANto a lONdr
he's going back to London soon

French often uses the present tense where English uses the future:

j'arrive dans une minute
jareev dON zOOn meenOOt
I'll be there in a minute

The actual future tense in French, used to say 'I will, you will' etc, is formed by making the following changes:

donner (to give) - I etc will give

je donnerai	donuhray	**nous donnerons**	donuhrON
tu donneras	donuhra	**vous donnerez**	donuhray
il / elle donnera	donuhra	**ils / elles donneront**	donuhrON

finir (to finish) - I etc will finish

je finirai	feeneeray	**nous finirons**	feeneerON
tu finiras	feeneera	**vous finirez**	feeneeray
il / elle finira	feeneera	**ils / elles finiront**	feeneerON

attendre (to wait) - I etc will wait

j'attendrai	atONdray	**nous attendrons**	atONdrON
tu attendras	atONdra	**vous attendrez**	atONdray
il / elle attendra	atONdra	**ils / elles attendront**	atONdrON

Some common irregular verbs:

être (to be) - I etc will be

je serai	suhray	**nous serons**	suhrON
tu seras	suhra	**vous serez**	suhray
il / elle sera	suhra	**ils / elles seront**	suhrON

avoir (to have) - I etc will have

j'aurai	joray	**nous aurons**	orON
tu auras	ora	**vous aurez**	oray
il / elle aura	ora	**ils / elles auront**	orON

aller (to go) - I **etc** will go

j'irai	jeeray	**nous irons**	eerON
tu iras	eera	**vous irez**	eeray
il / elle ira	eera	**ils / elles iront**	eerON

venir (to come) - I **etc** will come

je viendrai	v-yANdray	**nous viendrons**	v-yANdrON
tu viendras	v-yANdra	**vous viendrez**	v-yANdray
il / elle viendra	v-yANdra	**ils / elles viendront**	v-yANdrON

Some examples:

mes enfants arriveront demain
may zONfON areevuhrON duhmAN
my children will be arriving tomorrow

j'espère qu'il fera beau demain
jespair keel fuhra bo duhmAN
I hope it'll be fine tomorrow

Negatives

To express a negative in French – to say 'I don't know', 'it's not here' etc – you use the words ne ... pas placed around the verb:

j'ai faim jay fAN I'm hungry	**je n'ai pas faim** juh nay pa fAN I'm not hungry
il aime la glace eel em la glass he likes ice cream	**il n'aime pas la glace** eel nem pa la glass he doesn't like ice cream
elle a une voiture el a oon vwatoor she has a car	**elle n'a pas de voiture** el na pa duh vwatoor she doesn't have a car

If the verb is in the past tense (see Perfect Tense) the **ne ... pas** is used as follows:

je l'ai vu
juh lay voo
I saw him

je ne l'ai pas vu
juh nuh lay pa voo
I didn't see him

The following negatives work in the same way as ne ... pas:

ne ... jamais
nuh ... jamay
never

ne ... plus
nuh ... ploo
no more

ne ... rien
nuh ... ree-AN
nothing

je n'y suis jamais allé
juh nee swee jamay alay
I've never been there

il ne boit plus de bière
eel nuh bwa ploo duh bee-air
he doesn't drink beer any more

nous n'avons rien acheté
noo navON ree-AN ashtay
we didn't buy anything

If there is no verb, just use pas:

pas toi!
pa twa
not you!

comment vas-tu? – pas mal
komON va-too – pa mal
how are you? – not bad

In spoken French, the **ne** is often left out:

c'est pas possible!
say pa posseebl
impossible!

To say 'no' with nouns (no sugar, no cigarettes) use **pas de**:

pas de vin pour moi, merci
pa duh VAN poor mwa mairsee
no wine for me thanks

il n'y a pas d'eau chaude
eel nya pa do shohd
there is no (isn't any) hot water

Imperative

To express commands in French, remove the endings **-er**, **-ir** or **-re** and then add the following endings.

	tu	vous
donner	**donne**	**donnez**
(to give)	don	donay
	give	
finir	**finis**	**finissez**
(to finish)	feenee	feeneessay
	finish	
attendre	**attends**	**attendez**
(to wait)	atON	atONday
	wait	

Some examples:

regardez!
ruhgarday
look!

allez-vous-en!
alay-voo zON
go away!

dites-moi!
deet-mwa
tell me!

apporte-moi ça!
aport-mwa sa
bring me that!

To tell someone not to do something, to give a negative command, put the words **ne ... pas** around the forms as given above, for example:

n'attends pas
natON pa
don't wait

n'attendez pas
natONday pa

ne parlez pas si vite!
nuh parlay pa see veet
don't speak so quickly!

ne me regarde pas comme ça!
nuh muh ruhgard pa kom sa
don't look at me like that!

Some irregular forms:

ne sois / soyez pas en colère
nuh swa / swy-yay pa ON kolair
don't be angry

viens / venez avec moi!
v-yAN / vuhnay avek mwa
come with me!

On signs you might see the form:

ne pas toucher
nuh pa tooshay
do not touch

Questions

Often word order remains the same in a question, but the intonation changes – the voice should be raised at the end of the question.

vous parlez anglais?
voo parlay ONglay
do you speak English?

The word order can also be inverted to form a question. If the subject is a pronoun, subject and verb are inverted, and linked with a hyphen:

parlez-vous anglais?
parlay-voo ONglay
do you speak English?

If the subject is a noun, the verb is placed with the relevant pronoun after the subject, inserting **-t-** between verb and pronoun where the verb ends in a vowel:

le directeur parle-t-il anglais?
luh deerekturr parlteel ONglay
does the manager speak English?

Both the above types of question may be introduced by **est-ce que?** The word order then remains the same as that of a statement:

est-ce que vous parlez anglais?
eskuh voo parlay ONglay
do you speak English?

Dates

Use the numbers on pages 37-38 to express the date, except for the first, when **le premier** should be used:

le premier septembre
luh pruhm-yay septONbr
the first of September

le deux décembre
luh duh daysONbr
the second of December

le trois mars
luh trwa marss
the third of March

le vingt mai
luh vAN may
the twentieth of May

le vingt-et-un juin
luh vANtay-AN jwAN
the twenty-first of June

Time

a.m.		du matin	dꝏ matAN
p.m.	(afternoon)	de l'après-midi	duh lapray-meedee
	(evening)	du soir	dꝏ swahr

what time is it? quelle heure est-il? [kel urr eteel]
one o'clock une heure [ꝏn urr]
two o'clock deux heures [duh zur]
it's one o'clock il est une heure [eel ay ꝏn urr]
it's two o'clock il est deux heures [eel ay duh zurr]
it's ten o'clock il est dix heures [eel ay dee zurr]
five past one une heure cinq [ꝏn urr sANk]
ten past two deux heures dix [duh zurr deess]

quarter past one une heure et quart [ꝏn urr ay kar]
quarter past two deux heures et quart [duh zurr ay kar]
half past ten dix heures et demie [dee zurr ay duhmee]
twenty to ten dix heures moins vingt [dee zurr mwAN vAN]
quarter to two deux heures moins le quart [duh zurr mwAN luh kar]
at half past four à quatre heures et demie [a katr urr ay duhmee]
at eight o'clock à huit heures [a weet urr]
14.00 quatorze heures [katorz urr]
17.30 dix-sept heures trente [deesset urr trONt]
2 a.m. deux heures du matin [duh zurr dꝏ matAN]
2 p.m. deux heures de l'après-midi [duh zurr duh lapray-meedee]
6 a.m. six heures du matin [seez urr dꝏ matAN]
6 p.m. six heures du soir [seez urr dꝏ swahr]
noon midi [meedee]
midnight minuit [meenwee]
an hour une heure [ꝏn urr]
a minute une minute [ꝏn meenꝏt]
two minutes deux minutes [duh meenꝏt]
a second une seconde [ꝏn suhgONd]
a quarter of an hour un quart d'heure [AN kar durr]
half an hour une demi-heure [ꝏn duhmee urr]
three quarters of an hour trois quarts d'heure [trwa kar durr]

Numbers

0	zéro [zayro]	**10**	dix [deess]
1	un [AN]	**11**	onze [ONz]
2	deux [duh]	**12**	douze [dooz]
3	trois [trwa]	**13**	treize [trez]
4	quatre [katr]	**14**	quartorze [katorz]
5	cinq [sANk]	**15**	quinze [kANz]
6	six [seess]	**16**	seize [sez]
7	sept [set]	**17**	dix-sept [deesset]
8	huit [weet]	**18**	dix-huit [deez-weet]
9	neuf [nuhf]	**19**	dix-neuf [deez-nuhf]

20	vingt	[VAN]
21	vingt-et-un	[VANtay-AN]
22	vingt-deux	[VAN-duh]
23	vingt-trois	[VAN-trwa]
30	trente	[troNt]
31	trente-et-un	[troNtay-an]
40	quarante	[karONt]
50	cinquante	[SANkONt]
60	soixante	[swas-sONt]
70	soixante-dix	[swassONt-deess]
80	quatre-vingts	[katr-VAN]
90	quatre-vingt-dix	[katr-VAN-deess]
100	cent	[SON]
110	cent dix	[SON deess]
200	deux cents	[duh SON]
1,000	mille	[meel]
2,000	deux mille	[duh meel]
5,000	cinq mille	[SANk meel]
1,000,000	un million	[AN meel-yON]

In French, millions are written with spaces instead of commas, e.g. 1 500 000. Thousands are written without spaces or commas, e.g. 2700. Decimals are written with a comma, e.g. 3.5 would be 3,5 in French.

Ordinals

1st	premier	[pruhm-yay]
2nd	deuxième	[duhz-yem]
3rd	troisième	[trwaz-yem]
4th	quatrième	[katree-yem]
5th	cinquième	[SANk-yem]
6th	sixième	[seez-yem]
7th	septième	[set-yem]
8th	huitième	[weet-yem]
9th	neuvième	[nuhv-yem]
10th	dixième	[deez-yem]

Conversion Tables

1 centimetre = 0.39 inches

1 metre = 39.37 inches = 1.09 yards

1 kilometre = 0.62 miles = 5/8 mile

1 inch = 2.54 cm

1 foot = 30.48 cm

1 yard = 0.91 m

1 mile = 1.61 km

km	1	2	3	4	5	10	20	30	40	50	100
miles	0.6	1.2	1.9	2.5	3.1	6.2	12.4	18.6	24.8	31.0	62.1

miles	1	2	3	4	5	10	20	30	40	50	100
km	1.6	3.2	4.8	6.4	8.0	16.1	32.2	48.3	64.4	80.5	161

1 gram = 0.035 ounces

g	100	250	500
oz	3.5	8.75	17.5

1 kilo = 1000 g = 2.2 pounds

1 oz = 28.35 g

1 lb = 0.45 kg

kg	0.5	1	2	3	4	5	6	7	8	9	10
lb	1.1	2.2	4.4	6.6	8.8	11.0	13.2	15.4	17.6	19.8	22.0

kg	20	30	40	50	60	70	80	90	100
lb	44	66	88	110	132	154	176	198	220

lb	0.5	1	2	3	4	5	6	7	8	9	10	20
kg	0.2	0.5	0.9	1.4	1.8	2.3	2.7	3.2	3.6	4.1	4.5	9.0

1 litre = 1.75 UK pints / 2.13 US pints

1 UK pint = 0.57 l
1 US pint = 0.47 l

1 UK gallon = 4.55 l
1 US gallon = 3.79 l

centigrade / Celsius C = (F - 32) x 5/9

C	-5	0	5	10	15	18	20	25	30	36.8	38
F	23	32	41	50	59	64	68	77	86	98.4	100.4

Fahrenheit F = (C x 9/5) + 32

F	23	32	40	50	60	65	70	80	85	98.4	101
C	-5	0	4	10	16	18	21	27	29	36.8	38.3

English

→

French

A

a, an* un, une [AN, ooN]
about: about 20 environ vingt [ONveerON]
it's about 5 o'clock il est cinq heures environ
a film about France un film sur la France [soor]
above au-dessus de [o-duh-soo duh]
abroad à l'étranger [a laytrONjay]
absolutely (I agree) absolument [absolooMON]
accelerator l'accélérateur **m** [axaylayraturr]
accept accepter [axeptay]
accident l'accident **m** [axeedON]
there's been an accident il y a eu un accident [eelya oo]
accommodation le logement [lojmON]
see **hotel** and **room**
accurate précis [praysee]
ache la douleur [doolurr]
my back aches j'ai mal au dos [jay]
across: across the road de l'autre côté de la route [duh lohtr kohtay duh]
adapter l'adaptateur **m** [adaptaturr]
(plug) la prise multiple [preez moolteepl]
address l'adresse **f** [adress]
what's your address? quelle est votre adresse? [kel ay votr]
address book le carnet d'adresses [karnay dadress]
admission charge le droit d'entrée [drwa dONtray]
adult l'adulte **mf** [adoolt]
advance: in advance d'avance [davONss]
aeroplane l'avion **m** [av-yON]
after après [apray]
after you après toi/vous [twa/voo]
afternoon l'après-midi **m** [apray-meedee]
in the afternoon l'après-midi
this afternoon cet après-midi
aftershave l'après-rasage **m** [apray-razahj]
aftersun cream la crème après-soleil [krem apray-solay]
afterwards ensuite [ONsweet]
again de nouveau [duh noovo]
against contre [kONtr]
age l'âge **m** [ahj]
ago: a week ago il y a une semaine [eelya]
an hour ago il y a une heure
agree: I agree je suis d'accord [juh swee dakor]
AIDS le SIDA [seeda]
air l'air **m**
by air en avion [ON avyON]
air-conditioning la climatisation [kleemateezass-yON]
airmail: by airmail par avion [avyON]
airmail envelope l'enveloppe

par avion **f** [ONvlop par avyON]
airport l'aéroport **m** [a-airopor]
to the airport, please à l'aéroport, s'il vous plaît
airport bus la navette de l'aéroport [navet]
aisle seat la place côté couloir [plass kohtay koolwahr]
alarm clock le réveil [rayvay]
alcohol l'alcool **m** [alkol]
alcoholic alcoolisé [alkoleezay]
Algeria l'Algérie **f** [aljayree]
Algerian (adj) algérien [aljayree-AN]
all: all the boys tous les garçons [too]
all the girls toutes les filles [toot]
all of it tout [too]
all of them tous [tooss]
that's all, thanks c'est tout, merci
allergic: I'm allergic to ... je suis allergique à ... [juh swee alairjeek]
allowed: is it allowed? est-ce que c'est permis? [eskuh say pairmee]
all right d'accord [dakor]
I'm all right ça va [sa]
are you all right? ça va?
almond l'amande **f** [amONd]
almost presque [presk]
alone seul [surl]
alphabet l'alphabet **m** [alfabay]

a ah	h ash	o o	v vay
b bay	i ee	p pay	w doobl-vay
c say	j jee	q koo	x eeks
d day	k ka	r air	y ee-grek
e uh	l el	s ess	z zed
f ef	m em	t tay	
g jay	n en	u oo	

Alps les Alpes **fpl** [alp]
already déjà [dayja]
also aussi [o-see]
although bien que [b-yAN kuh]
altogether en tout [ON too]
always toujours [toojoor]
am*: I am je suis [juh swee]
a.m.: at seven a.m. à sept heures du matin [urr doo matAN]
amazing (surprising) étonnant [aytonON]
(very good) remarquable [ruhmark-abl]
ambulance l'ambulance **f** [ONbooIONss]
call an ambulance! appelez une ambulance! [aplay]

Call **Police Secours (17)** or the **Pompiers (18)** for an ambulance.

America l'Amérique **f** [amayreek]
American américain(e) [amayreekAN, -ken]
I'm American (man/woman) je suis américain/américaine
among parmi [parmee]
amount la quantité [kONteetay]

(money) la somme [som]
amp: a 13-amp fuse un fusible de 13 ampères [foozeebl ... ONpair]
amphitheatre l'amphithéâtre m [ONfeetay-ahtr]
and et [ay]
Andorra Andorre f [ONdor]
angry fâché [fashay]
animal l'animal m [aneemal]
ankle la cheville [shuhvee]
anniversary (wedding) l'anniversaire de mariage m [aneevairsair duh maree-ahj]
annoy: this man's annoying me cet homme m'importune [ANportoon]
annoying ennuyeux [ONwee-uh]
another un autre [ohtr]
can we have another room? est-ce que nous pouvons avoir une autre chambre? [eskuh noo poovON zavwa oon ohtr]
another beer, please encore une bière, s'il vous plaît [ONkor]
antibiotics les antibiotiques [ONteebeeoteek]
antifreeze l'antigel m [ONteejel]
antihistamine l'antihistaminique m [ONtee-eestameeneek]
antique: is it an antique? est-ce un objet d'époque? [ess AN objay daypok]
antique shop l'antiquaire m [ONteekair]
antiseptic le désinfectant [dayzANfektON]
any: have you got any bread/tomatoes? avez-vous du pain/des tomates? [avay-voo doo .../day]
do you have any change? avez-vous de la monnaie? [duh]
sorry, I don't have any désolé, je n'en ai pas [juh nON ay pa]
anybody quelqu'un [kelkAN]
does anybody speak English? est-ce qu'il y a quelqu'un qui parle anglais? [eskeel-ya]
there wasn't anybody there il n'y avait personne [pairson]
anything n'importe quoi

dialogues

anything else? désirez-vous autre chose? [dayzeeray-voo ohtr shohz]
nothing else, thanks c'est tout, merci [say too mairsee]

would you like anything to drink? veux-tu/voulez-vous boire quelque chose? [vuh-too/voolay-voo bwahr kelkuh-shohz]
I don't want anything, thanks je ne veux rien, merci [ree-AN]

apart from sauf [sohf]
apartment l'appartement m

[apartmON]
appendicitis l'appendicite **f** [apONdeesseet]
aperitif l'apéritif **m** [apayreeteef]
apology les excuses [exkOOz]
appetizer l'entrée **f** [ONtray]
apple la pomme [pom]
appointment le rendez-vous

dialogue

good afternoon, how can I help you? bonjour monsieur/madame, que puis-je faire pour vous? [kuh pweej fair poor voo]
I'd like to make an appointment j'aimerais prendre rendez-vous [jemray prONdr]
what time would you like? quelle heure vous conviendrait-elle? [kel urr voo KONvee-ANdrayt-el]
three o'clock trois heures
I'm afraid that's not possible, is four o'clock all right? cela ne va pas être possible, est-ce que quatre heures vous irait? [vooz eeray]
yes, that will be fine oui, cela ira parfaitement [eera parfetmON]
the name was ...? c'est monsieur/madame ...? [say]

apricot l'abricot **m** [abreeko]
April avril [avreel]
are*: we are nous sommes [noo som]
you are tu es/vous êtes [tOO ay, voo zet]
they are ils sont [eel sON]
area la région [rayjee-ON]
area code l'indicatif **m** [ANdeekateef]
arm le bras [bra]
arrange: will you arrange it for us? pouvez-vous vous en occuper? [poovay-voo voo zON okOOpay]
arrival l'arrivée **f** [areevay]
arrive arriver [areevay]
when do we arrive? à quelle heure arrivons-nous? [areevON-noo]
has my fax arrived yet? mon fax est-il arrivé? [areevay]
we arrived today nous sommes arrivés aujourd'hui
art l'art **m** [ar]
art gallery le musée d'art [mOOzay]
artist l'artiste **mf** [arteest]
as: as big as aussi gros que [ohsee gro kuh]
as soon as possible dès que possible [day]
ashtray le cendrier [sONdreeay]
ask demander [duhmONday]
I didn't ask for this ce n'est pas ce que j'ai commandé [suh nay pa suh kuy jay komONday]
could you ask him to ...? peux-tu/pouvez-vous lui

demander de ...? [puh-too/poovay-voo lwee ...]
asleep: she's asleep elle dort [dor]
aspirin l'aspirine **f** [aspeereen]
asthma l'asthme **m** [as-muh]
astonishing étonnant [aytonON]
at: at the hotel à l'hôtel [a]
at the station à la gare
at the café au café [o]
at six o'clock à six heures
at Paul's chez Paul [shay]
athletics l'athlétisme **m** [atlayteess-muh]
Atlantic l'Atlantique **m** [atlONteek]
attractive séduisant [saydweezON]
aubergine l'aubergine **f**
August août [oo]
aunt la tante [tONt]
Australia l'Australie **f** [ostralee]
Australian australien(ne) [ostralee-AN, -en]
I'm Australian (man/woman) je suis australien/australienne
Austria l'Autriche **f** [otreesh]
automatic (car) la voiture automatique [vwatoor otomateek]
autumn l'automne **m** [oton]
in the autumn en automne [ON]
avenue l'avenue **f**
average (not good) moyen [mwy-AN]
on average en moyenne [ON mwy-en]
awake: is he awake? est-il réveillé? [rayvay-yay]
away: go away! allez-vous en! [alay-voo zON]
is it far away? est-ce que c'est loin? [eskuh say lwAN]
awful affreux [afruh]
axle l'essieu **m** [ess-yuh]

B

baby le bébé [baybay]
baby food les aliments pour bébé [aleemON poor]
baby's bottle le biberon [beeberON]
baby-sitter le/la baby-sitter
back (of body) le dos [doh]
(back part) l'arrière **m** [aree-air]
at the back à l'arrière
can I have my money back? est-ce que vous pouvez me rendre mon argent? [eskuh voo poovay muh rONdr]
to come back revenir [ruh-veneer]
to go back rentrer [rONtray]
backache le mal de reins [duh rAN]
bad mauvais [movay]
a bad headache un violent mal de tête [veeolON]
badly mal
bag le sac
(handbag) le sac à main [mAN]
(suitcase) la valise [valeez]
baggage les bagages **mpl** [bagahj]

baggage check la consigne [kONseeñ]
baggage claim le retrait des bagages [ruhtray]
bakery la boulangerie [boolONjree]
balcony le balcon [balkON]
a room with a balcony une chambre avec balcon
bald chauve [shohv]
ball (large) le ballon [balON]
(small) la balle [bal]
ballet le ballet
banana la banane [banan]
band (musical) l'orchestre **m** [orkestr]
(pop, rock) le groupe
bandage le pansement [pONsmON]
Bandaids® les pansements **mpl** [pONsmON]
bank (money) la banque [bONk]

Banks are generally open from Monday to Friday, usually from 9 a.m. to noon, then again from 2 p.m. to 4 or 4.30 p.m. Branches of the **Banque de France** close on Mondays. A passport is sometimes required for transactions. The best rates for exchanging money or travellers' cheques are to be found in banks or post offices in larger cities, rather than in bureaux de change. What's more, the **Banque de France** and the post offices don't take a commission.

bank account le compte en banque [kONt ON bONk]
bar le bar

Bars sell hot drinks, soft and alcoholic drinks, and also savoury snacks. It's almost always cheaper if you stand at the bar to drink. A **bar-tabac** will have a special counter where you can buy cigarettes, stamps and phonecards.
see **café**

a bar of chocolate une tablette de chocolat [tablet duh shokola]
barber's le coiffeur pour hommes [kwafurr poor om]
basket le panier [pan-yay]
bath le bain [bAN]
can I have a bath? est-ce que je peux prendre un bain? [eskuh juh puh prONdr AN bAN]
bathroom la salle de bain [sal duh bAN]
with a private bathroom avec salle de bain
bath towel la serviette de bain
battery la pile [peel]
(for car) la batterie
bay la baie [bay]
be* être [etr]
beach la plage [plahj]
beach mat la natte [nat]
beach umbrella le parasol
beans les haricots [areeko]

runner beans les haricots à rames [ram]
broad beans les fèves [fev]
beard la barbe [barb]
beautiful beau, **f** belle [bo, bel]
because parce que [parss-kuh]
because of ... à cause de ... [a kohz duh]
bed le lit [lee]
I'm going to bed je vais me coucher [juh vay muh kooshay]
bed and breakfast la chambre avec petit déjeuner [shONbr avek puhtee dayjuhnay]

Prices of hotel rooms do not include breakfast.

bedroom la chambre à coucher [shONbr a kooshay]
beef le bœuf [burf]
beer la bière [bee-air]
two beers, please deux bières, s'il vous plaît [bee-air]

Some beer terms are:
blonde amber-coloured, light beer
rousse darker, maltier beer
brune [broon] dark beer
un panaché [panashay] a shandy
en bouteille [ON bootay] bottled
pression [press-yON] draught
un demi approximately half an imperial pint (250 cl)

before avant [avON]
begin: when does it begin? à quelle heure est-ce que ça commence? [sa kom-mONss]
beginner le débutant, la débutante [dayboOtON, -tONt]
beginning: at the beginning au début [o dayboo]
behind derrière [dairyair]
behind me derrière moi
beige beige [bej]
Belgian belge [belj]
(man/woman) le/la Belge
Belgium la Belgique [beljeek]
believe croire [krwahr]
below sous [soo]
belt la ceinture [sANtoor]
bend (in road) le virage [veerahj]
berth (on ship) la couchette [kooshet]
beside: beside the ... à côté du/de la ... [a kotay doo]
best le meilleur [may-yurr]
better mieux [m-yuh]
are you feeling better? est-ce que tu te sens/vous vous sentez mieux? [eskuh too tuh SON/voo voo SONtay]
between entre [ONtr]
beyond au delà [o duhla]
bicycle le vélo [vaylo]
big grand [grON]
too big trop grand
it's not big enough ce n'est pas assez grand [pa zassay]
bike le vélo [vaylo]
(motorbike) la moto
bikini le bikini
bill l'addition **f** [adeess-yON]
(US) le billet (de banque)

[bee-yay duh bONk]
could I have the bill, please? l'addition, s'il vous plaît

If you go out informally with a group, it is usual to share the bill equally. If someone intends to pay for everything, they will say **'c'est pour moi'** or **'c'est moi qui paie'**. If someone invites other people out, he or she is expected to pay.

bin la poubelle [poo-bel]
bin liners les sacs poubelle **mpl**
binding (ski) la fixation [feexass-yON]
bird l'oiseau **m** [wazo]
biro® le stylo-bille [steelo-bee]
birthday l'anniversaire **m** [aneevairsair]
happy birthday! bon anniversaire!
biscuit le biscuit [beeskwee]
bit: a little bit un peu [AN puh]
a big bit un gros morceau [gro morso]
a bit of ... un morceau de ...
a bit expensive un peu cher
bite (by insect) la piqûre [peekoor]
(by dog) la morsure [morsoor]
bitter (taste etc) amer [amair]
black noir [nwahr]
blanket la couverture [koovairtoor]
bleach (for toilet) l'eau de Javel **f** [ohd javel]
bless you! santé! [sONtay]
blind aveugle [avurgl]
blind (on window) le store [stor]
blister l'ampoule **f** [ONpool]
blocked (road, pipe, sink) bouché [booshay]
block of flats l'immeuble **m** [eemurbl]
blond(e) blond [blON]
blood le sang [sON]
high blood pressure l'hypertension **f** [eepairtONs-yON]
blouse le chemisier [shuhmeez-yay]
blow-dry le brushing
I'd like a cut and blow-dry je voudrais une coupe et un brushing
blue bleu [bluh]
blusher le rouge à joues [rooj a joo]
boarding house la pension [pONs-yON]
boarding pass la carte d'embarquement [dONbarkuh-mON]
boat le bateau [bato]
body le corps [kor]
boil (water) faire bouillir [fair booyeer]
(potatoes etc) faire cuire à l'eau [kweer a lo]
boiled egg l'œuf à la coque **m** [urf ala kok]
bone l'os **m** [oss]
bonnet (of car) le capot [kapo]
book le livre [leevr]
(verb) réserver [rayzairvay]

can I book a seat? est-ce que je peux réserver une place?

dialogue

I'd like to book a table for two j'aimerais réserver une table pour deux [jemray rayzairvay]
what time would you like it booked for? pour quelle heure voudriez-vous réserver? [poor kel urr voodree-ay-voo]
half past seven sept heures et demi
that's fine très bien
and your name? votre nom?

bookshop/bookstore la librairie [leebrairee]
boot (footwear) la botte [bot]
(of car) le coffre [kofr]
border (of country) la frontière [frONt-yair]
bored: I'm bored je m'ennuie [juh mON-nwee]
boring ennuyeux [ON-nwee-yuh]
born: I was born in Manchester je suis né à Manchester [juh swee nay]
I was born in 1960 je suis né en mille neuf cent soixante [ON meel nuhf sON swassONt]
borrow emprunter [ONprANtay]
may I borrow ...? puis-je emprunter ...?
both les deux [lay duh]
bother: sorry to bother you je suis désolé de vous déranger [juh swee dayzolay duh voo dayrON-jay]
bottle la bouteille [bootay]
a bottle of house red une bouteille de rouge maison [mezzON]
bottle-opener l'ouvre-bouteille **m** [oovr-bootay]
bottom (of person) le derrière [dairyair]
at the bottom of ... (hill etc) en bas de ... [ON ba duh]
box la boîte [bwat]
box office le guichet [geeshay]
boy le garçon [garsON]
boyfriend le petit ami [puhtee tami]
bra le soutien-gorge [soot-yAN-gorj]
bracelet le bracelet [braslay]
brake le frein [frAN]
brandy le cognac
bread le pain [pAN]
white bread du pain blanc [blON]
brown bread du pain noir [nwar]
wholemeal bread du pain complet [kONplay]
break casser [kassay]
I've broken the ... j'ai cassé le ... [jay kassay]
I think I've broken my wrist je crois que je me suis cassé le

poignet [juh muh swee]
breakdown la panne [pan]
I've had a breakdown je suis tombé en panne [juh swee tONbay ON]

If you are taking a car with you make sure that you take out breakdown insurance cover before you go.

breakdown service le service de dépannage [sairveess duh daypanahj]
breakfast le petit déjeuner [ptee day-juhnay]
English/full breakfast le petit déjeuner anglais [ONglay]
break-in: I've had a break-in il y a eu un cambriolage [eel ya oo AN kONbreeolahj]
breast le sein [SAN]
breathe respirer [respeeray]
breeze la brise [breez]
bridge (over river) le pont [pON]
brief court [koor]
briefcase la serviette
bright (light etc) clair
bright red rouge vif [veef]
brilliant (idea, person) génial [jayn-yal]
bring apporter [aportay]
I'll bring it back later je le rapporterai plus tard [raportuhray]
Britain la Grande-Bretagne [grONd-bruhtañ]
British britannique [breetaneek]
Brittany la Bretagne [bruhtañ]
brochure le prospectus [prospektooss]
broken cassé [kassay]
bronchitis la bronchite [brONsheet]
brooch la broche [brosh]
broom le balai [balay]
brother le frère [frair]
brother-in-law le beau-frère [bo-frair]
brown marron [marON]
(hair) brun [brAN]
bruise le bleu [bluh]
brush (for hair) la brosse [bross]
(artist's) le pinceau [pAN-so]
(for cleaning) le balai [balay]
Brussels Bruxelles [broossel]
bucket le seau [so]
buffet car le wagon-restaurant [vagON-restorON]
buggy (for child) le landau [lONdo]
building le bâtiment [bateemON]
bulb l'ampoule **f** [ONpool]
I need a new bulb j'ai besoin d'une nouvelle ampoule
bumper le pare-chocs [par-shok]
bunk la couchette [kooshet]
bureau de change le bureau de change
see **bank**
burglary le cambriolage [kONbreeolahj]
burn la brûlure [broolOOr]
(verb) brûler [broolay]
burnt: this is burnt c'est brûlé

[broolay]
burst: a burst pipe un tuyau crevé [twee-o kruhvay]
bus le bus [booss]
what number bus is it to ...? quel bus va à ...? [kel]
when is the next bus to ...? à quelle heure part le prochain bus pour ...? [a kel urr par luh proshAN]
what time is the last bus? à quelle heure passe le dernier bus? [dairn-yay]
could you let me know when we get there? est-ce que vous pourrez me dire quand on y sera? [eskuh voo pooray muh deer KON tON ee suhra]

In Paris, bus tickets are cheaper if bought in advance from newsstands, tobacconists or underground stations in a book of ten (**un carnet de tickets**) – they can also be bought on boarding the bus, but will be more expensive. Tickets have to be validated in the ticket-stamping machine on the bus. If travelling for more than two sections in Paris and some larger towns – as indicated on the route chart – you have to validate two tickets. Special day-tickets are also available which give you unlimited travel on the bus (and underground) for one day. In Paris, bus tickets can also be used in the underground.

dialogue

does this bus go to ...? est-ce que ce bus va à ...?
no, you need a number ... non, vous devez prendre le ... [prONdr]
where does it leave from? où est-ce que je le prends? [weskuh juh luh prON]

business les affaires **fpl** [lay zafair]
bus station la gare routière [gar root-yair]
bus stop l'arrêt d'autobus **m** [aray dotobooss]
bust la poitrine [pwatreen]
busy (person) occupé [okoopay]
the restaurant is very busy il y a beaucoup de monde dans le restaurant [eel ya bohkoo duh mONd]
I'm busy tomorrow demain, je suis pris(e) [duhmAN juh swee pree/preez]
but mais [may]
butcher's la boucherie [booshree]
butter le beurre [burr]
button le bouton [bootON]
buy acheter [ashtay]
where can I buy ...? où puis-je acheter ...? [oo pweej]
by: by bus/car en bus/voiture [ON]
written by ... écrit par ...
by the window près de la fenêtre [pray duh]

by the sea au bord de la mer [o bor]
by Thursday pour jeudi [poor]

bye au revoir [o ruh-vwa]

C

cabbage le chou [shoo]

cabin (on ship) la cabine [kabeen]

cable car le téléférique [taylayfayreek]

café le café

Every bar or café has to display its full price list (usually without the fifteen per cent service charge added). In addition to coffee, tea etc, cafés also serve alcoholic drinks and usually snacks or even simple dishes; they have waiter service, although drinks are cheaper at the bar (**comptoir**) than at a table (**en salle**) or outside (**en terrasse**). You normally pay just before you leave, rather than on ordering.

cagoule le K-way® [ka-way]

cake le gâteau [gato]

cake shop la pâtisserie

call appeler [aplay]
(to phone) téléphoner [taylayfonay]
what's it called? comment ça s'appelle? [komON sa sa-pel]
he/she is called ... il/elle s'appelle ...
please call the doctor appelez le docteur, s'il vous plaît [aplay]
please give me a call at 7.30 a.m. tomorrow pouvez-vous me réveiller à sept heures trente demain matin? [poovay-voo muh rayvayay]
please ask him to call me pouvez-vous lui demander de m'appeler?

call back: I'll call back later je reviendrai plus tard [ruhveeANdray]
(phone back) je rappelerai plus tard [rapelray]

call round: I'll call round tomorrow je passerai demain [passuhray]

camcorder le caméscope [kamayskop]

camera (for stills) l'appareil-photo **m** [aparay-]

camera shop le photographe [fotograf]

camp camper [kONpay]
can we camp here? est-ce qu'on peut camper ici? [eskON puh]

camping gas le butagaz

Camping gas canisters can be bought either from a **quincaillerie** (hardware store) or from campsite shops; you can't carry canisters on aeroplanes.

campsite le terrain de

camping [terrAN duh kONpeeng]

In France, campsites are classified in four categories, ranging from 1 to 4 stars according to the facilities they offer. Never camp rough on anyone's land without first asking permission of the landowner – farmers have been known to shoot before asking questions. In many parts of France, camping rough on public land is not tolerated at all, although Brittany is a notable exception.

can (tin) la boîte [bwat]
a can of beer une bière en boîte [bee-air ON]
can*: can you ...? peux-tu/pouvez-vous ...? [puh-too/poovay-voo]
can I have ...? est-ce que je peux avoir ...? [eskuh juh puh avwahr]
I can't ... je ne peux pas ... [juh nuh puh pa]
Canada le Canada
Canadian canadien(ne) [kanadee-AN, -ee-en]
I'm Canadian (man/woman) je suis canadien/canadienne
canal le canal
cancel annuler [anoolay]
candies les bonbons [bONbON]
candle la bougie [boo-jee]
canoe le canoë [kano-ay]
canoeing le canoë
can-opener l'ouvre-boîte **m** [oovr-bwat]
cap (hat) la casquette [kasket] (of bottle) la capsule
car la voiture [vwatoor]
by car en voiture
carafe une carafe
a carafe of house white, please une carafe de blanc maison, s'il vous plaît [mezzON]
caravan la caravane
caravan site le terrain de camping pour caravanes [terrAN duh kONpeeng poor]
carburettor le carburateur [karbooraturr]
card (birthday etc) la carte [kart]
here's my (business) card voici ma carte [vwa-see]
cardigan le gilet [jeelay]
cardphone le téléphone à carte [taylayfon a kart]
careful prudent [proodON]
be careful! faites attention! [fet zatONs-yON]
caretaker le/la concierge
car ferry le ferry
car hire la location de voitures [lokass-yON duh vwatoor] see **rent**
car park le parking [parkeeng]
carpet la moquette [moket]
carriage (of train) le wagon [vagON]
carrier bag le sac en plastique [ON plasteek]
carrot la carotte [karrot]
carry porter [portay]

carry-cot le porte-bébé [port-baybay]
carton (of orange juice etc) le carton [kartON]
carwash (place) le lave-auto [lav-oto]
case (suitcase) la valise [valeez]
cash l'argent liquide **m** [arjON leekeed]
(verb) encaisser
will you cash this for me? est-ce que vous pouvez encaisser cela pour moi? [eskuh voo poovay]
cash desk la caisse [kess]
cash dispenser le distributeur automatique de billets de banque [deestreebOOturr otomateek duh bee-yay duh bONk]
cashier (cash desk) la caisse [kess]
cassette la cassette
cassette recorder le magnétophone à cassettes [man-yetofon]
castle le château [shato]
casualty department le service des urgences [sairveess day zOOrjONss]
cat le chat [sha]
catch attraper [atrapay]
where do we catch the bus to ...? où est-ce qu'on peut prendre le bus pour ...? [weskON puh prONdr luh bOOss]
cathedral la cathédrale [katay-dral]
Catholic (adj) catholique [kato-leek]
cauliflower le chou-fleur [shoo-flurr]
cave la grotte [grot]
ceiling le plafond [plafON]
celery le céleri en branche [saylree ON brONsh]
cellar (for wine) la cave [kahv]
cemetery le cimetière [seemtee-air]
Centigrade* centigrade [sONteegrad]
centimetre* le centimètre [sONteemetr]
central central [sON-tral]
central heating le chauffage central [shofahj sON-tral]
centre le centre [sONtr]
how do we get to the city centre? comment va-t-on au centre-ville? [komON vatON o sONtr-veel]
it's in the city centre c'est dans le centre-ville
cereal les céréales [sayray-al]
certainly certainement [sairten-mON]
certainly not certainement pas [pa]
chair la chaise [shez]
champagne le champagne [shONpañ]
change (money) la monnaie [monay]
(verb) changer [shONjay]
can I change this for ...? j'aimerais échanger ceci contre ... [jemray ayshONjay suhsee]

Ca

I don't have any change je n'ai pas de monnaie [juh nay pa duh]
can you give me change for a 200-franc note? pouvez-vous me faire la monnaie sur un billet de deux cents francs? [muh fair]

dialogue

do we have to change (trains)? est-ce qu'il faut changer? [eskeel fo]
yes, change at Bordeaux oui, il faut changer à Bordeaux
no, it's direct non, c'est direct [deerekt]

changed: to get changed se changer [shONjay]
Channel la Manche [mONsh]
Channel Islands les îles Anglo-Normandes [eel ONglo-normONd]
Channel Tunnel le tunnel sous la Manche [toonel soo la mONsh]
chapel la chapelle [shapel]
charge (verb) faire payer
cheap bon marché [bON marshay]
do you have anything cheaper? avez-vous quelque chose de meilleur marché? [avay-voo kelkuh shohz duh may-yurr marshay]
check (US) le chèque [shek]
see **cheque**
(US: bill) l'addition **f** [adeess-yON]
see **bill**
(verb) vérifier [vayreef-yay]
could you check the ..., please? pouvez-vous vérifier ..., s'il vous plaît?
checkbook le chéquier [shaykee-ay]
check-in l'enregistrement des bagages **m** [ONrejeestruh-mON day bagahj]
check in (at airport) se faire enregistrer [suh fair ONrejeestray]
where do we have to check in? où est l'enregistrement?
checkout (in shop) la caisse [kess]
cheek (on face) la joue [joo]
cheerio! (bye-bye) au revoir! [o ruh-vwa]
cheers! (toast) santé! [sONtay]
(thanks) merci! [mairsee]
cheese le fromage [fromahj]

In France there are over 250 officially recognized types of cheeses, with each region having its own speciality. Cheese is served at nearly every meal, after or along with the green salad and before dessert.

chemist's (shop) la pharmacie [farmassee]

Chemist's are identified by a green cross sign. They are well-qualified to give you advice on minor ailments. There's an all-night chemist's in bigger towns and cities and they work on a rota system. You generally find the address of the one currently open on the door of any chemist's.

cheque le chèque [shek]
do you take cheques? est-ce que vous acceptez les chèques? [eskuh voo zaxeptay]
cheque book le chéquier [shaykee-ay]
cheque card la carte d'identité bancaire [kart deedONteetay bONkair]
cherry la cerise [suhreez]
chess les échecs [lay zayshek]
chest (body) la poitrine [pwatreen]
chewing gum le chewing-gum [shween-gom]
chicken la poule [pool]
(meat) le poulet [poolay]
chickenpox la varicelle [vareessel]
child l'enfant **mf** [ON-fON]
children les enfants
child minder le/la gardien(ne) d'enfants [gardee-AN, -ee-en]
children's pool la piscine pour enfants [peesseen]
children's portion la portion pour enfants [pors-yON]
chin le menton [mONtON]
china la porcelaine
Chinese chinois [sheenwa]
chips les frites [freet]
chocolate le chocolat [shokola]
milk chocolate le chocolat au lait [o lay]
plain chocolate le chocolat à croquer [a krokay]
a hot chocolate un chocolat chaud [sho]
choose choisir [shwazeer]
Christian name le prénom [praynON]
Christmas Noël [no-el]
Christmas Eve la veille de Noël [vay duh]
merry Christmas! joyeux Noël! [jwy-uh]
church l'église **f** [aygleez]
cider le cidre [seedr]
cigar le cigare [see-gar]
cigarette la cigarette [see-]

Cigarettes can be bought from the **bureaux de tabac** (tobacconists) which can be identified by a red diamond-shaped sign with **Tabac** written on it.

cigarette lighter le briquet [breekay]
cinema le cinéma [seenayma]
circle le cercle [sairkl]
(in theatre) le balcon [balkON]
city la ville [veel]
city centre le centre-ville [sONtr-veel]

clean (adj) propre [propr]
can you clean these for me? pouvez-vous me nettoyer ça? [poovay-voo muh net-wy-ay sa]
cleaning solution (for contact lenses) la solution de nettoyage [solOOss-yON duh net-wy-ahj]
cleansing lotion (cosmetic) la crème démaquillante [krem daymakeeyONt]
clear clair [klair]
clever intelligent [ANtayleejON]
cliff la falaise [falez]
climbing l'escalade **f**
cling film le cellophane [selofan]
clinic la clinique [kleeneek]
cloakroom (for coats) le vestiaire [vestee-air]
clock l'horloge **f** [orloj]
close fermer [fairmay]

dialogue

what time do you close? à quelle heure est-ce que vous fermez? [a kel urr eskuh voo fairmay]
we close at 8 pm on weekdays and 6 pm on Saturdays nous fermons à huit heures pendant la semaine et à six heures le samedi [noo fairmON]
do you close for lunch? est-ce que vous fermez pour déjeuner?
yes, between 1 and 3.30 pm oui, entre une heure et trois heures et demi

closed fermé [fairmay]
cloth (fabric) le tissu [teessOO]
(for cleaning etc) le chiffon [sheefON]
clothes les vêtements [vetmON]
clothes line la corde à linge [kord a lANj]
clothes peg la pince à linge [pANss]
cloud le nuage [nOO-ahj]
cloudy nuageux [nOO-ahjuh]
clutch l'embrayage **m** [ONbray-ahj]
coach (bus) le car
(on train) le wagon [vagON]
coach station la gare routière [gar rootee-air]
coach trip l'excursion en autocar **f** [exkOOrss-yON ON otokar]
coast la côte [koht]
on the coast sur la côte
coat (long coat) le manteau [mONto]
(jacket) la veste [vest]
coathanger le cintre [sANtr]
cockroach le cafard [kafar]
cocoa le cacao [kakow]
coconut la noix de coco [nwa duh]
code (when dialling) l'indicatif **m** [ANdeekateef]
what's the (dialling) code for outside Paris? quel est

l'indicatif pour la province? [kel ay lANdeekateef poor]

coffee le café

two coffees, please deux cafés, s'il vous plaît [kafay]

If you ask for **un café** you will be given an **express** (strong black coffee); you can also ask for one of the following:

- **un (café) crème** [krem] coffee with cream or milk
- **un (café) décaféiné** [day-kafeenay] decaffeinated coffee
- **un café serré** [serray] strong express

coin la pièce [p-yess]

Coke® le coca-cola

cold (weather, food etc) froid [frwa]

I'm cold j'ai froid [jay]

I have a cold je me suis enrhumé [juh muh swee zONrOOmay]

collapse: he's collapsed il s'est effondré [eel set ayfONdray]

collar le col

collect: **I've come to collect ...** je suis venu chercher ... [juh swee vuhnOO shairshay]

collect call une communication en PCV [-kass-yON ON pay-say-vay]

college l'université **f** [OOneevairseetay]

colour la couleur [koolurr]

do you have this in other colours? l'avez-vous en d'autres teintes? [lavay voo ON dohtr tANt]

colour film la pellicule couleur [pelikOOl]

comb le peigne [peñ]

come venir [vuhneer]

dialogue

where do you come from? d'où es-tu/êtes-vous? [doo ay-tOO/et-voo]

I come from Edinburgh je suis d'Édimbourg [juh swee]

come back revenir

I'll come back tomorrow je reviens demain [juh ruhv-yAN]

come in entrer [ONtray]

comfortable confortable [kONfort-abl]

compact disc le disque compact

company (business) la société [sos-yay-tay]

compartment (on train) le compartiment [kONparteemON]

compass la boussole [boossol]

complain se plaindre [suh plANdr]

complaint la réclamation [rayklamass-yON]

I have a complaint j'ai une réclamation à faire

completely complètement [kONpletmON]

computer l'ordinateur **m**

[ordeenaturr]
concert le concert [kONsair]
concussion la commotion cérébrale [komoss-yON sayray-bral]
conditioner (for hair) l'après-shampoing **m** [apray-shONpwAN]
condom le préservatif [prayzairvateef]
conference la conférence [kONfay-rONss]
confirm confirmer [kONfeermay]
congratulations! félicitations! [fayleesseetass-yON]
connecting flight le vol qui assure la correspondance [kee assoor la korespONdONss]
connection (in travelling) la correspondance
conscious conscient [kONs-yON]
constipation la constipation [kONsteepass-yON]
consulate le consulat [kONsoo-la]
contact contacter [kONtaktay]
contact lenses les lentilles de contact **fpl** [lONtee]
contraceptive le contraceptif [kONtrasepteef]
convenient (location) pratique [prateek]
(time) qui convient [kee kONvee-AN]
that's not convenient cela ne me convient pas
cook le cuisinier, la cuisinière [kweezeenee-ay, -yair]
not cooked (is underdone) pas cuit [pa kwee]
cooker la cuisinière [kweezeenyair]
cookie le biscuit [beeskwee]
cooking utensils les ustensiles de cuisine [oostONseel duh kweezeen]
cool (day, weather) frais, **f** fraîche [fray, fresh]
cork (in bottle) le bouchon [booshON]
corkscrew le tire-bouchon [teer-booshON]
corner: on the corner (of street) au coin de la rue [kwAN duh la roo]
in the corner dans le coin
cornflakes les cornflakes
correct (adj) correct, exact
corridor le couloir [koolwahr]
Corsica la Corse [korss]
Corsican (adj) corse
cosmetics les produits de beauté [prodwee duh bohtay]
cost coûter [kootay]
how much does it cost? combien ça coûte? [kONb-yAN sa koot]
cot (for baby) le lit d'enfant [lee dONfON]
cotton le coton [kotON]
cotton wool le coton hydrophile [kotON eedrofeel]
couch (sofa) le canapé [kanapay]
couchette la couchette

cough la toux [too]
cough medicine le sirop contre la toux [seero kONtr]
could: could you ...? pourriez-vous ...? [pooree-ay-voo]
could I have ...? j'aimerais ... [jemray]
I couldn't ... je ne pouvais pas ... [juh nuh poovay pa]
country (nation) le pays [payee]
(countryside) la campagne [kONpañ]
countryside la campagne
couple (man and woman) le couple [koopl]
a couple of ... quelques ... [kelkuh]
courier le/la guide [geed]
course (of meal) le plat [pla]
of course bien sûr [b-yAN soor]
of course not bien sûr que non [kuh nON]
cousin le cousin, la cousine [koozAN, koozeen]
cow la vache [vash]
crab le crabe [krab]
cracker (biscuit) le biscuit salé [beeskwee salay]
craft shop la boutique d'artisanat [arteezana]
crash la collision [koleez-yON]
I've had a crash j'ai eu un accident [jay oo AN axeedON]
crazy fou, **f** folle [foo, fol]
cream (on milk, in cake, lotion) la crème [krem]
(colour) crème
creche (for babies) la crèche
credit card la carte de crédit [kart duh kraydee]

Credit cards are widely accepted; just look out for the window stickers. Visa/Barclaycard – known as the **Carte Bleue** – is almost universally recognized. Access (known as Eurocard/Mastercard in France) ranks considerably lower – only the Crédit Agricole and the Crédit Mutuel banks provide facilities for the latter. Cash advances can be had at all banks – you should ask for a PIN number before you go.

dialogue

can I pay by credit card? est-ce que je peux payer par carte de crédit? [eskuh juh puh pay-ay]
which card do you want to use? avec quelle carte désirez-vous payer?
yes, sir oui monsieur
what's the number? quel est le numéro? [noomayro]
and the expiry date? et la date d'expiration?

crisps les chips **fpl** [cheeps]
crockery la vaisselle [vess-el]
crossing (by sea) la traversée [travairsay]

crossroads le carrefour [karfoor]
crowd la foule [fool]
crowded (streets, bars) bondé [bONday]
crown (on tooth) la couronne [kooron]
cruise (by ship) la croisière [krwaz-yair]
crutches les béquilles **fpl** [baykee]
cry pleurer [plurray]
cucumber le concombre [kONkONbr]
cup la tasse [tass]
a cup of ..., please une tasse de ..., s'il vous plaît
cupboard l'armoire **f** [armwahr]
curly (hair) frisé
current le courant [koorON]
curtains les rideaux **mpl** [reedo]
cushion le coussin [koossAN]
custom la coutume [kootoom]
Customs la douane [dwan]
cut la coupure [koopoor]
(hair) la coupe [koop]
(verb) couper [koopay]
I've cut myself je me suis coupé [juh muh swee koopay]
cutlery les couverts [kouvair]
cycling le cyclisme [seekleess-muh]
cyclist le/la cycliste [seekleest]

D

dad le papa
daily: they run daily il y en a tous les jours [eel yON a too lay joor]
a daily paper un (journal) quotidien [joornal koteedee-AN]
damage endommager [ONdoma-jay]
damaged abîmé [abeemay]
I'm sorry, I've damaged this je suis désolé, j'ai abimé ça [jay abeemay]
damn! zut! [zoot]
damp (adj) humide [oo-meed]
dance la danse [dONss]
(verb) danser [dONsay]
would you like to dance? veux-tu/voulez-vous danser avec moi? [vuh-too/voolay-voo – avek mwa]
dangerous dangereux [dONj-ruh]
Danish danois [danwa]
dark (adj: colour) foncé [fONsay]
(hair) brun [brAN]
it's getting dark il commence à faire sombre [eel komONss a fair sONbr]
date*: what's the date today? quel jour sommes-nous? [kel joor som-noo]
let's make a date for next Monday prenons rendez-vous pour lundi prochain [pruhnON]
dates (fruit) les dattes **fpl** [dat]

daughter la fille [fee]
daughter-in-law la belle-fille [bel-fee]
dawn l'aurore **f** [oror]
at dawn au lever du jour [o luhvay doo joor]
day le jour [joor]
the day after le lendemain [lONdmAN]
the day after tomorrow après-demain [apray-duhmAN]
the day before la veille [vay]
the day before yesterday avant-hier [avON-tee-air]
every day chaque jour
are you open all day? est-ce que vous êtes ouverts toute la journée? [toot la joornay]
in two days' time dans deux jours
have a nice day bonne journée [bon joornay]
day trip l'excursion d'une journée **f** [exkoors-yON doon joornay]
dead mort [mor]
deaf sourd [soor]
deal (business) l'affaire **f**
it's a deal d'accord! [dakor]
death la mort [mor]
decaffeinated coffee le café décaffeiné [daykafay-eenay]
December décembre [daysONbr]
decide décider [dayseeday]
we haven't decided yet nous n'avons pas encore décidé [noo navON pa zONkor dayseeday]
decision la décision [dayseez-yON]
deck (on ship) le pont [pON]
deckchair la chaise longue [shez lON-g]
deduct déduire [daydweer]
deep profond [profON]
definitely certainement [sairten-mON]
definitely not certainement pas [pa]
degree (qualification) le diplôme [deeplohm]
delay le retard [ruhtar]
deliberately exprès [expray]
delicatessen l'épicerie fine **f** [aypeesree feen]
delicious délicieux [dayleess-yuh]
deliver livrer [leevray]
delivery (of mail) la distribution [deestreeboossyON]
Denmark le Danemark [danmark]
dental floss le fil dentaire [feel dONtair]
dentist le/la dentiste [dON-teest]
see **doctor**

dialogue

it's this one here c'est celle-là [say sel-la]
this one? celle-ci? [sel-see]
no, that one non, celle-là
here? ici? [ee-see]
yes oui [wee]

dentures le dentier [dONt-yay]
deodorant le déodorant [dayodorON]
department le service [sairveess]
department store le grand magasin [grON magazAN]
departure le départ [daypar]
departure lounge le hall de départ [al duh]
depend: it depends ça dépend [sa daypON]
it depends on ... ça dépend de ...
deposit (as security) la caution [kohs-yON]
(as part payment) l'acompte **m** [akONt]
description la description [deskreeps-yON]
dessert le dessert [desair]
destination la destination [desteenass-yON]
develop développer [dayv-lopay]

When leaving your films to be developed, you will be asked if you want your photos **en mat ou brillant** (matt or glossy finish). If you don't specify, you're likely to get the matt finish.

dialogue

could you develop these films? pouvez-vous développer ces pellicules? [poovay-voo ... say peleekool]
when will they be ready? quand est-ce que ça sera prêt? [kON teskuh sa suhra pray]
tomorrow afternoon demain après-midi
how much is the four-hour service? combien coûte le service de développement en quatre heures?

diabetic le/la diabétique [dee-abayteek]
diabetic foods les aliments pour diabétiques [aleemON]
dial composer [kONpohzay]
dialling code l'indicatif **m** [ANdeekateef]

For direct international calls from France, dial 00, then the country code (given below), the area code (minus the first 0), and finally the subscriber number.
UK: 00 44
Australia: 00 61
Ireland: 00 353
New Zealand: 00 64
US & Canada: 00 1

diamond le diamant [dee-amON]
diaper la couche [koosh]
diarrhoea la diarrhée [dee-aray]
diary (business etc) l'agenda **m**

[ajANda]
(for personal experiences) le journal [joornal]
dictionary le dictionnaire [deex-yonair]
didn't* see **not**
die mourir [mooreer]
diesel (fuel) le gas-oil
diet le régime [ray-jeem]
I'm on a diet je suis au régime [juh swee zo]
I have to follow a special diet je dois suivre un régime spécial [dwa sweevr]
difference la différence [deefayrONss]
what's the difference? quelle est la différence? [kel ay]
different différent [deefayrON]
this one is different celui-ci est différent [suhlwee-see]
a different table une autre table [ohtr]
difficult difficile [deefeesseel]
difficulty la difficulté [deefeekooltay]
dinghy (rubber) le canot pneumatique [kano p-nuhmateek]
(sailing) le dériveur [dayreevurr]
dining room la salle à manger [sal a mONjay]
dinner (evening meal) le dîner [deenay]
to have dinner dîner
direct (adj) direct [deerekt]
is there a direct train? est-ce qu'il y a un train direct? [eskeel ya]
direction le sens [sONss]
which direction is it? dans quelle direction est-ce? [dON kel deereex-yON ess]
is it in this direction? est-ce par là?
directory enquiries les renseignements [rONsen-yuhmON]

The number for directory enquiries is 12. For international directory enquiries dial 00 33 12 followed by the appropriate country code. Most post offices also have **Minitel** terminals at the disposal of the public, which give you the telephone number and the address of the person you want to phone – all you need to use this is their name and the city or **département** they live in.

dirt la saleté [sal-tay]
dirty sale [sal]
disabled handicapé [ONdeekapay]
is there access for the disabled? est-ce que c'est aménagé pour les handicapés? [eskuh say amaynah-jay]
disappear disparaître [deesparetr]
it's disappeared (I've lost it) il/elle a disparu [deesparoo]
disappointed déçu [daysoo]

disappointing décevant [day-svON]
disaster le désastre [day-zastr]
disco la discothèque
discount le rabais [rabay]
disease la maladie [maladee]
disgusting dégoûtant [daygootON]
dish (meal, bowl) le plat [pla]
dishcloth le torchon à vaisselle [torshON a vess-el]
disinfectant le désinfectant [dayzANfek-tON]
disk (for computer) la disquette
disposable diapers les couches jetables **fpl** [koosh juhtahbl]
disposable nappies les couches jetables **fpl**
distance la distance [deestONss]
in the distance au loin [o lWAN]
distilled water l'eau distillée **f** [o deesteelay]
district le quartier [kart-yay]
disturb déranger [dayrONjay]
diversion (detour) la déviation [dayvee-ass-yON]
diving board le plongeoir [plON-jwahr]
divorced divorcé [deevorsay]
dizzy: I feel dizzy j'ai la tête qui tourne [jay la tet kee toorn]
do faire [fair]
what shall we do? qu'est-ce qu'on fait? [keskON fay]
how do you do it? comment est-ce qu'on fait? [komON eskON fay]
will you do it for me? est-ce que tu peux/vous pouvez le faire pour moi? [eskuh too puh/voo poovay]

dialogues

how do you do? comment vas-tu/allez-vous? [va-too/alay-voo]
nice to meet you enchanté [ONshONtay]
what do you do? (work) qu'est-ce que tu fais/vous faites dans la vie? [kes kuh too fay/voo fet dON la vee]
I'm a teacher, and you? je suis enseignant(e), et toi/vous? [twa]
I'm a student je suis étudiant(e)
what are you doing this evening? qu'est-ce que tu fais/vous faites ce soir? [suh swahr]
we're going out for a drink, do you want to join us? nous allons prendre un verre, veux-tu te/voulez-vous vous joindre à nous? [vuh-too tuh/voolay-voo voo jwANdr]

do you want cream? voulez-vous de la crème?
I do, but she doesn't moi oui, mais pas elle [mwa]

doctor le médecin [maydsAN]
we need a doctor nous avons besoin d'un médecin
please call a doctor appelez un médecin, s'il vous plaît [aplay]

Citizens of all EC countries are entitled to take advantage of each others' health services under the same terms as the residents of the country, if they have the correct documentation. British citizens need form E111 (obtainable from post offices in the UK) – this will enable you to get subsidized treatment and pay for prescriptions at the local rate. Non-EC citizens should take out health insurance. In France, every hospital visit, doctor's consultation and prescribed medicine is charged for. Although all employed French people are entitled to a refund of 75-80 per cent of their medical expenses, this can still leave a hefty shortfall. To find a doctor, stop at any **pharmacie** and ask for an address. The doctor should give you a **Feuille de soins** (Statement of Treatment) for later documentation of insurance claims. The medicines you buy will have **vignettes** (stickers) attached to them which you must remove and attach to your Feuille de soins, together with the prescription itself.

dialogue

where does it hurt? où est-ce que ça fait mal? [weskuh sa fay]
right here ici [ee-see]
does that hurt now? est-ce que ça fait mal là?
yes oui [wee]
take this to the chemist emmenez ça chez le pharmacien [ONmuhnay sa shay luh farmass-yAN]

document le document [dokOOmON]
dog le chien [shee-AN]
doll la poupée [poopay]
domestic flight le vol intérieur [ANtayree-urr]
don't!* non! [nON] see **not**
don't do that! ne faites pas ça! [nuh fet pa sa]
door (of room) la porte [port]
(of train, car) la portière [port-yair]
doorman le portier [port-yay]
double double [doobl]
double bed le grand lit [grON lee]
double room la chambre pour deux personnes [shONbr poor duh pairson]
doughnut le beignet [benyay]
down en bas [ON ba]
put it down over there posez-le là [pohzay-luh]
it's down there on the right c'est par là sur la droite

it's further down the road c'est plus loin sur cette route [ploo lwAN soor set root]

downhill skiing le ski de descente [duh duhsONt]

downmarket (restaurant etc) simple [sANpl]

downstairs en bas [ON ba]

dozen la douzaine [doozen]

half a dozen une demi-douzaine [duhmee-]

drain le tuyau d'écoulement [twee-yo day-koolmON]

draught beer la bière pression [bee-air press-yON]

draughty: it's draughty il y a un courant d'air [eelya AN koorON dair]

drawer le tiroir [teer-wa]

drawing le dessin [duh-sAN]

dreadful épouvantable [aypoovONtabl]

dream le rêve [rev]

dress la robe [rob]

dressed: to get dressed s'habiller [sabeeyay]

dressing (for cut) le pansement [pONsmON]
(for salad) la vinaigrette

dressing gown la robe de chambre [rob duh shONbr]

drink la boisson [bwassON]
(verb) boire [bwahr]

a cold drink une boisson fraîche [fresh]

can I get you a drink? tu prends/vous prenez un verre? [too prON/voo pruhnay zAN vair]

what would you like (to drink)? qu'est-ce que tu veux/vous voulez boire? [keskuh]

no thanks, I don't drink non merci, je ne bois pas [juh nuh bwa pa]

I'll just have a drink of water un verre d'eau, c'est tout [vair do say too]

drinking water l'eau potable **f** [o pot-abl]

is this drinking water? est-ce que cette eau est potable? [eskuh]

Public water supplies are safe, although in some cities tap water (**l'eau du robinet**) doesn't taste wonderful and you might prefer to drink mineral water (**de l'eau minérale**).

drive conduire [kONdweer]

we drove here nous sommes venus en voiture [noo som vuhnoo en vwatoor]

I'll drive you home je vais te/vous reconduire [juh vay tuh/voo ruhkONdweer]

EC and US driving licences are valid, though an International Driver's Licence makes life easier if you get a policeman unwilling to peruse a document in English. The vehicle registration documents and the insurance papers must be carried with you. If your car is right-hand drive, you are required by law to fit headlight or beam converters (available from car accessory shops) to redirect the beams to the right. A rule of the road to remember in France is that you must often give way to traffic coming from a minor road on the right – the law of **priorité à droite**. Look out along the roadside for the yellow diamond on a white background that gives you right of way – until you see the same sign crossed out which indicates that vehicles emerging from the right have priority. Speed limits are: 130km/hr (80mph) on the tolled motorways; 110km/hr (68mph) on two-lane highways; 90km/hr (56mph) on other roads; and 60km/hr (37mph) or less in towns.

driver (of car) le conducteur [kONdookturr]
(of bus) le chauffeur
driving licence le permis de conduire [pairmee duh kONdweer]
drop: just a drop, please (of drink) une petite goutte, s'il vous plaît [oon puhteet goot]
drug (medical) le médicament [maydeekamON]
drugs (narcotics) la drogue [drog]
drunk (adj) ivre [eevr]
drunken driving la conduite en état d'ivresse [kONdweet ON ayta deevress]

The legal limit for alcohol in the blood for drivers is 0.5%. Don't drink and drive. If you are found to be over the limit, you will be fined and if you are over 0.8%, you are also liable to a term of imprisonment and points on your licence.

drunkenness l'ivresse **f** [eevress]
dry (adj) sec, **f** sèche [sek, sesh]
dry-cleaner le teinturier [tANtooree-ay]
duck le canard [kanar]
due: he was due to arrive yesterday il devait arriver hier [eel duhvay]
when is the train due? quand est-ce que le train doit arriver? [dwa]
dull (pain) sourd [soor]
(weather) sombre [sONbr]
dummy (baby's) la tétine [tayteen]
during pendant [pONdON]
dust la poussière [pooss-yair]
dusty poussiéreux [pooss-yayruh]
dustbin la poubelle [poo-bel]
Dutch hollandais [olONday]
duty-free hors taxes [or tax]
duty-free shop la boutique hors taxes
duvet la couette [kwet]

E

each (every) chaque **[shak]**
how much are they each? combien est-ce qu'ils sont la pièce? **[KONb-yAN eskeel SON la p-yess]**
ear l'oreille **f [oray]**
earache: I have earache j'ai mal à l'oreille **[jay mal a loray]**
early tôt **[toh]**
early in the morning tôt le matin
I called by earlier je suis passé tout à l'heure **[toot a lurr]**
earring la boucle d'oreille **[bookl doray]**
east l'est **m [est]**
in the east à l'est
Easter Pâques **[pak]**
easy facile **[fasseel]**
eat manger **[mONjay]**
we've already eaten, thanks nous avons déjà mangé, merci **[noo zavON dayja mONjay]**

eating habits
The French usually have three meals a day: a light breakfast, consisting of **café** or **café au lait** and bread/ **croissants**, butter and jam; a substantial lunch, with a first course of **charcuterie** or salad, a second course of meat or fish and vegetables (vegetarianism still hasn't made a great impact on France), followed by cheese and/or dessert, then coffee (the majority of people still have a large lunch-time meal, although in cities, snacks and sandwiches are popular among office workers); the evening meal (similar courses to lunch) is normally quite substantial as well. It is quite common to have an **apéritif** (drink and snack) before lunch and dinner.

eau de toilette l'eau de toilette **f**
EC CE **f [say uh]**
economy class la classe économique **[klass aykonomeek]**
egg l'œuf **m [urf]**
eggplant l'aubergine **f [obairjeen]**
either: either ... or ... soit ... soit ... **[swa]**
either of them soit l'un soit l'autre
elastic l'élastique **m [aylasteek]**
elastic band l'élastique **m**
elbow le coude **[kood]**
electric électrique **[aylektreek]**
electrical appliances les appareils électriques **mpl [aparay]**
electric fire le radiateur électrique **[rad-yaturr]**
electrician l'électricien **m [aylektreess-yAN]**
electricity l'électricité **f [aylektreesseetay]**
see **voltage**
elevator l'ascenseur **m**

[asONsurr]
else: something else autre chose [ohtr shohz]
somewhere else ailleurs [ī-yurr]

dialogue

would you like anything else? désirez-vous autre chose?
no, nothing else, thanks non, c'est tout, merci [say too]

embassy l'ambassade **f** [ONbasad]
emergency l'urgence **f** [oorjONss]
this is an emergency! c'est une urgence! [sayt oon]
emergency exit la sortie de secours [sortee duh suhkoor]
empty vide [veed]
end la fin [fAN]
(verb) finir [feeneer]
at the end of the street au bout de la rue [o boo duh la roo]
when does it end? quand est-ce que ça finit? [kONteskuh sa feenee]
engaged (toilet, telephone) occupé [okoopay]
(to be married) fiancé [f-yONsay]
engine (car) le moteur [moturr]
England l'Angleterre **f** [ONgluhtair]
English anglais [ONglay]
I'm English (man/woman) je suis anglais/anglaise [-ez]
do you speak English? parlez-vous l'anglais? [parlay voo]
enjoy: to enjoy oneself s'amuser [samoozay]

dialogue

how did you like the film? comment as-tu trouvé le film? [komON atoo troovay]
I enjoyed it very much j'ai beaucoup aimé [jay bo-koo paymay]

enjoyable très agréable [tray zagrayabl]
enlargement (of photo) l'agrandissement **m** [agrONdeesmON]
enormous énorme [aynorm]
enough assez [assay]
there's not enough il n'y a pas assez [eel nya pa]
it's not big enough ce n'est pas assez grand
that's enough ça suffit [sa soofee]
entrance l'entrée **f** [ONtray]
envelope l'enveloppe **f** [ONvlop]
epileptic épileptique [aypeelepteek]
equipment (for climbing etc) l'équipement **m** [aykeepmON]
error l'erreur **f** [air-rurr]

especially spécialement [spays-yalmON]
essential essentiel [aysONs-yel]
it is essential that ... il est essentiel que ...
EU (European Union) l'Union Européenne **f** [oon-yON urropay-en]
euro l'euro **m** [urro]
Eurocheque l'Eurochèque **m** [urroshek]
Eurocheque card la carte Eurochèque [kart]
Europe l'Europe **f** [urrop]
European européen(ne) [urropay-AN, -en]
even même [mem]
evening le soir [swahr]
this evening ce soir
in the evening le soir
evening meal le repas du soir [ruhpa]
eventually finalement [feenalmON]
ever jamais [jamay]

dialogue

have you ever been to Cannes? est-ce que vous êtes déjà allé à Cannes? [eskuh voo zet dayja alay a]
yes, I was there two years ago oui, j'y suis allé il y a deux ans

every chaque [shak]
every day chaque jour
everyone tout le monde [too luh mONd]
everything tout [too]
everywhere partout [partoo]
exactly! exactement! [exaktuhmON]
exam l'examen **m** [examAN]
example l'exemple **m** [exONpl]
for example par exemple
excellent excellent [exsaylON]
excellent! parfait! [parfay]
except sauf [sohf]
excess baggage l'excédent de bagages **m** [exsaydON duh bagahj]
exchange rate le cours du change [koor doo shONj]
exciting passionnant [pass-yonON]
excuse me (to get past, to get attention) pardon [par-dON] (to say sorry) excusez-moi, pardon
exhaust (pipe) le tuyau d'échappement [twee-o dayshapmON]
exhausted (tired) épuisé [aypweezay]
exhibition l'exposition **f** [expozeess-yON]
exit la sortie [sortee]
where's the nearest exit? où se trouve la sortie la plus proche?
expect attendre [atONdr]
expensive cher [shair]
experienced expérimenté [expayreemONtay]
explain expliquer [expleekay]
can you explain that?

pouvez-vous expliquer cela? [poovay-voo]
express (mail) par exprès [express]
(train) express
extension le poste [posst]
extension 21, please poste vingt-et-un, s'il vous plaît
extension lead la rallonge [ralONj]
extra: can we have an extra one? pouvons-nous en avoir un/une supplémentaire? [poovON-noo zON avwahr AN/oon sooplaymONtair]
do you charge extra for that? est-ce qu'il faut payer un supplément pour ça? [eskeel fo pay-ay AN sooplaymON poor sa]
extraordinary (strange) extraordinaire
extremely extrêmement [extrem-mON]
eye l'œil **m** [uh-ee]
will you keep an eye on my suitcase for me? est-ce que vous pouvez surveiller ma valise? [eskuh voo poovay soorvay-ay]
eyebrow pencil le crayon à sourcils [soorsee]
eye drops les gouttes pour les yeux [goot poor lay z-juh]
eyeglasses les lunettes [loonet]
eyeliner l'eye-liner **m**
eye make-up remover le démaquillant pour les yeux [daymalee-yON]
eye shadow l'ombre à paupière **f** [ONbr a pohp-yair]

F

face le visage [veezahj]
factory l'usine **f** [oozeen]
Fahrenheit* fahrenheit [faren-ī-t]
faint s'évanouir [sayvanweer]
she's fainted elle s'est évanouie [el set ayvanwee]
I feel faint je me sens mal [juh muh sON]
fair la foire [fwahr]
(adj) juste [joost]
fairly (quite) assez [assay]
fake le faux [fo]
fall l'automne **m** [oton]
see **autumn**
fall (verb) tomber [tONbay]
she's had a fall elle est tombée [eel ay tONbay]
false faux, **f** fausse [fo, fohss]
family la famille [famee]
famous célèbre [saylebr]
fan (electrical) le ventilateur [vONteelaturr]
(hand held) l'éventail **m** [ayvONt-ī]
(sports) le/la fan [fan]
fan belt la courroie du ventilateur [koorwa doo]
fantastic fantastique [fONtasteek]
far loin [lwAN]

dialogue

is it far from here? c'est loin d'ici? [say lwAN dee-see]
no, not very far non, pas très loin
it's about 20 kilometres c'est à vingt kilomètres environ [ONveerON]

fare le prix (du billet) [pree (doo beeyay)]
farm la ferme [fairm]
fashionable à la mode [mod]
fast rapide [rapeed]
fat (person) gros, **f** grosse [gro, gross]
(on meat) le gras [gra]
father le père [pair]
father-in-law le beau-père [bo-pair]
faucet le robinet [robeenay]
fault le défaut [dayfo]
sorry, it was my fault désolé, c'est de ma faute [say duh ma foht]
it's not my fault ce n'est pas de ma faute
faulty (equipment) défectueux [dayfektoo-uh]
favourite préféré [prayfay-ray]
fax le fax
(verb) (person) envoyer un fax à [ONvwy-ay]
(document) faxer [faxay]
February février [fayvree-ay]
feel sentir [sONteer]
I feel hot j'ai chaud [jay sho]
I feel unwell je ne me sens pas bien [juh nuh muh sON pa b-yAN]
I feel like going for a walk j'ai envie d'aller me promener [jay ONvee]
how are you feeling? comment te sens-tu/vous sentez-vous? [komON tuh sON-too/voo sONtay-voo]
I'm feeling better je me sens mieux [juh muh sON m-yuh]
felt-tip pen le stylo-feutre [steelo-furtr]
fence la barrière [baree-air]
fender le pare-chocs [par-shok]
ferry le ferry
festival le festival [festeeval]
fetch aller chercher [alay shairshay]
I'll fetch him j'irai le chercher [jeeray]
will you come and fetch me later? est-ce que tu peux/vous pouvez venir me chercher plus tard? [eskuh too puh/voo poovay vuh-neer muh]
feverish fiévreux [fee-evruh]
few: a few quelques-uns, quelques-unes [kelkuh-zAN, kelkuh-zoon]
a few days quelques jours
fiancé le fiancé [fee-ONsay]
fiancée la fiancée [fee-ONsay]
field le champ [shON]
fight la bagarre [bagar]
fill remplir [rONpleer]
fill in remplir [rONpleer]

do I have to fill this in? est-ce que je dois remplir ceci? [eskuh juh dwa]
fill up remplir [rONpleer]
fill it up, please le plein, s'il vous plaît [luh plAN]
filling (in cake, sandwich) la garniture
(in tooth) le plombage [plONbahj]
film (movie) le film [feelm]
(for camera) la pellicule [peleekOOl]

dialogue

do you have this kind of film? avez-vous ce genre de pellicule? [avay-voo]
yes, how many exposures? oui, avec combien de poses? [kONb-yAN duh pohz]
36 trente-six

film processing le développement de la pellicule [dayv-lopmON]
filter coffee le café filtre [feeltr]
filter papers les filtres **mpl**
filthy crasseux [krassuh]
find trouver [troovay]
I can't find it je n'arrive pas à le retrouver [juh nareev pa a luh ruh-]
I've found it je l'ai trouvé [lay troovay]
find out découvrir [daykoovreer]
could you find out for me? pourriez-vous vous renseigner pour moi? [pooree-ay-voo voo rONsen-yay poor mwa]
fine (weather) beau [bo]
(punishment) l'amende **f** [amOND]

dialogues

how are you? comment vas-tu/allez-vous? [komON vatOO/alay-voo]
I'm fine thanks bien, merci [b-yAN]
and you? et toi/vous? [twa]

is that OK? est-ce que ça ira? [eskuh sa eera]
that's fine thanks ça ira très bien comme cela, merci [tray b-yAN kom suhla]

finger le doigt [dwa]
finish terminer [tairmeenay]
I haven't finished yet je n'ai pas encore terminé [juh nay pa zONkor tairmeenay]
when does it finish? à quelle heure est-ce que ça finit? [a kel urr eskuh sa feenee]
fire le feu [fuh]
can we light a fire here? pouvons-nous faire du feu ici? [poovON-noo fair dOO]
it's on fire il a pris feu [eel a pree]

fire alarm l'avertisseur d'incendie **m** [avairteessurr dANSONdee]
fire brigade les pompiers [pONp-yay]

In the event of a fire, phone 18.

fire escape la sortie de secours [sortee duh suhkoor]
fire extinguisher l'extincteur **m** [extANKturr]
first premier [pruhm-yay]
I was first je suis arrivé avant vous [juh sweez areevay avON voo]
at first tout d'abord [too dabor]
the first time la première fois [pruhm-yair fwa]
first on the left la première à gauche
first aid les premiers secours [pruhm-yay suhkoor]
first aid kit la trousse de premiers secours [trooss duh]
first class (compartment etc) de première (classe) [duh pruhm-yair klass]
first floor le premier [pruhm-yay]
(US) le rez-de-chaussée [rayd-shoh-say]
first name le prénom [praynON]
fish le poisson [pwassON]
fishing village le village de pêcheurs [veelahj duh peshurr]
fishmonger's la poissonnerie [pwassonnuh-ree]
fit (attack) l'attaque **f** [atak]
(verb) **it doesn't fit me** ce n'est pas la bonne taille [suh nay pa la bon tī]
fitting room la cabine d'essayage [kabeen dessay-ahj]
fix réparer [rayparay]
can you fix this? pouvez-vous réparer ceci? [poovay-voo]
fizzy gazeux [gazuh]
flag le drapeau [drapo]
flannel le gant de toilette [gON duh twalet]
flash (for camera) le flash
flat (apartment) l'appartement **m** [apartmON]
(adj) plat [pla]
I've got a flat tyre j'ai un pneu à plat [jay un pnuh]
flavour l'arôme **m** [arohm]
flea la puce [pooss]
flight le vol
flight number le numéro de vol [noomay-ro]
flippers les palmes **fpl** [pal-m]
flood l'inondation **f** [eenONdass-yON]
floor (of room) le plancher [plONshay]
(storey) l'étage **m** [aytahj]
on the floor par terre [tair]
florist le/la fleuriste [flurreest]
flour la farine [fareen]
flower la fleur [flurr]
flu la grippe [greep]
fluent: he speaks fluent

French il parle couramment le français [kooramON]
fly la mouche [moosh]
(verb) voler [volay]
fly in arriver en avion [arrevay en av-yON]
fly out partir en avion [parteer]
fog le brouillard [broo-yar]
foggy: it's foggy il y a du brouillard [eelya doo broo-yar]
folk dancing les danses folkloriques [dONss]
folk music la musique folklorique [moozeek]
follow suivre [sweevr]
follow me suivez-moi [sweevay-mwa]
food la nourriture [nooreetoor]
food poisoning l'intoxication alimentaire **f** [ANtoxeekass-yON aleemONtair]
food shop/store le magasin d'alimentation [magazAN daleemONtass-yON]
foot* le pied [p-yay]
on foot à pied
football (game) le football
(ball) le ballon de football [balON]
football match le match de football
for pour [poor]
do you have something for ...? (headache/diarrhoea etc) avez-vous quelque chose contre ...? [avay-voo kelkuh-shohz KONtr]

dialogues

who's the chocolate mousse for? la mousse au chocolat, c'est pour qui?
that's for me c'est pour moi [mwa]
and this one? et l'autre?
that's for her c'est pour elle

where do I get the bus for Gare de l'Est? où dois-je prendre le bus pour aller à la gare de l'Est? [oo dwaj prONdr luh booss poor alay]
the bus for Gare de l'Est leaves from rue de Rivoli le bus qui va à la gare de l'Est part de la rue de Rivoli

how long have you been here? ça fait combien de temps que vous êtes ici? [sa fay KONb-yAN duh tON kuh voo zet ee-see]
I've been here for two days, how about you? je suis ici depuis deux jours, et vous? [juh swee zee-see duhpwee]
I've been here for a week je suis ici depuis une semaine

forehead le front [frON]
foreign étranger [aytrONjay]
foreigner l'étranger **m**,

l'étrangère **f** [aytrONjay, -jair]
forest la forêt [foray]
forget oublier [ooblee-ay]
I forget, I've forgotten j'ai oublié [jay ooblee-ay]
fork (for eating) la fourchette [foorshet]
(in road) l'embranchement **m** [ONbrONshmON]
form (document) le formulaire
formal dress la tenue de soirée [tuhnoo duh swahray]
fortnight la quinzaine [kANzen]
fortunately heureusement [urrurzmON]
forward: could you forward my mail? est-ce que vous pouvez faire suivre mon courrier? [eskuh voo poovay fair sweevr mON koor-yay]
forwarding address l'adresse pour faire suivre le courrier **f**
foundation cream le fond de teint [fON duh tAN]
fountain la fontaine [fONten]
foyer (of hotel) le hall [awl]
(of theatre) le foyer
fracture la fracture [fraktoor]
France la France [frONss]
free libre [leebr]
(no charge) gratuit [gratwee]
is it free (of charge)? est-ce que c'est gratuit? [eskuh say]
freeway l'autoroute **f** [otoroot]
freezer le congélateur [kONjaylaturr]
French français, **f** française [frONsay, -ez]
French fries les frites **fpl** [freet]
Frenchman le Français [frONsay]
Frenchwoman la Française [frONsez]
frequent fréquent [fraykON]
how frequent is the bus to Marseilles? à quels intervalles y a-t-il un bus pour Marseille? [a kel ANtairval yateel]
fresh frais, **f** fraîche [fray, fresh]
fresh orange l'orange pressée **f** [orONj pressay]
Friday vendredi [vONdruhdee]
fridge le frigo [freego]
fried frit [free]
fried egg l'œuf sur le plat **m** [urf soor luh pla]
friend l'ami **m**, l'amie **f** [amee]
friendly amical [ameekal]
from de [duh]
when does the next train from Lyons arrive? à quelle heure arrive le prochain train en provenance de Lyon? [ON provuhnONss]
from Monday to Friday du lundi au vendredi [doo ... o]
from next Thursday à partir de jeudi prochain [a parteer]

dialogue

where are you from? d'où es-tu/êtes-vous? [doo ay-too/et-voo]
I'm from Slough je suis de Slough [juh swee]

front l'avant **m** [avON]
in front devant [duhvON]
in front of the hotel devant l'hôtel
at the front à l'avant
frost le gel [jel]
frozen gelé [juhlay]
frozen food les aliments surgelés [aleemON sOOrjuhlay]
fruit les fruits **mpl** [frwee]
fruit juice le jus de fruit [joo duh frwee]
fry frire [freer]
frying pan la poêle [pwal]
full plein [plAN]
it's full of ... c'est plein de ...
I'm full j'ai trop mangé [jay tro mONjay]
full board la pension complète [pONs-yON kONplet]
fun: it was fun on s'est bien amusé [ON say b-yAN amOOzay]
funny (strange, amusing) drôle
furniture les meubles **mpl** [murbl]
further plus loin [ploo lwAN]
it's further down the road c'est plus loin sur cette route [root]

dialogue

how much further is it to Figeac? il y a encore combien de kilomètres pour arriver à Figeac? [eelya ONkor kONb-yAN duh keelometr]
about 5 kilometres environ cinq kilomètres [ONveerON]

fuse le fusible [foozeebl]
the lights have fused les plombs ont sauté [lay plON ON sohtay]
fuse box la boîte à fusibles [bwat]
fuse wire le fusible
future le futur [footoor]
in future à l'avenir [a lavneer]

G

gallon* le gallon [galON]
game (cards etc) le jeu [juh]
(match) la partie [partee]
(meat) le gibier [jeeb-yay]
garage (for fuel) la station d'essence [stass-yON dessONss]
(for repairs, parking) le garage [garahj]

Although motorway and big city garages are open 24 hours seven days a week, those situated on smaller roads and in small towns usually close all day Sunday and at 7.30-8 p.m. on other days. Nowadays, most garages are self-service – only in smaller garages will the pump assistant fill the tank for you or clean the windscreen and check the water, oil and tyres.

garden le jardin [jardAN]
garlic l'ail **m** [ī]
gas le gaz
(US) l'essence **f** [essONss]
gas cylinder (camping gas) la bouteille de gaz [bootay]
gasoline (US) l'essence **f** [essONss]
see **petrol**
gas permeable lenses les lentilles semi-rigides **fpl** [lontee suhmee-reejeed]
gas station la station-service [stass-yON-sairveess]
gate le portail [port-ī]
(at airport) la porte [port]
gay homosexuel
gay bar le bar d'homosexuels
gears les vitesses **fpl** [veetess]
gearbox la boîte de vitesses [bwat]
gear lever le levier de vitesses [luhv-yay]
general (adj) général [jaynay-ral]
Geneva Genève [juhnev]
gents (toilet) les toilettes pour hommes [twalet poor om]
genuine (antique etc) authentique [otONteek]
German allemand [almON]
German measles la rubéole [rOObay-ol]
Germany l'Allemagne **f** [almañ]
get (fetch) obtenir [obtuhneer]
will you get me another one, please? est-ce que vous pouvez m'en apporter un autre, s'il vous plaît? [eskuh voo poovay mON aportay AN ohtr]
how do I get to ...? pouvez-vous m'indiquer comment aller à ...? [poovay-voo mANdeekay komON talay]
do you know where I can get them? est-ce que vous savez où je peux en trouver? [eskuh voo savay oo juh puh zON troovay]

dialogue

can I get you a drink? puis-je t'offrir/vous offrir un verre? [pweej tofreer ...]
no, I'll get this one, what would you like? non, celui-là c'est pour moi, que voudrais-tu/voudriez-vous? [suhlwee-la say poor mwa]
a glass of red wine un verre de vin rouge

get back (return) rentrer [rONtray]

get in (arrive) arriver [areevay]
get off descendre [duhsONdr]
where do I get off? où dois-je descendre? [oo dwaj]
get on (to train etc) monter [mONtay]
get out (of car etc) descendre [duhsONdr]
get up (in the morning, stand up) se lever [suh luhvay]
gift le cadeau [kado]
gift shop la boutique de cadeaux
gin le gin [djeen]
a gin and tonic, please un gin-tonic, s'il vous plaît
girl la fille [fee]
girlfriend la petite amie [puhteet amee]
give donner [donay]
can you give me some change? pouvez-vous me donner de la monnaie? [poovay-voo]
I gave it to him je le lui ai donné [juh luh lwee ay donay]
will you give this to ...? pouvez-vous donner ceci à ...?

dialogue

how much do you want for this? combien en voulez-vous? [kONb-yAN ON voolay-voo]
100 francs cent francs
I'll give you 90 francs je vous en donne 90 francs [juh voo zON don]

give back rendre [rONdr]
glad content [kONtON]
glass le verre [vair]
a glass of wine un verre de vin
glasses (spectacles) les lunettes [loonet]
gloves les gants **mpl** [gON]
glue la colle [kol]
go aller [alay]
we'd like to go to the cathedral nous aimerions aller à la cathédrale [noo zemree-ON alay a]
where are you going? où vas-tu/allez-vous? [oo vatoo/alay voo]
where does this bus go? où va ce bus?
let's go! allons-y! [alONzee]
she's gone (left) elle est partie [partee]
where has he gone? où est-il allé? [alay]
I went there last week j'y suis allé la semaine dernière
hamburger to go hamburger à emporter [ONportay]
go away partir [parteer]
go away! va t'en!/allez-vous-en! [vatON/alay-voo-zON]
go back (return) retourner [ruhtoornay]
go down descendre [duhsONdr]
(price) baisser [bessay]
go in entrer [ONtray]
go out (in the evening) sortir [sorteer]
do you want to go out

tonight? veux-tu/voulez-vous sortir ce soir? [vuh-too/voolay-voo]
go through traverser [travairsay]
go up monter [mONtay]
goat la chèvre [shevr]
goat's cheese le fromage de chèvre [fromahj]
God Dieu [d-yuh]
goggles (ski) les lunettes de ski [loonet]
gold l'or **m**
golf le golf
golf course le terrain de golf [terrAN]
good bon, **f** bonne [bON, bon]
good! bien! [b-yAN]
it's no good ça ne va pas [sa nuh va pa]
goodbye au revoir [o ruh-vwa]
good evening bonsoir [bON-swa]
Good Friday le Vendredi Saint [vONdruhdee sAN]
good morning bonjour [bON-joor]
good night bonne nuit [bon nwee]
goose l'oie **f** [wa]
got: we've got to leave il faut que nous partions [eel fo kuh]
I've got to ... il faut que je ...
have you got any ...? est-ce que tu as/vous avez des/du ...? [eskuh too a/voo zavay ...]
government le gouvernement [goovairnuhmON]
gradually peu à peu [puh a puh]
grammar la grammaire
gram(me) le gramme
granddaughter la petite-fille [puhteet-fee]
grandfather le grand-père [grON-pair]
grandmother la grand-mère [grON-mair]
grandson le petit-fils [puhtee-feess]
grapefruit le pamplemousse [pONpluh-mooss]
grapefruit juice le jus de pamplemousse [joo]
grapes le raisin [rez-AN]
grass l'herbe **f** [airb]
grateful reconnaissant [ruhkonessON]
gravy la sauce au jus de viande [sohss o joo duh vee-ONd]
great (excellent) fantastique [fONtasteek]
that's great! c'est formidable! [say formee-dabl]
a great success un grand succès [grON sook-say]
Great Britain la Grande-Bretagne [grONd-bruhtañ]
Greece la Grèce [gress]
greedy gourmand [goormON]
Greek grec
green vert [vair]
green card (car insurance) la carte verte [kart vairt]
greengrocer's le marchand de légumes [marshON duh

laygoom]
grey gris [gree]
grill le grill
grilled grillé [gree-yay]
grocer's l'épicerie **f** [aypeesree]
ground le sol
on the ground par terre [tair]
ground floor le rez-de-chaussée [rayd-shoh-say]
group le groupe [groop]
guarantee la garantie [garONtee]
is it guaranteed? y a-t-il une garantie? [yateel]
guest l'invité(e) [ANveetay]
guesthouse la pension [pONs-yON]
see **hotel**
guide le guide [geed]
guidebook le guide
guided tour la visite guidée [veezeet geeday]
guitar la guitare [geetar]
gum (in mouth) la gencive [jONseev]
gun le fusil [foozee]
gym le gymnase [jeemnaz]

H

hair les cheveux **mpl** [shuhvuh]
hairbrush la brosse à cheveux [bross]
haircut la coupe de cheveux [koop]
hairdresser le coiffeur [kwafurr]
hairdryer le sèche-cheveux [sesh-shuhvuh]
hair gel le gel (pour les cheveux) [jel]
hairgrips les pinces à cheveux **fpl** [pANss]
hair spray la laque [lak]
half* la moitié [mwatee-ay]
half an hour une demi-heure [duhmee-urr]
half a litre un demi-litre
about half that la moitié
half board la demi-pension [duhmee-pONs-yON]
half-bottle la demi bouteille [bootay]
half fare le demi-tarif [tareef]
half price moitié prix [mwatee-ay pree]
ham le jambon [jONbON]
hamburger le hamburger [ONboorgair]
hammer le marteau [marto]
hand la main [mAN]
handbag le sac à main
handbrake le frein à main [frAN]
handkerchief le mouchoir [mooshwahr]
handle la poignée [pwAN-yay]
hand luggage les bagages à main **mpl** [bagahj]
hang-gliding le deltaplane [-plahn]
hangover la gueule de bois [gurl duh bwa]
I've got a hangover j'ai la gueule de bois

happen arriver [areevay]
what's happening? qu'est-ce qui se passe? [kes-kee suh pass]
what has happened? qu'est-ce qui s'est passé? [say passay]
happy heureux [ur-ruh]
I'm not happy about this ça ne me plaît pas [sa nuh muh play pa]
harbour le port [por]
hard dur [door]
(difficult) difficile [deefeesseel]
hard-boiled egg l'œuf dur **m** [urf]
hard lenses les lentilles dures **fpl** [lONtee door]
hardly à peine [a pen]
hardly ever presque jamais [presk jamay]
hardware shop la quincaillerie [kAN-ky-ree]
hat le chapeau [shapo]
hate détester [daytestay]
have* avoir [avwahr]
can I have a ...? j'aimerais ... [jemray]
do you have ...? as-tu/avez-vous ...? [atoo/avay-voo]
what'll you have? qu'est-ce que tu prends/vous prenez? [keskuh too prON/voo pruhnay]
I have to leave now je dois partir maintenant [juh dwa]
do I have to ...? est-ce que je dois ...? [eskuh]
can we have some ...? est-ce que nous pouvons avoir du ...?
we don't have any left nous n'en avons plus [noo nON avON ploo]
hayfever le rhume des foins [room day fwAN]
hazelnuts les noisettes **fpl** [nwazet]
he* il [eel]
head la tête [tet]
headache le mal de tête
headlights les phares **mpl** [far]
headphones les écouteurs **mpl** [aykooturr]
health food shop le magasin de produits diététiques **m** [magazAN duh prodwee dee-aytayteek]
healthy (food, climate) bon pour la santé [sONtay]
(person) bien portant [b-yAN portON]
hear entendre [ONtONdr]

dialogue

can you hear me? m'entendez-vous? [mONtONday-voo]
I can't hear you, could you repeat that? je ne vous entends pas, pouvez-vous répéter? [juh nuh voo zONtON pa poovay-voo raypaytay]

hearing aid l'audiophone **m** [odeeo-fon]
heart le cœur [kurr]
heart attack la crise

cardiaque [kreez kard-yak]
heat la chaleur [shalurr]
heater (in room) le radiateur [rad-yaturr]
(in car) le chauffage [shohfahj]
heating le chauffage
heavy lourd [loor]
heel le talon [talON]
could you heel these? pouvez-vous refaire les talons? [poovay-voo ruhfair]
heelbar le talon-minute [talON-meenoot]
height (of person) la taille [tī]
(of mountain) l'altitude **f**
helicopter l'hélicoptère **m** [ayleekoptair]
hello bonjour [bONjoor]
(in the evening) bonsoir [bONswahr]
(answer on phone) allô
helmet (for motorcycle) le casque [kask]
help l'aide **f** [ed]
(verb) aider [ayday]
help! au secours! [o suhkoor]
can you help me? est-ce que vous pouvez m'aider? [eskuh voo poovay]
thank you very much for your help merci de votre aide
helpful (person) serviable [sairvee-abl]
(objects) utile [ooteel]
hepatitis l'hépatite **f** [aypateet]
her*: I haven't seen her je ne l'ai pas vue
to her à elle [el]
for/with her pour/avec elle
that's her c'est elle
her towel sa serviette
herbal tea la tisane [teezahn]
herbs les fines herbes **fpl** [feen zairb]
here ici [ee-see]
here is/are ... voici ... [vwa-see]
here you are (offering) voilà [vwala]
hers*: that's hers c'est à elle [set a el]
hey! hé! [hay]
hi! (hello) salut! [saloo]
hide cacher [kashay]
high haut [o]
highchair la chaise haute [shez oht]
highway l'autoroute **f** [otoroot]
hill la colline [koleen]
him*: I haven't seen him je ne l'ai pas vu
to him à lui [lwee]
with him avec lui
for him pour lui
that's him c'est lui
hip la hanche [ONsh]
hire: for hire à louer [loo-ay]
(verb) louer
where can I hire a bike? où y a-t-il des vélos à louer? [oo yateel]
see also **rent**
his*: it's his car c'est sa voiture
it's his bike c'est son vélo [sON]
that's his c'est à lui [set a lwee]

hit frapper **[frapay]**
hitch-hike faire de l'autostop **[fair duh lotostop]**
hobby le hobby **[obbee]**
hockey le hockey **[ockee]**
hold tenir **[tuhneer]**
hole le trou **[troo]**
holiday les vacances **fpl** **[vakONss]**
on holiday en vacances **[ON]**
Holland la Hollande **[ollONd]**
home la maison **[mezzON]**
at home (in my house etc) chez moi **[shay mwa]**
(in my country) dans mon pays **[dON mON payee]**
we go home tomorrow nous rentrons demain **[rONtrON duhmAN]**
honest honnête **[onnet]**
honey le miel **[mee-el]**
honeymoon la lune de miel **[loon]**
hood (US) le capot **[kapo]**
hope espérer **[espayray]**
I hope so j'espère que oui **[jespair kuh wee]**
I hope not j'espère que non
hopefully: hopefully he'll arrive soon espérons qu'il arrive bientôt **[espairON]**
horn (of car) le klaxon
horrible horrible **[oreebl]**
horse le cheval **[shuhval]**
horse riding l'équitation **f** **[aykeetass-yON]**
hospital l'hôpital **m** **[opee-tal]**
hospitality l'hospitalité **f** **[-eetay]**
thank you for your hospitality merci de votre hospitalité

If you are invited to someone's home, you can take a bunch of flowers (but not chrysanthemums which are used in cemeteries) or a plant, or a box of chocolates. Unlike in the UK, it is not very common to take a bottle of wine as a present when invited for a meal. If you are staying at someone's house, you may want to take presents such as whisky, tea, etc.

hot chaud **[sho]**
(spicy) épicé **[aypeessay]**
I'm hot j'ai chaud **[jay]**
it's hot today il fait chaud aujourd'hui **[eel fay]**
hotel l'hôtel **m** **[otel]**

Most French hotels are graded from zero to five stars. The price more or less corresponds to the number of stars, although the system is a little haphazard. Ungraded and single-star hotels are often very good. Remember that the price displayed is the price for the room only, excluding breakfast. In rural areas, you'll also find **chambres d'hôte** – bed and breakfast accommodation in someone's house or farm. These vary in standard but are rarely an inexpensive option. If you are planning to stay a week or more in any one place it might be worth considering renting accommodation (**gîte**). You can do this by checking adverts in British Sunday newspapers or trying one of the numerous holiday firms that market accommodation/travel packages. It's easier, however, to use the London office of the official French government service **Gîtes de France**.

hotel room: in my hotel room dans ma chambre d'hôtel [shONbr]
hour l'heure **f** [urr]
house la maison [mezzON]
house wine la cuvée du patron [koovay doo]

In most restaurants, **le vin maison** will be a good-value quality wine. You can ask for **une carafe** (4-5 glasses) or **une demi-carafe** (2-3 glasses).

hovercraft l'aéroglisseur **m** [a-ayro-gleessurr]
how comment [komON]
how many? combien? [kONb-yAN]
how do you do? enchanté! [ONshONtay]

dialogues

how are you? comment vas-tu/allez-vous? [komON va-too/alay-voo]
fine, thanks, and you? bien, merci, et toi/vous? [twa]

how much is it? c'est combien?
... francs ... francs
I'll take it je le prends [juh luh prON]

humid humide [oomeed]
humour l'humour **m** [oomoor]
hungry: I'm hungry j'ai faim [jay fAN]
are you hungry? est-ce que tu as/vous avez faim? [eskuh too a/voo zavay]
hurry se dépêcher [suh daypeshay]
I'm in a hurry je suis pressé [juh swee pressay]
there's no hurry ce n'est pas pressé [suh nay pa]
hurry up! dépêche-toi!/dépêchez-vous! [daypesh-twa/daypeshay-voo]
hurt faire mal
it really hurts ça fait vraiment mal [sa fay vraymON]
husband le mari [maree]
hydrofoil l'hydrofoil **m** [eedro-]
hypermarket l'hypermarché **m** [eepairmarshay]

I

I je [juh]
ice la glace [glass]
with ice avec des glaçons [glassON]
no ice, thanks pas de glaçons, merci
ice cream la glace [glass]
ice-cream cone le cornet de glace [kornay]
iced coffee le café glacé [glassay]
ice lolly l'esquimau **m** [eskeemo]
ice rink la patinoire [pateenwahr]
ice skates les patins à glace **mpl** [patAN a glass]
idea l'idée **f** [eeday]
idiot l'idiot **m** [eedee-o]
if si [see]
ignition l'allumage **m** [alσσmahj]
ill malade [malad]
I feel ill je ne me sens pas bien [juh nuh muh sON pa b-yAN]
illness la maladie [maladee]
imitation (leather etc) l'imitation **f** [eemeetass-yON]
immediately immédiatement [eemaydee-atmON], tout de suite [toot sweet]
important important [ANportON]
it's very important c'est très important [say trayz]
it's not important ça ne fait rien [sa nuh fay ree-AN]
impossible impossible [ANposs-eebl]
impressive impressionnant [ANpress-yonON]
improve améliorer [amayleeoray]
I want to improve my French je veux améliorer mon français [juh vuh]
in: it's in the centre c'est au centre [o sONtr]
in my car dans ma voiture [dON]
in Dijon à Dijon
in two days from now d'ici deux jours
in May en mai [ON]
in English en anglais
in French en français
is he in? il est là? [eel ay la]
in five minutes dans cinq minutes
inch* le pouce [pooss]
include inclure [ANkloor]
does that include meals? est-ce que les repas sont compris? [eskuh lay ruhpa sON kONpree]
is that included? est-ce que c'est compris?
inconvenient inopportun [eenoportAN]
incredible (very good, amazing) incroyable [ANkrwy-abl]
Indian indien, **f** indienne [ANdee-AN, -en]
indicator (on car) le clignotant [kleen-yotON]

indigestion l'indigestion **f** [ANdeejest-yON]
indoor pool la piscine couverte [peesseen koovairt]
indoors à l'intérieur [lANtay-ree-urr]
inexpensive bon marché [bON marshay]
infection l'infection **f** [ANfex-yON]
infectious contagieux [kONtahj-yuh]
inflammation l'inflammation **f** [ANflamass-yON]
informal simple [sAN-pl]
information les renseignements **mpl** [rONsen-yuhmON]
 do you have any information about ...? est-ce que vous avez des renseignements sur ...? [eskuh voo zavay]
information desk les renseignements [rONsen-yuhmON]
injection la piqûre [pee-kOOr]
injured blessé [blessay]
 she's been injured elle est blessée
in-laws les beaux-parents [bo-parON]
inner tube la chambre à air [shONbr]
innocent innocent [eenosON]
insect l'insecte **m** [ANsekt]
insect bite la piqûre d'insecte [peekOOr]
 do you have anything for insect bites? est-ce que vous avez quelque chose contre les piqûres d'insecte? [eskuh voo zavay kelkuh shohz]
insect repellent la crème anti-insecte [krem ONtee-ANsekt]
inside à l'intérieur [lANtayree-urr]
 inside the hotel dans l'hôtel [dON]
 let's sit inside allons nous asseoir à l'intérieur
insist insister [ANseestay]
 I insist j'insiste [jANseest]
insomnia l'insomnie **f** [ANsomnee]
instant coffee le café soluble [solOObl]
instead à la place [plass]
 give me that one instead donnez-moi celui-ci à la place [donay-mwa suhlwee-see]
 instead of ... au lieu de ... [o l-yuh duh]
insulin l'insuline **f** [ANsOOleen]
insurance l'assurance **f** [assOOrONss]
intelligent intelligent [ANtayleejON]
interested: I'm interested in ... je m'intéresse à ... [mANtay-ress]
interesting intéressant [ANtayressON]
 that's very interesting c'est très intéressant
international international [ANtairnass-yonal]
interpret faire l'interprète

[fair lANtairpret]
interpreter l'interprète **mf** [ANtairpret]
intersection le carrefour [karfoor]
interval (at theatre) l'entracte **m** [ONtrakt]
into dans [dON]
I'm not into ... je n'aime pas ... [juh nem pa]
introduce présenter [prayzONtay]
may I introduce ...? puis-je vous présenter ...? [pweej voo]
invitation l'invitation **f** [ANveetass-yON]
invite inviter [ANveetay]
Ireland l'Irlande **f** [eerlONd]
Irish irlandais [eerlONday]
I'm Irish (man/woman) je suis irlandais/irlandaise [-ez]
iron (for ironing) le fer à repasser [fair a ruh-passay]
can you iron these for me? pouvez-vous me repasser ces vêtements? [vetmON]
is* est [ay]
island l'île **f** [eel]
it* ça [sa]; il [eel]; elle [el]
it is ... c'est ... [say]
is it ...? est-ce ...? [ess]
where is it? où est-ce que c'est? [weskuh say]
it's him c'est lui
it was ... c'était ... [saytay]
Italian italien [eetalyAN]
Italy l'Italie **f** [eetalee]
itch: it itches ça me démange [sa muh daymONj]

J

jack (for car) le cric [kreek]
jacket la veste [vest]
jar le pot [po]
jam la confiture [kONfeetoor]
jammed: it's jammed c'est coincé [say kwANsay]
January janvier [jONvee-ay]
jaw la mâchoire [mashwahr]
jazz le jazz
jealous jaloux [jaloo]
jeans le jean
jellyfish la méduse [maydooz]
jersey le tricot [treeko]
jetty la jetée [juhtay]
Jewish juif, **f** juive [jweef, jweev]
jeweller's la bijouterie [beejootuhree]
jewellery les bijoux [beejoo]
job le travail [trav-ī]
jogging le jogging
to go jogging faire du jogging [fair]
joke la plaisanterie [plezzONtree]
journey le voyage [vwy-ahj]
have a good journey! bon voyage!
jug le pot [po]
a jug of water une carafe d'eau [do]
juice le jus [joo]
July juillet [jwee-yay]
jump sauter [sohtay]

jumper le pull [pool]
jump leads les câbles de démarrage [kahbl duh daymarahj]
junction le croisement [krwazmON]
June juin [jwAN]
just (only) seul [surl]
just two seulement deux [surlmON]
just for me seulement pour moi [poor mwa]
just here juste ici [joost ee-see]
not just now pas maintenant [pa]
we've just arrived nous venons d'arriver [noo vuhnON dareevay]

K

keep garder [garday]
keep the change gardez la monnaie [garday la monay]
can I keep it? est-ce que je peux le garder? [eskuh juh puh]
please keep it gardez-le
ketchup le ketchup
kettle la bouilloire [boo-ee-wahr]
key la clé [klay]
the key for room 201, please la clé de la chambre deux cent un, s'il vous plaît
key ring le porte-clé [port-klay]
kidneys (in body) les reins mpl [rAN]
(food) les rognons mpl [rON-yON]
kill tuer [too-ay]
kilo* le kilo
kilometre* le kilomètre [keelo-metr]
how many kilometres is it to ...? combien y a-t-il de kilomètres pour aller à ...? [kONb-yAN yateel]
kind aimable [em-abl]
that's very kind c'est très aimable

dialogue

which kind do you want? de quel type voulez-vous?
I want this/that kind c'est de ce type que je veux

king le roi [rwa]
kiosk le kiosque
kiss le baiser [bezzay]
(verb) embrasser [ONbrassay]

It is customary to greet friends and relatives by kissing them on both cheeks. The exception to this is when men greet each other, when they generally shake hands instead. The number of kisses can be two or four depending on which region you are in.

kitchen la cuisine [kweezeen]

kitchenette le coin-cuisine [kwAN-kweezeen]
Kleenex® les kleenex **mpl**
knee le genou [juh-noo]
knickers le slip [sleep]
knife le couteau [kooto]
knitwear les tricots [treeko]
knock frapper [frapay]
knock down renverser [rONvairsay]
he's been knocked down il s'est fait renverser [eel say fay]
knock over renverser [rONvairsay]
know (somebody, a place) connaître [konetr]
(something) savoir [savwahr]
I don't know je ne sais pas [juh nuh say pa]
I didn't know that je ne savais pas [savay]
do you know where I can find ...? savez-vous où je peux trouver ...? [savay-voo]

L

label l'étiquette **f** [ayteeket]
ladies' (room) les toilettes (pour dames) [twalet poor dam]
ladies' wear les vêtements pour femmes [vetmON poor fam]
lady la dame [dam]
lager la bière [bee-air]
see **beer**
lake le lac
lamb l'agneau **m** [an-yo]
lamp la lampe [lONp]
lane (on motorway) la voie [vwa]
(small road) le chemin [shuhmAN]
language la langue [lONg]
language course le cours de langue [koor duh lONg]
large grand [grON]
last dernier [dairn-yay]
last week la semaine dernière [suhmen dairn-yair]
last Friday vendredi dernier
last night hier soir [yair swahr]
what time is the last train to Nancy? à quelle heure part le dernier train pour Nancy? [kel urr par]
late tard [tar]
sorry I'm late je suis désolé d'être en retard [juh swee dayzolay detr ON ruhtar]
the train was very late le train avait beaucoup de retard [avay bo-koo duh]
we'll be late nous allons arriver en retard [noo zalON areevay]
it's getting late il se fait tard [eel suh fay]
later plus tard [plOO tar]
I'll come back later je reviendrai plus tard [juh ruhvee-ANdray]
see you later à tout à l'heure [a toota lurr]
later on plus tard
latest dernier [dairn-yay]

by Wednesday at the latest d'ici mercredi au plus tard [o ploo tar]
laugh rire [reer]
launderette/ laundromat la laverie automatique [lavree otomateek]
laundry (clothes) le linge sale [lANj sal]
(place) la blanchisserie [blONsheesree]
lavatory les toilettes [twalet]
law la loi [lwa]
lawn la pelouse [puhlooz]
lawyer l'avocat **m** [avoka]
laxative le laxatif [laxateef]
lazy paresseux [paressuh]
lead (electrical) le fil (électrique) [feel aylektreek]
(verb) mener à [muhnay]
where does this lead to? où cette route mène-t-elle? [oo set root mentel]
leaf la feuille [fuh-ee]
leaflet le dépliant [daypleeON]
leak la fuite [fweet]
(verb) fuir [fweer]
the roof leaks il y a une fuite dans le toit [eelya]
learn apprendre [aprONdr]
least: not in the least pas du tout [pa doo too]
at least au moins [o mwAN]
leather le cuir [kweer]
leave (go away) partir [parteer]
I am leaving tomorrow je pars demain [juh par]
he left yesterday il est parti hier [eel ay partee]
when does the bus for Avignon leave? à quelle heure part le bus pour Avignon? [par]
may I leave this here? puis-je laisser ceci ici? [pweej lessay suhsee ee-see]
I left my coat in the bar j'ai oublié ma veste au bar [jay ooblee-ay]
leeks les poireaux **mpl** [pwahro]
left la gauche [gohsh]
on the left à gauche
to the left sur la gauche [soor]
turn left tournez à gauche
there's none left il n'y en a plus [eel n-yON a ploo]
left-handed gaucher [gohshay]
left luggage (office) la consigne [kONseeñ]
leg la jambe [jONb]
lemon le citron [seetrON]
lemonade la limonade [leemonad]
lemon tea le thé citron [tay seetrON]
lend prêter [pretay]
will you lend me your ...? pourrais-tu/pourriez-vous me prêter ton/votre ...? [pooray-too/pooree-ay-voo muh]
lens (of camera) l'objectif **m** [objekteef]
lesbian la lesbienne
less moins [mwAN]
less than moins que
less expensive moins cher

lesson la leçon [luhsON]
let laisser [lessay]
will you let me know? pouvez-vous me le faire savoir? [poovay-voo muh luh fair savwahr]
I'll let you know je te/vous préviendrai [juh tuh/voo prayvee-ANdray]
let's go for something to eat allons manger un morceau [alON mONjay]
let off laisser descendre [lessay duhsONdr]
will you let me off at ...? pouvez-vous me laisser descendre à ..., s'il vous plaît? [poovay-voo]
letter la lettre [letr]
do you have any letters for me? est-ce qu'il y a du courrier pour moi? [eskeel ya doo kooree-ay poor mwa]
letterbox la boite à lettres [bwat a letr]

Letterboxes in France are yellow. They usually have one slot for mail within the city or **département** you're in, and another one for **autres destinations** (for mail going everywhere else).

lettuce la laitue [letoo]
lever le levier [luhv-yay]
library la bibliothèque
licence le permis [pairmee]
lid le couvercle [koovairkl]
lie (tell untruth) mentir [mONteer]
lie down s'étendre [saytONdr]
life la vie [vee]
lifebelt la bouée de sauvetage [boo-ay duh sohvtahj]
lifeguard le maître nageur [metr nahjurr]
life jacket le gilet de sauvetage [jeelay duh sohvtahj]
lift (in building) l'ascenseur **m** [asONsurr]
could you give me a lift? pouvez-vous m'emmener? [poovay-voo mONmuhnay]
would you like a lift? est-ce que je peux vous déposer quelque part? [eskuh juh puh voo daypohzay kelkuh par]
lift pass le forfait de remonte-pente [forfay duh ruhmONt-pONt]
a daily/weekly lift pass un forfait de remonte-pente d'une journée/d'une semaine
light la lumière [loom-yair]
(not heavy) léger [lay-jay]
do you have a light? avez-vous du feu? [avay-voo doo fuh]
light green vert clair
light bulb l'ampoule **f** [ONpool]
lighter (cigarette) le briquet [breekay]
lightning les éclairs [ayklair]
like aimer [aymay]
I like it ça me plaît [sah muh play]
I like going for walks j'aime bien aller me promener

[jem b-yAN]
I like you tu me plais [tOO muh play]
I don't like it ça ne me plaît pas
do you like ...? est-ce que tu aimes/vous aimez ...? [tOO em/voo zaymay]
I'd like a beer je voudrais une bière [juh voodray]
I'd like to go swimming j'aimerais nager [jemray]
would you like a drink? veux-tu/voulez-vous boire quelque chose? [vuh-tOO/voolay-voo]
would you like to go for a walk? veux-tu/voulez-vous aller faire une promenade?
what's it like? comment est-ce? [komON ess]
one like this un comme ça [kom]
lime le citron vert [seetrON vair]
lime cordial le jus de citron vert [jOO]
line la ligne [leeñ]
could you give me an outside line? pouvez-vous me donner une ligne extérieure? [poovay-voo]
lip la lèvre [levr]
lip salve la pommade pour les lèvres [pomahd]
lipstick le rouge à lèvres [rooj]
liqueur la liqueur [leekurr]
listen écouter [aykootay]
litre* le litre [leetr]
a litre of white wine un litre de vin blanc
little peu [puh]
just a little, thanks un tout petit peu, s'il vous plaît [AN too puhtee puh]
a little milk un peu de lait
a little bit more un petit peu plus [plOOss]
live vivre [veevr]
we live together nous vivons ensemble [noo veevON zONsONbl]

dialogue

where do you live? où est-ce que tu habites/vous habitez? [weskuh tOO abeet/voo zabeetay]
I live in London je vis à Londres [vee]

lively vivant [veevON]
liver le foie [fwa]
loaf le pain [pAN]
lobby (in hotel) le hall [al]
lobster la langouste [lONgoost]
local local
a local wine/restaurant un vin de la région/un restaurant dans le quartier [duh la rayjON/... dON luh kart-yay]
lock la serrure [sair-rOOr]
(verb) fermer à clé [fairmay a klay]
it's locked c'est fermé à clé [fairmay]
lock in enfermer à clé

[ONfairmay]
lock out enfermer dehors [duh-or]
I've locked myself out je me suis enfermé dehors [juh muh swee ZONfairmay]
locker (for luggage etc) le casier [kaz-yay]
lollipop la sucette [sOOsset]
London Londres [lONdr]
long long, **f** longue [lON, lON-g]
how long will it take to fix it? combien de temps est-ce que ça prendra pour le réparer? [kONb-yAN duh tON]
how long does it take? combien de temps est-ce que ça prend? [eskuh sa prON]
a long time longtemps [lONtON]
one day/two days longer un jour/deux jours en plus [ON plOOss]
long-distance call l'appel longue-distance **m**
loo les toilettes [twalet]
look regarder [ruhgarday]
I'm just looking, thanks je ne fais que regarder, merci [juh nuh fay kuh]
you don't look well tu n'as pas l'air dans ton assiette [tOO na pa lair dON tON ass-yet]
look out! attention! [atONs-yON]
can I have a look? puis-je regarder? [pweej]
look after garder [garday]
look at regarder [ruhgarday]
look for chercher [shairshay]
I'm looking for ... je cherche ... [juh shairsh]
look forward to: I'm looking forward to it je m'en réjouis à l'avance [juh mON rayjwee a lavONss]
loose (handle etc) lâche [lahsh]
lorry le camion [kam-yON]
lose perdre [pairdr]
I've lost my way je suis perdu [juh swee pairdOO]
I'm lost, I want to get to ... je suis perdu, je voudrais aller à ...
I've lost my (hand)bag j'ai perdu mon sac à main [jay]
lost property (office) les objets trouvés [objay troovay]
lot: a lot, lots beaucoup [bo-koo]
not a lot pas beaucoup [pa]
a lot of people beaucoup de monde
a lot bigger beaucoup plus gros
I like it a lot ça me plaît beaucoup
lotion la lotion [lohss-yON]
loud fort [for]
lounge le salon
(in airport) la salle d'embarquement [sal dONbarkmON]
love l'amour **m** [amoor]
(verb) aimer [aymay]
I love Corsica j'aime la Corse [jem]
lovely (view, present etc)

ravissant [ravee-sON]
(meal) délicieux [dayleess-yuh]
(weather) magnifique [mAN-yeefeek]
low bas [ba]
luck la chance [shONss]
good luck! bonne chance! [bon]
luggage les bagages **mpl** [bagahj]
luggage trolley le chariot à bagages [sharee-o]
lump (on body) la grosseur [grossurr]
lunch le déjeuner [dayjuhnay]
lungs les poumons **mpl** [poomON]
Luxembourg le Luxembourg [lOOxONboor]
luxurious luxueux [lOOxOO-uh]
luxury le luxe [lOOx]

M

machine la machine
mad (insane) fou, **f** folle [foo, fol]
(angry) furieux [fOOree-uh]
magazine le magazine
maid (in hotel) la femme de chambre [fam duh shONbr]
maiden name le nom de jeune fille [nON duh jurn fee]
mail le courrier [kooree-ay]
(verb) poster [posstay]
is there any mail for me? est-ce qu'il y a du courrier pour moi? [eskeel ya dOO]
see **post**
mailbox la boite à lettres [bwat a letr]
see **letterbox**
main principal [prANseepal]
main course le plat principal [pla]
main post office la poste principale [posst]
main road (in town) la rue principale [rOO]
(in country) la grande route [grONd root]
mains switch le disjoncteur [deesjONkturr]
make (brand name) la marque [mark]
(verb) faire [fair]
I make it 500 francs d'après mes calculs, ça fait cinq cents francs [dapray may kalkOOl sa fay]
what is it made of? en quoi est-ce? [ON kwa ess]
make-up le maquillage [makee-ahj]
man l'homme **m** [om]
manager le patron [pa-trON]
can I see the manager? puis-je parler au patron? [pweej parlay o]
manageress la directrice [deerektreess]
manual (car) la voiture à embrayage manuel [vwatOOr a ONbrī-ahj mONOOel]
many beaucoup [bo-koo]
not many pas beaucoup [pa]
map (of city) le plan [plON]

(road map, geographical) la carte [kart]
March mars [marss]
margarine la margarine [marghareen]
market le marché [marshay]
marmalade la confiture d'oranges [kONfeetOOr dorONj]
married: I'm married je suis marié [juh swee maree-ay]
are you married? êtes-vous marié? [et-voo]
mascara le mascara
match (football etc) le match
matches les allumettes **fpl** [alOOmet]
material (fabric) le tissu [teessOO]
matter: it doesn't matter ça ne fait rien [sa nuh fay ree-AN]
what's the matter? qu'est-ce qu'il y a? [keskeel ya]
mattress le matelas [matla]
May mai [may]
may: may I have another one? puis-je en avoir un autre? [pweej]
may I come in? puis-je entrer?
may I see it? puis-je le/la voir?
may I sit here? est-ce que je peux m'asseoir ici? [eskuh juh puh masswahr]
maybe peut-être [puht-etr]
mayonnaise la mayonnaise
me* moi [mwa]
that's for me c'est pour moi
send it to me envoyez-le moi
me too moi aussi [o-see]
meal le repas [ruhpa]

dialogue

did you enjoy your meal? est-ce que vous avez fait un bon repas? [eskuh voo zavay fay tAN bON]
it was excellent, thank you c'était excellent, merci [saytay]

mean signifier [seen-yeefee-ay]
what do you mean? qu'est-ce que vous voulez dire? [keskuh-voo voolay deer]

dialogue

what does this word mean? que signifie ce mot? [kuh seen-yeefee suh mo]
it means ... in English ça veut dire ... en anglais [sa vuh deer]

measles la rougeole [roojol]
meat la viande [veeONd]
mechanic le mécanicien [maykaneess-yAN]
medicine le médicament [maydeekamON]
Mediterranean la Méditerranée [maydeetairanay]
medium (size) moyen [mwy-AN]
medium-dry (wine) demi-sec

[duhmee-sek]
medium-rare (steak) à point [pwAN]
medium-sized moyen [mwy-AN]
meet rencontrer [rONkONtray]
nice to meet you enchanté [ONshONtay]
where shall I meet you? où nous retrouverons-nous? [oo noo ruhtroovuhrON-noo]
meeting la réunion [rayOOn-yON]
meeting place le point de rendez-vous [pwAN duh]
melon le melon [muhlON]
men les hommes [om]
mend réparer [rayparay]
could you mend this for me? pouvez-vous me réparer ça? [poovay-voo]
menswear les vêtements pour hommes [vetmON poor om]
mention mentionner [mONs-yONay]
don't mention it je vous en prie [juh voo zON pree]
menu la carte [kart]
may I see the menu, please? puis-je voir la carte, s'il vous plaît? [pweej vwahr]
see **Menu Reader** page 231
message le message [messahj]
are there any messages for me? est-ce que quelqu'un a laissé un message pour moi? [eskuh kelkAN a lessay]
I want to leave a message for ... je voudrais laisser un message pour ... [juh voodray]
metal le métal [may-tal]
metre* le mètre [metr]
microwave le micro-ondes [meekro-OND]
midday midi [meedee]
at midday à midi
middle: in the middle au milieu [o meel-yuh]
in the middle of the night au milieu de la nuit
the middle one celui du milieu
midnight minuit [meenwee]
at midnight à minuit
might: I might want to stay another day il est possible que je reste encore un jour [eel ay posseebl kuh]
I might not leave tomorrow il est possible que je ne parte pas demain
migraine la migraine [meegren]
mild (taste, weather) doux, **f** douce [doo, dooss]
mile* le mille [meel]
milk le lait [lay]
milkshake le milk-shake
millimetre* le millimètre [meelee-metr]
minced meat la viande hachée [veeONd ashay]
mind: never mind tant pis [tON pee]
I've changed my mind j'ai changé d'avis [jay shONjay davee]

dialogue

do you mind if I open the window? ça vous dérange si j'ouvre la fenêtre? [sa voo dayrONj see]
no, I don't mind non, ça ne me dérange pas [sa nuh muh]

mine*: it's mine c'est à moi [set a mwa]
mineral water l'eau minérale **f** [o meenayral]
mint-flavoured à la menthe [mONt]
mint cordial la menthe à l'eau [a lo]
mints (sweets) les bonbons à la menthe **mpl**
minute la minute [meenOOt]
in a minute dans un instant [dON zAN ANstON]
just a minute un instant
mirror le mirroir [meer-wahr]
Miss Mademoiselle [mad-mwazel]
miss rater
I missed the bus j'ai raté le bus [jay ratay]
missing: to be missing manquer [mONkay]
one of my ... is missing il me manque un de mes ... [eel muh mONk]
there's a suitcase missing il manque une valise
mist la brume [brOOm]
mistake l'erreur **f** [air-rurr]
I think there's a mistake je crois qu'il y a une erreur [juh krwa keelya]
sorry, I've made a mistake désolé, j'ai fait une erreur
misunderstanding le malentendu [malONtONdOO]
mix-up: sorry, there's been a mix-up désolé, il y a une erreur [dayzolay eelya OOn air-rurr]
modern moderne [modairn]
modern art gallery la galerie d'art moderne [dar]
moisturizer la crème hydratante [krem eedratONt]
moment: I'll be back in a moment je reviens dans un instant [juh ruhv-yan dON zAN ANstON]
Monday lundi [lANdee]
money l'argent **m** [arjON]
month le mois [mwa]
monument le monument [monOOmON]
moon la lune [lOOn]
moped la mobylette [mobeelet]
more* plus [plOOss]
can I have some more water, please? est-ce que je peux avoir encore un peu d'eau, s'il vous plaît? [eksuh juh puh avwahr ONkor]
more expensive/interesting plus cher/intéressant [plOO shair]
more than 50 plus de cinquante

more than that plus que ça [plooss kuh sa]
a lot more beaucoup plus [bo-koo]

dialogue

would you like some more? est-ce que vous en voulez encore? [eskuh voo ZON voolay]
no, no more for me, thanks non, pas pour moi, merci
how about you? et vous?
I don't want any more, thanks je n'en veux plus, merci

morning le matin [matAN]
this morning ce matin
in the morning le matin
Moroccan marocain [marokAN]
Morocco le Maroc
mosquito le moustique [moosteek]
mosquito repellent le produit anti-moustiques [prodwee ONtee-]
most: I like that most of all c'est ce que je préfère [say suh kuh juh prayfair]
most of the time la plupart du temps [plOOpar]
most tourists la plupart des touristes
mostly principalement [prANseepal-mON]
mother la mère [mair]
motorbike la moto
motorboat le bateau à moteur [bato a moturr]
motorway l'autoroute **f** [otoroot]
mountain la montagne [mONtañ]
in the mountains à la montagne
mountaineering l'alpinisme **m** [alpeeneess-muh]
mouse la souris [sooree]
moustache la moustache [mooss-tash]
mouth la bouche [boosh]
mouth ulcer l'aphte **m** [afft]
move bouger [boojay]
he's moved to another room il a changé de chambre [eel a shONjay duh shONbr]
could you move your car? est-ce que vous pouvez déplacer votre voiture? [eskuh voo poovay dayplassay votr vwatOOr]
could you move up a little? est-ce que vous pouvez vous pousser un peu? [poossay]
where has it moved to? où se trouve-t-il maintenant? [oo suh troovteel mANtuhnON]
movie le film [feelm]
movie theater le cinéma [seenayma]
Mr Monsieur [muhss-yuh]
Mrs Madame [ma-dam]
Ms Madame; Mademoiselle [ma-dam, mad-mwazel]
much beaucoup [bo-koo]

much better/much worse beaucoup mieux/bien pire
much hotter beaucoup plus chaud
not much pas beaucoup [pa]
not very much pas tellement [telmON]
I don't want very much je n'en veux pas beaucoup [juh nON vuh pa]
mud la boue [boo]
mug (for drinking) la tasse [tass]
I've been mugged j'ai été dévalisé [jay aytay dayvaleezay]
mum la maman [ma-mON]
mumps les oreillons [oray-ON]
museum le musée [mOOzay]

Museums are not very generous with their hours, tending to open at around 10 a.m., close for lunch at noon until 2 p.m. or 3 p.m., and then run through only until 5 or 6 p.m. The usual closing day for museums and galleries is Monday, although some close on Tuesday.

mushrooms les champignons **mpl** [shONpeen-yON]
music la musique [mOOzeek]
musician le musicien, la musicienne [mOOzeess-yAN, -yen]
Muslim musulman [mOOzOOlmON]
mussels les moules **fpl** [mool]
must*: **I must** je dois [juh dwa]
I mustn't drink alcohol il ne faut pas que je boive d'alcool [eel nuh fo pa juh]
mustard la moutarde [mootard]
my*: **my room** ma chambre
my passport mon passeport [mON]
my parents mes parents [may]
myself: **I'll do it myself** je le ferai moi-même [mwa-mem]
by myself tout seul [too surl]

N

nail (finger) l'ongle **m** [ONgl]
(metal) le clou [kloo]
nail varnish le vernis à ongles [vairnee]
name le nom [nON]

First names are only used in informal relationships, between friends and relatives, or in semi-formal relationships (e.g. to shopkeepers, bar staff etc) provided you use the polite vous form of address. In formal situations **monsieur**, **madame** ou **mademoiselle** (Mr, Mrs or Ms) + surname are used.
see **you**

my name's John je m'appelle John [juh ma-pel]
what's your name? comment tu t'appelles/vous appelez-

vous? [komON too ta-pel/voo zaplay-voo]
what is the name of this street? comment s'appelle cette rue? [sa-pel]
napkin la serviette [sairv-yet]
nappy la couche [koosh]
narrow (street) étroit [aytrwa]
nasty (person, taste) désagréable [dayzagray-abl] (weather, accident) mauvais [mo-vay]
national national [nass-yonal]
nationality la nationalité [nass-yonaleetay]
natural naturel [natoo-rel]
nausea la nausée [no-zay]
navy (blue) (bleu) marine [bluh mareen]
near près [pray]
is it near the city centre? est-ce que c'est près du centre? [eskuh say]
do you go near the harbour? est-ce que vous allez vers le port? [vair]
where is the nearest ...? où est le/la ... le/la plus proche? [ploo prosh]
nearby tout près [too pray]
nearly presque [presk]
necessary nécessaire [naysessair]
neck le cou [koo]
necklace le collier [kol-yay]
necktie la cravate
need: I need ... j'ai besoin de ... [jay buhzwAN duh]
do I need to pay? est-ce que je dois payer? [eskuh juh dwa]
needle l'aiguille **f** [aygwee]
negative (film) le négatif [naygateef]
neither: neither (one) of them ni l'un ni l'autre [nee lAN nee lohtr]
neither ... nor ... ni ... ni ...
nephew le neveu [nuhvuh]
net (in sport) le filet [feelay]
Netherlands les Pays-Bas [payee-ba]
network map le plan du réseau [plON doo rayzo]
never jamais [jamay]

dialogue

have you ever been to Monaco? êtes-vous déjà allé à Monaco? [et-voo dayja alay]
no, never, I've never been there non, jamais, je n'y suis jamais allé [juh nee swee]

new nouveau, **f** nouvelle [noovo, noovel]
news (radio, TV etc) les informations [ANformass-yON]
newsagent's le marchand de journaux [marshON duh joorno]
newspaper le journal [joor-nal]
newspaper kiosk le kiosque à journaux [keeosk]
New Year le Nouvel An [noovel ON]

The French normally celebrate New Year with friends, either by organizing a party at somebody's house or by going out to a dance or dinner-dance. It is customary to wish people **bonne année** and **bonne santé**. People spend the next day visiting all the friends and relatives who weren't celebrating with them the night before.

Happy New Year! bonne année! [bon anay]
New Year's Eve la Saint-Sylvestre [sAN seelvestr]
New Zealand la Nouvelle-Zélande [noovel zaylOND]
New Zealander: I'm a New Zealander je suis Néo-Zélandais [nayozaylONday]
next prochain [proshAN]
the next on the left la prochaine à gauche [proshen a gohsh]
at the next stop au prochain arrêt
next week la semaine prochaine
next to à côté de [a kotay duh]
nice (food) bon [bON]
(looks, view etc) joli [jolee]
(person) sympathique, gentil [sANpateek, jONtee]
niece la nièce [nee-ess]
night la nuit [nwee]
at night la nuit
good night bonne nuit [bon]

dialogue

do you have a single room for one night? est-ce que vous avez une chambre pour une personne pour une nuit? [eskuh voo zavay ooN shONbr poor ooN pairson]
yes, madam oui Madame
how much is it per night? combien est-ce par nuit? [kONb-yAN ess]
it's 300 francs for one night c'est trois cents francs la nuit
thank you, I'll take it d'accord, je la prends [juh la prON]

nightclub la boîte de nuit [bwat duh nwee]
nightdress la chemise de nuit [shuhmeez]
night porter le gardien de nuit [gardee-AN]
no non [nON]
I've no change je n'ai pas de monnaie [juh nay pa duh]
there's no ... left il n'y a plus de ... [eel nya ploo]
no way! pas question! [pa kest-yON]
oh no! (upset) ce n'est pas possible! [suh nay pa posseebl]
nobody personne [pairson]
there's nobody there il n'y a personne [eel nya]
noise le bruit [brwee]
noisy: it's too noisy c'est trop

bruyant [say tro brwee-yON]
non-alcoholic sans alcool [sON zalkol]
none aucun [o-kAN]
nonsmoking compartment le compartiment non-fumeurs [kONparteemON nON-foomurr]
noon midi [meedee]
no-one personne [pairson]
nor: nor do I moi non plus [mwa nON ploo]
normal normal [nor-mal]
north le nord [nor]
in the north dans le nord
north of Paris au nord de Paris [o]
northeast le nord-est [nor-est]
northern du nord [doo]
northwest le nord-ouest [nor-west]
Northern Ireland l'Irlande du Nord **f** [eerlOND]
Norway la Norvège [norvej]
Norwegian (adj) norvégien [nor-vayj-yAN]
nose le nez [nay]
nosebleed le saignement de nez [sen-yuh-mON]
not** pas [pa]
no, I'm not hungry non, je n'ai pas faim [juh nay pa]
I don't want any, thank you je n'en veux pas, merci [nON vuh]
it's not necessary ce n'est pas nécessaire
I didn't know that je ne savais pas
not that one – this one pas celui-là – celui-ci [suhlwee-la suhlwee-see]
note (banknote) le billet (de banque) [bee-yay (duh bONk)]
notebook le cahier [ky-yay]
notepaper (for letters) le papier à lettres [pap-yay a letr]
nothing rien [ree-AN]
nothing for me, thanks pour moi rien, merci [poor mwa]
nothing else rien d'autre [dohtr]
novel le roman [romON]
November novembre [no-vONbr]
now maintenant [mANtnON]
number le numéro [noomayro]
I've got the wrong number j'ai fait un mauvais numéro [jay fay AN]
what is your phone number? quel est votre numéro de téléphone? [kel ay votr]
number plate la plaque minéralogique [plak meenay-ralojeek]
nurse (female) l'infirmière **f** [ANfeerm-yair]
(male) l'infirmier **m** [ANfeerm-yay]
nursery slope la piste pour débutants [peest poor dayb0otON]
nut (for bolt) l'écrou **m** [aykroo]
nuts les noisettes **fpl** [nwazet]

O

o'clock*: it's 10 o'clock il est dix heures [urr]
occupied (toilet) occupé [okOOpay]
October octobre [oktobr]
odd (strange) étrange [aytrONj]
of* de [duh]
off (lights) éteint [aytAN]
it's just off the Champs Elysées c'est tout près des Champs Elysées [too pray day]
we're off tomorrow (leaving) nous partons demain [noo partON]
offensive (language, behaviour) choquant [shokON]
office le bureau [bOOro]
officer (said to policeman) monsieur l'agent [muhss-yuh lajON]
often souvent [soovON]
not often pas souvent [pa]
how often are the buses? à quel intervalle les bus passent-ils? [kel ANtairval]
oil l'huile **f** [weel]
ointment la pommade [pomahd]
OK d'accord [dakor]
are you OK? ça va? [sa va]
is that OK with you? est-ce que ça te/vous va? [eskuh sa tuh/voo]
is it OK to ...? est-ce qu'on peut ...? [puh]
that's OK thanks (it doesn't matter) merci, ça va [mairsee]
I'm OK (nothing for me, I've got enough) ça va comme ça
(I feel OK) ça va
is this train OK for ...? ce train va bien à ...? [b-yAN]
I said I'm sorry, OK? j'ai dit pardon, ça ne suffit pas? [sa nuh sOOfee pa]
old vieux, **f** vieille [v-yuh, v-yay]

dialogue

how old are you? quel âge as-tu/avez-vous? [kel ahj atOO/avay-voo]
I'm twenty-five j'ai vingt-cinq ans [jay]
and you? et vous?

old-fashioned démodé [daymoday]
old town (old part of town) la vieille ville [v-yay veel]
in the old town dans la vieille ville
olive oil l'huile d'olive **f** [weel doleev]
olives les olives **fpl** [oleev]
black/green olives les olives noires/vertes
omelette l'omelette **f**
on* sur [sOOr]
on the street/beach dans la rue/à la plage [dON]
is it on this road? est-ce que c'est sur cette route?

on the plane dans l'avion
on Saturday samedi
on television à la télévision
I haven't got it on me je ne l'ai pas sur moi [juh nuh lay pa sOOr mwa]
this one's on me (drink) c'est ma tournée [say ma toornay]
the light wasn't on la lumière n'était pas allumée [alOOmay]
what's on tonight? qu'est-ce qu'il y a ce soir? [keskeel-ya suh swahr]
once une fois [OOn fwa]
at once (immediately) tout de suite [toot sweet]
one* un, une [AN, OOn]
the white one le blanc, la blanche
one-way ticket: a one-way ticket to ... un aller simple pour ... [alay SANpl poor]
onion l'oignon **m** [on-yON]
only seulement [surlmON]
only one seulement un(e)
only just à peine [pen]
it's only 6 o'clock il n'est que six heures [eel nay kuh]
I've only just got here je viens d'arriver [juh v-yAN dareevay]
on/off switch l'interrupteur de marche/arrêt **m** [ANtairOOpturr duh marsh/aray]
open (adj) ouvert [oovair]
(verb) ouvrir [oovreer]
when do you open? à quelle heure est-ce que vous ouvrez? [a kel urr eskuh voo zoovray]
I can't get it open je n'arrive pas à l'ouvrir [juh nareev pa]
in the open air en plein air [ON plAN air]
opening times les heures d'ouverture [urr doovairtOOr]
open ticket le billet open [bee-yay]
opera l'opéra **m** [opayra]
operation l'opération **f** [opayrass-yON]
operator (telephone) le/la standardiste [stONdardeest]
opposite: the opposite direction le sens inverse [anvairss]
opposite my hotel en face de mon hôtel [ON fass duh]
the bar opposite le bar d'en face
optician l'opticien **m** [opteess-yAN]
or ou [oo]
orange (fruit) l'orange **f** [orONj]
(colour) orange
orange juice le jus d'orange [jOO]
orchestra l'orchestre **m** [orkestr]
order: can we order now? est-ce que nous pouvons commander? [eskuh noo poovON komONday]
I've already ordered, thanks j'ai déjà commandé, merci [jay dayja komONday]
I didn't order this ce n'est pas ce que j'ai commandé

[suh nay pa suh kuh]
out of order hors service [or sairveess]
ordinary ordinaire [ordeenair]
other autre [ohtr]
the other one l'autre
the other day (recently) l'autre jour
I'm waiting for the others j'attends les autres [lay zohtr]
do you have any others? est-ce que vous en avez d'autres? [eskuh voo zON avay dohtr]
otherwise sinon [seenON]
our* notre, pl nos
ours* le/la nôtre [nohtr]
out: he's out il est sorti [eel ay sortee]
three kilometres out of town à trois kilomètres de la ville
outdoors en plein air [ON plAN air]
outside (preposition) à l'extérieur de [extayree-urr duh]
can we sit outside? est-ce que nous pouvons nous mettre dehors? [eskuh noo poovON noo metr duh-or]
oven le four [foor]
over: over here par ici [ee-see]
over there là-bas [laba]
over 500 plus de cinq cents [ploo duh]
it's over (finished) c'est fini [say feenee]
overcharge: you've overcharged me il y a une erreur dans la note [eelya oon air-rurr dON la not]
overcoat le pardessus [parduhsoo]
overnight (travel) de nuit [duh nwee]
overtake doubler [dooblay]
owe: how much do I owe you? qu'est-ce que je vous dois? [keskuh juh voo dwa]
own: my own ... mon propre ... [propr]
are you on your own? êtes-vous seul? [et-voo surl]
I'm on my own je suis seul
owner le/la propriétaire [propree-aytair]

P

pack: a pack of ... un paquet de ... [pakay duh]
(verb) faire ses bagages [fair say bagahj]
package (at post office) le colis [kolee]
package holiday les vacances organisées [vakONss organeezay]
packed lunch le casse-croûte [kass-kroot]
packet: a packet of cigarettes un paquet de cigarettes [pakay]
padlock le cadenas [kadna]
page (of book) la page [pahj]
could you page Mr ...? pouvez-vous faire appeler M. ...? [poovay-voo fair aplay]

pain la douleur [doolurr]
I have a pain here j'ai mal ici [jay mal ee-see]
painful douloureux [doolooruh]
painkillers les analgésiques **mpl** [an-aljayzeek]
paint la peinture [pANtoor]
painting (picture) le tableau [tablo]
pair: a pair of ... une paire de ... [pair duh]
Pakistani pakistanais [-ay]
palace le palais [palay]
pale pâle [pahl]
pale blue bleu clair
pan la poêle [pwal]
panties le slip [sleep]
pants (underwear) le slip (US) le pantalon [pONtalON]
pantyhose le collant [kollON]
paper le papier [papyay] (newspaper) le journal [joor-nal]
a piece of paper un bout de papier [boo]
paper handkerchiefs les kleenex® **mpl**
parcel le colis [kolee]
pardon? (didn't understand) pardon? [par-dON]
parents: my parents mes parents [parON]
parents-in-law les beaux-parents [bo-]
park le parc (verb) se garer [suh garay]
can I park here? est-ce que je peux me garer ici?
parking lot le parking [parkeeng]
part une partie [partee]
partner (boyfriend, girlfriend) le/la partenaire [partuhnair]
party (group) le groupe (celebration) la fête [fet]
pass (in mountains) le col
passenger le passager, la passagère [passahjay, -jair]
passport le passeport [pass-por]
past*: in the past autrefois [ohtruh-fwa]
just past the information office tout de suite après le centre d'information [toot sweet apray]
path le sentier [sONt-yay]
pattern le motif [moteef]
pavement le trottoir [trotwahr]
on the pavement sur le trottoir
pavement café le café en terrasse [ON tairass]
pay (verb) payer [pay-ay]
can I pay, please? l'addition, s'il vous plaît [ladeess-yON]
it's already paid for ça a déjà été réglé [sa a day-ja aytay rayglay]

dialogue

who's paying? qui est-ce qui paie? [kee eskee pay]
I'll pay c'est moi qui paie [say mwa]
no, you paid last time, I'll pay non, tu as payé la

dernière fois, cette fois c'est mon tour [too a pay-ay la dairn-yair fwa set fwa say mON toor]

pay phone la cabine téléphonique [kabeen taylayfoneek]
peaceful paisible [pezzeebl]
peach la pêche [pesh]
peanuts les cacahuètes **fpl** [kaka-wet]
pear la poire [pwahr]
peas les petits pois **mpl** [puhtee pwa]
peculiar (taste, custom) bizarre
pedestrian crossing le passage pour piétons [passahj poor p-yaytON]
pedestrian precinct la zone piétonne [zohn p-yaytON]
peg (for washing) la pince à linge [pANss a lANj]
(for tent) le piquet [peekay]
pen le stylo [steelo]
pencil le crayon [kray-ON]
penfriend le correspondant [-dON], la correspondante [-dONt]
penicillin la pénicilline [payneesseeleen]
penknife le canif [kaneef]
pensioner le retraité, la retraitée [ruhtraytay]
people les gens [jON]
the other people les autres [lay zohtr]
too many people trop de monde [tro duh mOND]
pepper (spice) le poivre [pwahvr]
(vegetable) le poivron [pwahvrON]
peppermint (sweet) le bonbon à la menthe [bONbON ala mONt]
per: per night par nuit
how much per day? quel est le prix par jour? [kel ay]
per cent pour cent [poor sON]
perfect parfait [parfay]
perfume le parfum [parfAN]
perhaps peut-être [puht-etr]
perhaps not peut-être que non [kuh nON]
period (of time) la période [payree-od]
(menstruation) les règles [regl]
perm la permanente [pairmanONt]
permit l'autorisation **f** [otoreezass-yON]
person la personne [pairson]
personal stereo le baladeur [baladurr]
petrol l'essence **f** [essONss]

Petrol is substantially more expensive on the motorway, so make sure you fill up your tank beforehand. The best prices are normally to be found in supermarket petrol stations. The following are available: **super** (4-star), **ordinaire** (2-star), **sans plomb** (unleaded) and **gas-oil** (diesel).

petrol can le bidon d'essence

[beedON dessONss]
petrol station la station-service [stass-yON-sairveess]
pharmacy la pharmacie [farmasee]
see **chemist's**
phone le téléphone [taylay-]
(verb) téléphoner
could you phone the police? pourriez-vous téléphoner à la police? [pooree-ay-voo]

You can make domestic and international calls from any box (or **cabine**) and receive calls where there's a blue logo of a ringing bell. Most call boxes only take phonecards (**télécarte**), obtainable from post offices, petrol stations and some tobacconists (**tabac**). In central Paris a phonecard is indispensable. The least expensive is 40F. Coin-only payphones are still common in cafés, bars and in rural areas. They take 50 centimes, 1F, 5F and 10F coins. International calls are cheaper between 10 p.m. and 8 a.m. and on Saturday after 1 p.m. and all day Sunday.
see **speak**

phone box la cabine téléphonique [kabeen taylayfoneek]
phonecard la télécarte [taylay-kart]
phone directory l'annuaire du téléphone **m** [anOOair dOO taylayfon]
phone number le numéro de téléphone [nOOmayro]
photo la photographie [foto-grafee]
excuse me, could you take a photo of us? pourriez-vous nous prendre en photo? [pooree-ay-voo noo prONdr ON]
phrasebook le manuel de conversation [manOOel duh kONvairsass-yON]
piano le piano
pickpocket le/la pickpocket
pick up: will you be there to pick me up? est-ce que vous viendrez me chercher? [eskuh voo vee-ANdray muh shairshay]
picnic le pique-nique [peek-neek]
picture l'image **f** [eemahj]
pie (meat) le pâté en croûte [patay ON kroot]
(fruit) la tarte
piece le morceau [morso]
a piece of ... un morceau de ...
pill la pilule [peelOOl]
I'm on the pill je prends la pilule [juh prON]
pillow l'oreiller **m** [oray-yay]
pillow case la taie d'oreiller [tay]
pin l'épingle **f** [aypANgl]
pineapple l'ananas **m** [anana]
pineapple juice le jus d'ananas [jOO]
pink rose [roz]

pipe (for smoking) la pipe [peep]
(for water) le tuyau [twee-o]
pity: it's a pity c'est dommage [say domahj]
pizza la pizza
place l'endroit **m** [ONdrwa]
is this place taken? est-ce que cette place est prise? [eskuh set plass ay preez]
at your place chez toi/vous [shay twa/voo]
at his place chez lui [lwee]
plain (not patterned) uni [oonee]
plane l'avion **m** [av-yON]
by plane en avion
plant la plante [plONt]
plaster cast le plâtre [plahtr]
plasters les pansements **mpl** [pONsmON]
plastic le plastique [plass-teek]
(credit cards) les cartes de crédit [kart duh kray-dee]
plastic bag le sac en plastique [ON plass-teek]
plate l'assiette **f** [ass-yet]
platform le quai [kay]
which platform is it for Paris? c'est quelle voie pour Paris? [say kel vwa]

In French stations a **quai** will have two **voies**, the voie being the side of the quai where a train comes in.

play (verb) jouer [joo-ay]
(in theatre) la pièce de théâtre [p-yess duh tay-atr]
playground (for children) le terrain de jeux [terrAN duh juh]
pleasant agréable [agray-abl]
please s'il vous plaît [seel voo play]
(if using 'tu' form) s'il te plaît [seel tuh]
yes please oui, merci [wee mairsee]
could you please ...? pourriez-vous ..., s'il vous plaît? [pooree-ay-voo]
please don't wait for me ce n'est pas la peine de m'attendre [suh nay pa la pen]
pleased to meet you enchanté [ONshONtay]
pleasure le plaisir [plezzeer]
my pleasure tout le plaisir est pour moi [too luh ... ay poor mwa]
plenty: plenty of ... beaucoup de ... [bo-koo duh]
we've plenty of time nous avons largement le temps [noo zavON larj-mON luh tON]
that's plenty, thanks merci, ça suffit [sa soofee]
pliers la pince [pANss]
plug (electrical) la prise [preez]
(for car) la bougie [boojee]
(in sink) le bouchon [booshON]
plumber le plombier [plONb-yay]
p.m.* de l'après-midi [duh lapray-meedee]
(in the evening) du soir [doo swahr]
poached egg l'œuf poché **m** [urf poshay]

pocket la poche [posh]
point: two point five deux virgule cinq [... veergool ...]
there's no point ça ne sert à rien [sa nuh sair a ree-AN]
points (in car) les vis platinées [veess plateenay]
poisonous toxique
police la police
call the police! appelez la police! [aplay]

There are two types of French police (popularly know as **les flics**): the **Police Nationale** and the **Gendarmerie Nationale.** For all practical purposes they are indistinguishable; if you need to report a theft or other incident you can go to either. The phone number for the police is 17.

policeman l'agent de police **m** [ajON]
police station le commissariat [komeessaree-a]
policewoman la femme agent [fam ajON]
polish le cirage [seerahj]
polite poli [polee]
polluted pollué [poloo-ay]
pony le poney [ponay]
pool (for swimming) la piscine [peesseen]
poor (not rich) pauvre [pohvr]
(quality) médiocre [maydeeokr]
pop music la musique pop [moozeek]
pop singer le chanteur/la chanteuse de musique pop [shONturr/shONturz duh]
population la population [popoolass-yON]
pork le porc [por]
port (for boats) le port [por]
(drink) le porto
porter (in hotel) le portier [port-yay]
portrait le portrait [portray]
Portugal le Portugal
Portuguese (adj) portugais [portoogay]
posh (restaurant, people) chic [sheek]
possible possible [posseebl]
is it possible to ...? est-ce qu'on peut ...? [eskON puh]
as ... as possible aussi ... que possible [o-see]
post (mail) le courrier [kooree-ay]
(verb) poster [posstay]
could you post this for me? pourriez-vous me poster cette lettre? [pooree-ay-voo muh posstay set letr]
postbox la boîte aux lettres [bwat o letr]
see **letterbox**
postcard la carte postale [kart poss-tal]
poster l'affiche **f** [afeesh]
post office la poste [posst]

Post offices are generally open from Monday to Friday from 9 a.m. to noon and from 2 to 5-6 p.m.; on Saturdays they are only open in the morning. However, in larger towns main post offices often don't close for lunch, while in villages, lunch hours and closing times can vary enormously. To register a letter send it **en recommandé**, and send your urgent letters or parcels **en urgent**. Post offices also sell phonecards (**télécarte**) and cardboard boxes for your parcels. Major post offices change money, generally at a good rate and without charging a commission.

poste restante la poste restante
potato la pomme de terre [pom duh tair]
potato chips les chips **fpl** [cheeps]
pots and pans les casseroles [kassuhrohl]
pottery (objects) la poterie [potree]
pound (money) la livre (sterling) [leevr (stairleeng)]
(weight) la livre
power cut la coupure de courant [koopoor duh koorON]
power point la prise (de courant) [preez]
practise: I want to practise my French je veux m'exercer à parler français [juh vuh mexairsay a parlay]
prawns les crevettes **fpl** [kruhvet]
prefer: I prefer ... je préfère ... [juh prayfair]
pregnant enceinte [ONSANt]
prescription (for chemist) l'ordonnance **f** [ordonONss]
present (gift) le cadeau [kado]
president le président [prayzeedON]
pretty joli [jolee]
it's pretty expensive c'est plutôt cher [say plooto shair]
price le prix [pree]
priest le prêtre [pretr]
prime minister le Premier ministre [pruhm-yay meeneestr]
printed matter l'imprimé **m** [ANpreemay]
priority (in driving) la priorité [preeoreetay]
prison la prison [preezON]
private privé [preevay]
private bathroom la salle de bain particulière [sal duh bAN parteekool-yair]
probably probablement [prob-abluhmON]
problem le problème [prob-lem]
no problem! pas de problème! [pa duh]
program(me) le programme [prog-ram]
promise: I promise je te/vous le promets [juh tuh/voo luh promay]
pronounce: how is this pronounced? comment est-ce que ça se prononce? [komON teskuh sa suh pronONss]

properly (repaired, locked etc) bien [b-yAN]
protection factor l'indice de protection **m** [ANdeess duh protex-yON]
Protestant protestant [-tON]
public holiday le jour férié [joor fayree-ay]
public toilets les toilettes publiques [twalet pOObleek]
pudding (dessert) le dessert [dessair]
pull tirer [teeray]
pullover le pull [pOOl]
puncture la crevaison [kruhvezzON]
purple violet [veeolay]
purse (for money) le porte-monnaie [port-monay]
(US) le sac à main [mAN]
push pousser [poossay]
pushchair la poussette [poosset]
put mettre [metr]
where can I put ...? où est-ce que je peux mettre ...? [weskuh juh puh]
could you put us up for the night? pourriez-vous nous héberger pour la nuit? [pooree-ay-voo noo zaybairjay poor la nwee]
pyjamas le pyjama [peejama]
Pyrenees les Pyrénées [peeraynay]

Q

quality la qualité [kaleetay]
quarantine la quarantaine [karONten]
quarter le quart [kar]
quayside: on the quayside sur les quais [sOOr lay kay]
question la question [kest-yON]
queue la queue [kuh]
quick rapide [rapeed]
that was quick tu as/vous avez fait vite [tOO a/voo zavay fay veet]
what's the quickest way there? quel est le chemin le plus court? [kel ay luh shuhmAN luh plOO koor]
fancy a quick drink? tu as/vous avez le temps de prendre un verre? [tOO a/voo zavay luh tON duh prONdr AN vair]
quickly vite [veet]
quiet (place, hotel) tranquille [trONkeel]
quiet! silence! [seelONss]
quite (fairly) assez [assay]
(very) très [tray]
that's quite right c'est tout à fait juste [say too ta fay jOOst]
quite a lot pas mal [pa]

R

rabbit le lapin [lapAN]
race (for runners, cars) la course [koorss]

racket (tennis, squash etc) la raquette [raket]
radiator (of car, in room) le radiateur [rad-yaturr]
radio la radio [ra-deeo]
on the radio à la radio
rail: by rail en train [ON trAN]
railway le chemin de fer [shuhmAN duh fair]
rain la pluie [plwee]
in the rain sous la pluie [soo]
it's raining il pleut [eel pluh]
raincoat l'imperméable **m** [ANpairmay-abl]
rape le viol [veeol]
rare (steak) saignant [sen-yON]
rash (on skin) l'éruption **f** [ayrOOps-yON]
raspberry la framboise [frONbwahz]
rat le rat [ra]
rate (for changing money) le taux [toh]
rather: it's rather good c'est assez bon [say tassay bON]
I'd rather ... je préfère ... [juh prayfair]
razor le rasoir [razwahr]
razor blades les lames de rasoir **fpl** [lahm duh razwahr]
read lire [leer]
ready prêt [pray]
are you ready? est-ce que tu es/vous êtes prêt? [eskuh tOO ay/voo zet]
I'm not ready yet je ne suis pas encore prêt [juh nuh swee pa zONkor]

dialogue

when will it be ready? quand est-ce que ce sera prêt? [kONteskuh suh suhra]
it should be ready in a couple of days ça devrait être prêt dans un ou deux jours [sa duhvray]

real véritable [vayreet-abl]
really vraiment [vraymON]
that's really great c'est vraiment formidable
really? (doubt) vraiment? (polite interest) ah bon?
rearview mirror le rétroviseur [raytroveezurr]
reasonable raisonnable [rezzON-abl]
receipt le reçu [ruhsOO]
recently récemment [ray-samON]
reception (for guests, in hotel) la réception [ray-seps-yON]
at reception à la réception
reception desk le bureau de réception
receptionist le/la réceptionniste [rayseps-yoneest]
recognize reconnaître [ruhkonetr]
recommend: could you recommend ...? pourriez-vous me recommander ...? [pooree-ay-voo muh ruhkomONday]
record (music) le disque [deesk]

red rouge [rooj]
red wine le vin rouge [VAN]
refund le remboursement [rONboorss-mON]
can I have a refund? est-ce que je serai remboursé? [eskuh juh suhray rONboorsay]
region la région [rayjeeON]
registered: by registered mail en recommandé [ON ruhkomONday]
registration number le numéro d'immatriculation [nOOmayro deematreekOOlass-yON]
relative le parent [parON]
religion la religion [ruhleejeeON]
remember: I don't remember je ne me souviens pas [juh nuh muh soov-yAN pa]
I remember je m'en souviens [juh mON]
do you remember? tu te souviens?/vous souvenez-vous? [tOO tuh .../voo soovnay-voo]
rent (for apartment etc) le loyer [lwy-ay]
(verb) louer [loo-ay]
for rent à louer

dialogue

I'd like to rent a car j'aimerais louer une voiture [jemray]
for how long? pour combien de temps? [poor KONb-yAN duh tON]
two days deux jours
this is our range voici notre gamme
I'll take the ... je vais prendre la ... [juh vay prONdr]
is that with unlimited mileage? est-ce que ça comprend un kilométrage illimité? [eskuh sa KONprON AN keelomaytrahj eeleemeetay]
it is oui [wee]
can I see your licence please? puis-je voir votre permis de conduire, s'il vous plaît? [pweej vwahr votr pairmee duh KONdweer]
and your passport et votre passeport [pass-por]
is insurance included? est-ce que l'assurance est comprise? [eskuh lassOOrONss ay KONpreez]
yes, but you pay the first 600 francs oui, mais vous payez les six cents francs de départ [voo pay-ay lay see SON frON duh daypar]
can you leave a deposit of ...? pouvez-vous me laisser une caution de ...? [kohss-yON]

rented car la voiture de location [vwatOOr duh lokass-yON]
repair (verb) réparer [rayparay]
can you repair it? est-ce que

vous pouvez réparer ça? [eskuh voo poovay]

repeat répéter [raypaytay]

could you repeat that? pourriez-vous répéter? [pooree-ay-voo]

reservation la réservation [rayzairvass-yON]

I'd like to make a reservation je voudrais faire une réservation [juh voodray fair]

dialogue

I have a reservation j'ai réservé [jay rayzairvay]

yes sir, what name please? certainement monsieur, à quel nom s'il vous plaît? [sairten-mON muh-syuh a kel nON]

reserve réserver [rayzairvay]

dialogue

can I reserve a table for tonight? j'aimerais réserver une table pour ce soir [jemray]

yes madam, for how many people? certainement madame, pour combien de personnes? [sairten-mON ... poor kONb-yAN duh pairson]

for two pour deux

and for what time? et pour quelle heure? [kel urr]

for eight o'clock pour huit heures

and could I have your name please? pourrais-je avoir votre nom s'il vous plaît? [poorayj avwahr]

see **alphabet**

rest: I need a rest j'ai besoin de repos [jay buh-zwAN duh ruhpo]

the rest of the group le reste du groupe [rest]

restaurant le restaurant [restorON]

There's often no difference between **restaurants** (or **auberges** or **relais** as they sometimes call themselves) and **brasseries** in terms of quality or price range. The distinction is that brasseries, which resemble cafés, serve quicker meals at most hours of the day, while restaurants tend to stick to the traditional meal times. Meals are usually served from 12 to 3 p.m. and from 7.30 to 11.30 p.m. Booking is only required in very busy or upmarket places. Restaurants will normally have a **plat du jour** (dish of the day) and various **menus fixes** (set-price menus) which are good value for money, but you can eat **à la carte** (single dishes chosen from the menu) and this is invariably more expensive. In small towns it may be impossible to get anything other than a sandwich after 10 p.m.; in major cities, town centre brasseries will serve until 11 p.m. or midnight and one or two may be open all night.

dialogue

what's the dish of the day?
quel est le plat du jour?
[kel ay luh pla doo joor?]
I'll take the 75 franc menu
je vais prendre le menu à soixante-quinze francs
[juh vay prONdr]

restaurant car le wagon-restaurant [vagON]
rest room les toilettes [twalet]
see **toilet**
retired: I'm retired je suis retraité(e) [ruhtretay]
return (ticket) l'aller-retour **m** [alay-ruhtoor]

Return tickets in France are calculated as twice the price of a single ticket – there is no reduction.

reverse charge call le PCV [pay-say-vay]
reverse gear la marche arrière [marsh aree-air]
revolting dégoûtant [daygootON]
rib la côte [koht]
rice le riz [ree]
rich (person) riche [reesh]
(food) lourd [loor]
ridiculous ridicule [reedeekool]
right (correct) juste [joost]
(not left) droit [drwa]
you were right vous aviez raison [voo zaveeay rezzON]
that's right c'est juste [say joost]
this can't be right ce n'est pas possible [suh nay pa posseebl]
right! d'accord! [dakor]
is this the right road for ...? est-ce bien la route de ...? [ess b-yAN la root]
on the right à droite [drwat]
turn right tournez à droite [toornay]
right-hand drive la conduite à droite [kONdweet a drwat]
ring (on finger) la bague [bag]
I'll ring you je vous appellerai [juh vooz apelray]
ring back rappeler
ripe (fruit) mûr [moor]
rip-off: it's a rip-off c'est de l'arnaque [say duh larnak]
rip-off prices les prix exorbitants [pree exorbeetON]
risky risqué [reeskay]
river la rivière [reev-yair]
road la route [root]
is this the road for ...? est-ce la bonne route pour aller à ...? [ess la bon root poor alay]
it's just down the road c'est

tout près d'ici [say too pray dee-see]
road accident l'accident de la circulation m [axeedon duh la seerkoolass-yON]
road map la carte routière [kart root-yair]
roadsign le panneau de signalisation [pano duh seen-yaleezass-yON]
rob: I've been robbed j'ai été dévalisé [jay aytay dayvaleezay]
rock le rocher [roshay]
(music) la musique rock [moozeek]
on the rocks (with ice) avec des glaçons [avek day glassON]
roll (bread) le petit pain [puhtee pAN]
roof le toit [twa]
roof rack la galerie [galree]
room la chambre [shONbr]
in my room dans ma chambre [dON]

dialogue

do you have any rooms? est-ce que vous avez des chambres? [eskuh voo zavay day]
for how many people? pour combien de personnes? [poor kONb-yAN duh pairson]
for one/for two pour une personne/deux personnes
yes, we have rooms free oui, nous avons des chambres libres [leebr]
for how many nights will it be? ce serait pour combien de nuits? [suh suhray – duh nwee]
just for one night pour une nuit seulement [surlmON]
how much is it? combien est-ce? [ess]
400 francs with bathroom and 350 francs without bathroom quatre cents francs avec salle de bain et trois cent cinquante francs sans salle de bain [sal duh bAN]
can I see a room with bathroom? est-ce que je pourrais voir une chambre avec salle de bain? [eskuh juh pooray vwahr]
OK, I'll take it d'accord, je la prends [dakor juh la prON]

room service le service en chambre [sairveess ON shONbr]
rope la corde [kord]
rosé (wine) le rosé [rozzay]
roughly (approximately) environ [ONveerON]
round: it's my round c'est ma tournée [say ma toornay]
roundabout (for traffic) le rond-point [rON-pwAN]
round trip ticket l'aller-retour m [alay-ruhtoor]
see **return ticket**

route l'itinéraire **m** [eeteenay-rair]
what's the best route? quel itinéraire nous conseillez-vous? [noo KONsay-ay-voo]
rubber (material) le caoutchouc [ka-oochoo]
(eraser) la gomme [gom]
rubber band l'élastique **m** [aylasteek]
rubbish (waste) les ordures [ordoor]
(poor-quality goods) la camelote [kamlot]
rubbish! (nonsense) n'importe quoi! [nANport kwa]
rucksack le sac à dos [do]
rude grossier [gross-yay]
ruins les ruines **fpl** [rooeen]
rum le rhum [rum]
rum and coke un rhum coca
run (person) courir [kooreer]
how often do the buses run? à quels intervalles les bus passent-ils? [kel zANtairval lay booss pasteel]
I've run out of money je n'ai plus d'argent [juh nay ploo darjON]
rush hour les heures de pointe [urr duh pwANt]

S

sad triste [treest]
saddle (for bike, horse) la selle [sel]
safe (not in danger) en sécurité [ON saykooreetay]
(not dangerous) sûr [soor]
safety pin l'épingle de sûreté **f** [aypANgl duh soortay]
sail la voile [vwal]
sailboard la planche à voile [plONsh a vwal]
sailboarding la planche à voile
salad la salade [sa-lad]
salad dressing la vinaigrette
sale: for sale à vendre [vONdr]
salmon le saumon [so-mON]
salt le sel
same: the same le/la même [mem]
the same as he has le/la même que lui
the same again, please la même chose, s'il vous plaît [shohz seel voo play]
it's all the same to me ça m'est égal [sa met aygal]
sand le sable [sabl]
sandals les sandales **fpl** [sON-dal]
sandwich le sandwich [sONd-weetch]
sanitary napkin la serviette hygiénique [eejee-ayneek]
sanitary towel la serviette hygiénique
sardines les sardines **fpl**
Saturday samedi [samdee]
sauce la sauce [sohss]
saucepan la casserole
saucer la soucoupe [sookoop]
sauna le sauna [sona]
sausage la saucisse [soseess]

say: how do you say ... in French? comment dit-on ... en français? [komON deet-ON]
what did he say? qu'est-ce qu'il a dit? [keskeel a dee]
he said ... il a dit ...
I said ... j'ai dit ... [jay]
could you say that again? pourriez-vous répéter? [pooree-ay-voo raypaytay]
scarf (for neck) l'écharpe **f** [aysharp]
(for head) le foulard [foolar]
scenery le paysage [payee-zahj]
schedule (US) l'horaire **m** [orair]
scheduled flight le vol de ligne [vol duh leeñ]
school l'école **f** [aykol]
scissors: a pair of scissors une paire de ciseaux [seezo]
scotch le whisky
Scotch tape® le scotch
Scotland l'Écosse **f** [aykoss]
Scottish écossais [aykossay]
I'm Scottish (man/woman) je suis écossais/écossaise [aykossez]
scrambled eggs les œufs brouillés [uh broo-yay]
scratch l'éraflure **f** [ayraflOOr]
screw la vis [veess]
screwdriver le tournevis [toornuhveess]
scrubbing brush la brosse [bross]
sea la mer [mair]
by the sea au bord de la mer [o bor]
seafood les fruits de mer [frwee duh mair]
seafood restaurant le restaurant de fruits de mer
seafront le bord de la mer [bor duh la mair]
on the seafront au bord de la mer
seagull la mouette [mwet]
search chercher [shairshay]
seashell le coquillage [kokee-yahj]
seasick: I feel seasick j'ai le mal de mer [jay luh mal duh mair]
I get seasick je suis sujet au mal de mer [juh swee sOOjay]
seaside: by the seaside au bord de la mer [o bor duh la mair]
seat le siège [see-ej]
is this anyone's seat? est-ce que cette place est prise? [eskuh set plass ay preez]
seat belt la ceinture de sécurité [sANtOOr duh saykOOreetay]
sea urchin l'oursin **m** [oorsAN]
seaweed les algues [alg]
secluded isolé [eezolay]
second (adj) second [suhgON]
(of time) la seconde [suhgONd]
just a second! une seconde!
second class (travel) en seconde [ON suhgONd]
second floor le deuxième [duhz-yem]; (US) le premier [pruhm-yay]
second-hand d'occasion

[dokaz-yON]
see voir [vwahr]
can I see? est-ce que je peux voir? [eskuh juh puh]
have you seen ...? est-ce que tu as/vous avez vu ...? [too a/voo zavay voo]
I saw him this morning je l'ai vu ce matin [juh lay]
see you! à bientôt! [b-yANto]
I see (I understand) je vois [juh vwa]
self-catering apartment l'appartement (de vacances) **m** [apartmON (duh vakONss)]
self-service le self-service [-sairveess]
sell vendre [vONdr]
do you sell ...? est-ce que vous vendez ...? [eskuh voo vONday]
Sellotape® le scotch
send envoyer [ONvwy-ay]
I want to send this to England j'aimerais envoyer ceci en Angleterre [jemray]
senior citizen la personne du troisième âge [pairson doo trwaz-yem ahj]
separate séparé [sayparay]
separated: I'm separated je suis séparé [juh swee sayparay]
separately (pay, travel) séparément [sayparay-mON]
September septembre [septONbr]
septic infecté [ANfektay]
serious (person, situation, problem) sérieux [sayree-uh]
(illness) grave [grahv]
service charge (in restaurant) le service [sairveess]
service station la station-service [stass-yON sairveess]
serviette la serviette [sair-]
set menu le menu (à prix fixe) [muhnoo (a pree feex)]
several plusieurs [plooz-yurr]
sew coudre [koodr]
could you sew this back on? pouvez-vous recoudre ceci? [poovay-voo ruhkoodr suhsee]
sex le sexe
sexy sexy
shade: in the shade à l'ombre [lONbr]
shake: let's shake hands serrons-nous la main [sairrON-noo la mAN]
shallow (water) peu profond [puh profON]
shame: what a shame! quel dommage! [kel domahj]
shampoo le shampoing [shONpwAN]
shampoo and set le shampoing-mise en plis [ON plee]
share (room, table etc) partager [partajay]
sharp (knife) tranchant [trONshON]
(taste, pain) piquant, âpre [apr]
shattered (very tired) épuisé [aypweezay]
shaver le rasoir [razwahr]
shaving foam la mousse à raser [razay]

shaving point la prise pour rasoirs [preez poor razwahr]
she* elle [el]
sheet (for bed) le drap [dra]
shelf l'étagère **f** [aytajair]
shellfish les crustacés [kroostassay]
sherry le sherry
ship le bateau [bato]
 by ship en bateau
shirt la chemise [shuhmeez]
shit! merde! [maird]
shock le choc [shok]
 I got an electric shock from the ... j'ai reçu une décharge en touchant ... [jay ruhsoo oon daysharj ON tooshON]
shock-absorber l'amortisseur **m** [amorteessurr]
shocking scandaleux [skONdaluh]
shoe la chaussure [shoshoor]
 a pair of shoes une paire de chaussures
shoelaces les lacets **mpl** [lassay]
shoe polish le cirage [seerahj]
shoe repairer le cordonnier [kordon-yay]
shop le magasin [magazAN]

Shops generally open between 8.30 and 9.30 a.m. and normally close for lunch around 12.30, re-opening at 2 or 2.30 p.m. They then remain open until 7 or 8 p.m. **Boulangeries** (baker's shops) usually open earlier than other shops. Some shops and all large department stores and supermarkets are open at lunchtime. Shops in holiday resorts don't always close for lunch and often remain open until very late at night. Nearly all shops are closed on Sunday and for many shops Monday is the additional weekly closing day.

shopping: I'm going shopping je vais faire des courses [juh vay fair day koorss]
shopping centre le centre commercial [sONtr komairs-yal]
shop window la vitrine [veetreen]
shore (of sea, lake) le rivage [reevahj]
short (time, journey) court [koor] (person) petit [puhtee]
shortcut le raccourci [rakoorsee]
shorts le short
should: what should I do? que dois-je faire? [kuh dwaj fair]
 he shouldn't be long il devrait revenir bientôt [eel duhvray]
 you should have told me vous auriez dû me le dire [voo zoreeay doo]
shoulder l'épaule **f** [aypol]
shout crier [kree-ay]
show (in theatre) le spectacle [spekt-akl]
 could you show me? pourrais-tu/pourriez-vous me montrer? [pooray-

too/pooree-ay-voo muh mONtray]
shower (in bathroom) la douche [doosh]
with shower avec douche
shower gel le gel douche
shut fermer [fairmay]
when do you shut? à quelle heure fermez-vous? [kel urr fairmay-voo]
when do they shut? à quelle heure est-ce que ça ferme? [eskuh sa fairm]
they're shut c'est fermé [say fairmay]
I've shut myself out je me suis enfermé dehors [juh muh swee zONfairmay duh-or]
shut up! tais-toi/taisez-vous! [tay-twa/tezzay-voo]
shutter (on camera) l'obturateur **m** [obtooraturr]
(on window) le volet [volay]
shy timide [teemeed]
sick (US) malade [malad]
I'm going to be sick (vomit) j'ai envie de vomir [jay ONvee duh vomeer]
see **ill**
side le côté [kotay]
the other side of town l'autre côté de la ville
side lights les feux de position **mpl** [fuh duh pozeess-yON]
side salad la salade [sa-lad]
side street la petite rue [puhteet roo]
sidewalk le trottoir [trotwahr]
see **pavement**
sight: the sights of ... les endroits à voir à ... [lay zONdrwa a vwahr]
sightseeing: we're going sightseeing nous allons visiter la ville [noo zalON veezeetay]
sightseeing tour l'excursion **f** [exkoors-yON]
sign (roadsign etc) le panneau de signalisation [pano duh seen-yaleezass-yON]
signal: he didn't give a signal (driver) il n'a pas mis son clignotant [eel na pa mee SON kleen-yotON]
(cyclist) il n'a pas fait signe qu'il allait tourner [fay seeñ keel alay toornay]
signature la signature [seen-yatoor]
signpost le poteau indicateur [poto ANdeekaturr]
silence le silence [seelONSS]
silk la soie [swa]
silly idiot [eed-yo]
silver l'argent **m** [arjON]
silver foil le papier d'argent [papyay]
similar semblable [sONbl-abl]
simple simple [SAN-pl]
since: since yesterday depuis hier [duhp-wee]
since I got here depuis que je suis arrivé [areevay]
sing chanter [shONtay]
singer le chanteur, la chanteuse [shONturr, -urz]
single: a single to ... un aller

simple pour ... [alay sAN-pl]
I'm single je suis célibataire [juh swee sayleebatair]
single bed le lit d'une personne [lee dOOn pairson]
single room la chambre pour une personne [shONbr poor OOn pairson]
sink (in kitchen) l'évier **m** [ayv-yay]
sister la sœur [surr]
sister-in-law la belle-sœur [bel-surr]
sit: can I sit here? est-ce que je peux m'asseoir ici? [eskuh juh puh masswahr ee-see]
sit down s'asseoir
sit down assieds-toi/asseyez-vous [ass-yay-twa/asay-ay-voo]
is anyone sitting here? est-ce que cette place est prise? [eskuh set plass ay preez]
size la taille [tī]
ski le ski
(verb) skier [skee-ay]
a pair of skis une paire de skis
ski boots les chaussures de ski **fpl** [shohsOOr]
skiing le ski
we're going skiing nous allons faire du ski [noo zalON fair]
ski instructor le moniteur (de ski) [moneeturr]
ski-lift le remonte-pente [ruhmONt-pONt]
skin la peau [po]
skin-diving la plongée sous-marine [plONjay soo-mareen]
skinny maigre [megr]
ski-pants le fuseau [fOOzo]
ski-pass le forfait de ski [forfay]
ski pole le bâton de ski [bahtON]
skirt la jupe [jOOp]
ski run la piste de ski
ski slope la pente de ski [pONt]
ski wax le fart [far]
sky le ciel [s-yel]
sleep dormir [dormeer]
did you sleep well? tu as/vous avez bien dormi? [tOO a/voo zavay b-yAN dormee]
I need a good sleep j'ai besoin d'une bonne nuit de sommeil [jay buh-zwAN dOOn bon nwee duh somay]
sleeper (rail) le wagon-lit [vagON-lee]
sleeping bag le sac de couchage [kooshahj]
sleeping car le wagon-lit [vagON-lee]
sleeping pill le somnifère [somneefair]
sleepy: I'm feeling sleepy j'ai sommeil [jay somay]
sleeve la manche [mONsh]
slide (photographic) la diapositive [dee-apozeeteev]
slip (under dress) la combinaison [kONbeenezzON]
slippery glissant [gleessON]
slow lent [lON]
slow down! (driving, speaking)

moins vite! [mwAN veet]
slowly lentement [lONtmON]
could you say it slowly? pourriez-vous parler plus lentement? [pooree-ay-voo parlay plOO]
very slowly très lentement
small petit [puhtee]
smell: it smells ça sent mauvais [mo-vay]
smile sourire [sooreer]
smoke la fumée [fOOmay]
do you mind if I smoke? est-ce que ça vous dérange si je fume? [eskuh sa voo dayrONj see juh fOOm]
I don't smoke je ne fume pas
do you smoke? tu fumes/vous fumez? [tOO fOOm/voo fOOmay]
snack: I'd just like a snack j'aimerais manger un petit quelque chose [jemray mONjay AN puhtee kelkuh shohz]
sneeze l'éternuement **m** [aytairnOOmON]
snorkel le tuba
snow la neige [nej]
so: it's so good c'est tellement bien [telmON]
not so fast pas si vite!
so am I moi aussi [mwa o-see]
so do I moi aussi
so-so comme ci, comme ça [kom see, kom sa]
soaking solution (for contact lenses) la solution de trempage [solOOss-yON duh trONpahj]
soap le savon [savON]
soap powder la lessive [lesseev]
sober sobre [sobr]
sock la chaussette [sho-set]
socket (electrical) la prise de courant [preez duh kooroN]
soda (water) le soda
sofa le canapé, le divan [deevON]
soft doux, **f** douce [doo, dooss]
soft-boiled egg l'œuf à la coque **m** [urf a la kok]
soft drink la boisson non-alcoolisée [bwassON nON-alkoleezay]
soft lenses les lentilles souples **fpl** [lONtee soopl]
sole (of shoe, of foot) la semelle [suhmel]
could you put new soles on these? pourriez-vous ressemeler ces chaussures? [pooree-ay-voo ruh-suhmuhlay say shohsOOr]
some: can I have some water/peanuts? j'aimerais de l'eau/des cacahuètes, s'il vous plaît [jemray duh lo/day]
can I have some? est-ce que je peux en avoir? [eskuh juh puh ON avwahr]
somebody, someone quelqu'un [kel-kAN]
something quelque chose [kelkuh shohz]
something to drink quelque chose à boire

sometimes parfois [parfwa]
somewhere quelque part [kelkuh par]
son le fils [feess]
song la chanson [shONSON]
son-in-law le beau-fils [bo-feess]
soon bientôt [b-yANto]
I'll be back soon je reviens bientôt
as soon as possible dès que possible [day kuh]
sore: it's sore ça fait mal [sa fay mal]
sore throat le mal de gorge
sorry: (I'm) sorry je suis désolé, excusez-moi [juh swee dayzolay, eskOOzay-mwa]
sorry? (didn't understand) pardon? [par-dON]
sort: what sort of ...? quel genre de ...? [kel jONr duh]
soup le potage [potahj]
sour (taste) acide [aseed]
south le sud [sOOd]
in the south dans le sud
South Africa l'Afrique du Sud **f** [afreek dOO sOOd]
South African (adj) sud-africain [sOOd afreekAN]
I'm South African (man/woman) je suis sud-africain/sud-africaine [-ken]
southeast le sud-est [sOOd-est]
South of France le Midi
southwest le sud-ouest [sOOd-west]
souvenir le souvenir
Spain l'Espagne **f** [españ]
Spanish espagnol [espan-yol]
spanner la clé anglaise [klay ONglez]
spare part la pièce de rechange [p-yes duh ruhshONj]
spare tyre le pneu de rechange [p-nuh duh ruhshONj]
spark plug la bougie [boojee]
speak: do you speak English? parlez-vous l'anglais? [parlay-voo]
I don't speak ... je ne parle pas ... [juh nuh parl pa]

dialogue

can I speak to Marc? j'aimerais parler à Marc [jemray parlay]
who's calling? c'est de la part de qui? [say duh la par duh kee]
it's Patricia c'est Patricia
I'm sorry, he's not in, can I take a message? désolé, il n'est pas là, est-ce que je peux prendre un message [prONdr un messahj]
no thanks, I'll call back later non merci, je rappellerai plus tard [mairsee juh rapeluhray plOO tar]
please tell him I called dites-lui que j'ai appelé, s'il vous plaît [deet-lwee kuh jay apelay seel voo play]

spearmint la menthe verte [mONt vairt]

speciality la spécialité [spayss-yaleetay]
spectacles les lunettes [loonet]
speed la vitesse [veetess]
speed limit la limite de vitesse [leemeet]
speedometer le compteur [kONturr]
spell: how do you spell it? comment est-ce que ça s'écrit? [komON teskuh sa saykree]
see **alphabet**
spend dépenser [daypONsay]
spider l'araignée **f** [aren-yay]
spin-dryer l'essoreuse **f** [esorurz]
splinter l'écharde **f** [ayshard]
spoke (in wheel) le rayon [ray-ON]
spoon la cuillère [kwee-yair]
sport le sport [spor]
sprain: I've sprained my ... je me suis foulé ... [juh muh swee foolay]
spring (season) le printemps [prANtON]
(of car, seat) le ressort [ruhsor]
square (in town) la place [plass]
stairs l'escalier **m** [eskal-yay]
stale (taste) pas frais, **f** pas fraîche [pa fray, pa fresh]
(bread) rassis [rassee]
stall: the engine keeps stalling le moteur cale sans arrêt [moturr kal sON zaray]
stamp le timbre [tANbr]

dialogue

a stamp for England, please un timbre pour l'Angleterre, s'il vous plaît
what are you sending? qu'est-ce que vous envoyez? [keskuh voo zONvwy-yay]
it's for this postcard c'est pour cette carte postale

Stamps can either be bought at a post office or at tobacconists' shops (which can be identified by a red diamond-shaped sign with **Tabac** written on it), and sometimes from stalls and shops selling postcards.

standby le vol en stand-by [ON]
star l'étoile **f** [aytwal]
(in film) la star
start le début [dayboo]
(verb) commencer [kom-ONssay]
when does it start? quand est-ce que ça commence? [kONteskuh sa kom-mONss]
the car won't start la voiture refuse de démarrer [ruhfooz duh daymaray]
starter (of car) le démarreur [daymarurr]
(food) l'entrée **f** [ONtray]
state (in country) l'état **m** [ayta]
the States (USA) les États-

Unis [ayta-zoonee]
station la gare [gar]
statue la statue
stay: where are you staying? où logez-vous? [oo lojay-voo]
I'm staying at ... je loge au ... [juh loj o]
I'd like to stay another two nights j'aimerais rester deux nuits de plus [jemray restay]
steak le steak
steal voler [volay]
my bag has been stolen on m'a volé mon sac [ON ma volay]
steep (hill) raide [red]
steering la direction [deereks-yON]
step: on the steps sur les marches [soor lay marsh]
stereo stéréo [stayray-o]
sterling la livre sterling [leevr stairleeng]
steward (on plane) le steward
stewardess l'hôtesse de l'air **f** [otess]
sticking plaster le sparadrap [-dra]
still: I'm still waiting j'attends toujours [toojoor]
is he still there? est-ce qu'il est toujours là? [eskeel ay]
keep still! ne bouge/bougez pas! [nuh booj/boojay pa]
sting: I've been stung j'ai été piqué (par un insecte) [jay aytay peekay (par AN ANsekt)]
stockings les bas **mpl** [ba]
stomach le ventre, l'estomac **m** [vONtr, estoma]
stomach ache les maux d'estomac [mo destoma]
stone (rock) la pierre [p-yair]
stop s'arrêter [sa-retay]
to stop the car arrêter la voiture
please, stop here (to taxi driver etc) arrêtez-moi ici, s'il vous plaît [aretay-mwa ee-see]
do you stop near ...? est-ce que vous vous arrêtez près de ...? [eskuh voo voo zaretay]
stop doing that! arrêtez!
stopover la halte [alt]
storm la tempête [tON-pet]
straight: it's straight ahead c'est tout droit [say too drwa]
a straight whisky un whisky sec
straightaway tout de suite [toot sweet]
strange (odd) bizarre, étrange [aytrONj]
stranger l'étranger **m**, l'étrangère **f** [aytrONjay, -jair]
I'm a stranger here je ne suis pas d'ici [juh nuh swee pa dee-see]
strap (on watch) le bracelet [braslay]
(on dress) la bretelle [bruhtel]
(on suitcase) la sangle [sONgl]
strawberry la fraise [frez]
stream le ruisseau [rwee-so]
street la rue [roo]
on the street dans la rue
streetmap le plan de ville [plON duh veel]

string la ficelle [feessel]
strong fort [for]
stuck coincé [kwANsay]
the key's stuck le clé est coincée
student (male/female) l'étudiant **m**, l'étudiante **f** [aytood-yON, -yONt]
stupid stupide [stoopeed]
suburb le faubourg [fo-boor]
subway (US) le métro [maytro]
suddenly tout d'un coup [too dAN koo]
suede le daim [dAN]
sugar le sucre [sookr]
suit le costume
it doesn't suit me (colour etc) ça ne me va pas [sa nuh muh va pa]
it suits you (colour etc) ça vous va bien [b-yAN]
suitcase la valise [valeez]
summer l'été **m** [aytay]
in the summer en été
sun le soleil [solay]
in the sun au soleil [o]
out of the sun à l'ombre [lONbr]
sunbathe prendre un bain de soleil [prONdr AN bAN duh solay]
sunblock (cream) l'écran total **m** [aykrON toh-tal]
sunburn le coup de soleil [koo duh solay]
sunburnt: I'm sunburnt j'ai pris un coup de soleil [pree AN]
Sunday dimanche [deemONsh]
sunglasses les lunettes de soleil [loonet duh solay]
sun lounger la chaise longue [shez lON-g]
sunny ensoleillé [ONsolay-yay]
it's sunny il fait soleil [eel fay solay]
sun roof (in car) le toit ouvrant [twa oovrON]
sunset le coucher de soleil [kooshay duh solay]
sunshade le parasol
sunshine le soleil [solay]
sunstroke l'insolation **f** [ANsolass-yON]
suntan le bronzage [brONzahj]
suntan lotion le lait solaire [lay solair]
suntanned bronzé [brONzay]
suntan oil l'huile solaire **f** [weel solair]
super super [soopair]
we had a super time c'était super [saytay]
supermarket le supermarché [soopairmarshay]
supper le dîner [deenay]
supplement (extra charge) le supplément [sooplaymON]
sure: are you sure? vous êtes sûr? [voo zet soor]
sure! d'accord! [dakor]
surname le nom de famille [nON duh famee]
swearword le juron [jooron]
sweater le pullover
sweatshirt le sweatshirt
Sweden la Suède [swed]
Swedish (adj) suédois [swaydwa]

sweet (taste) sucré [sOOkray]
(dessert) le dessert [dessair]
sweets les bonbons **mpl**
[bONbON]
swelling l'enflure **f** [ONflOOr]
swim nager [nahjay]
I'm going for a swim je vais me baigner [juh vay muh benyay]
let's go for a swim allons nous baigner
swimming costume le maillot de bain [my-o duh bAN]
swimming pool la piscine [peesseen]
swimming trunks le slip de bain [sleep duh bAN]
Swiss (adj) suisse [sweess]
(man) le Suisse
(woman) la Suissesse [sweessess]
switch l'interrupteur **m** [ANtairOOpturr]
switch off (TV, lights) éteindre [aytANdr]
(engine) arrêter [aretay]
switch on (TV, lights) allumer [alOOmay]
(engine) mettre en marche [metr ON marsh]
Switzerland la Suisse [sweess]
swollen enflé [ONflay]

T

table la table [tahbl]
a table for two une table pour deux
tablecloth la nappe [nap]
table tennis le ping-pong
table wine le vin ordinaire [vAN ordeenair]
tailback (of traffic) le bouchon [booshON]
tailor le tailleur [tī-urr]
take (lead) prendre [prONdr]
(accept) accepter [axeptay]
can you take me to the airport? est-ce que vous pouvez m'emmener à l'aéroport? [eskuh voo poovay mONmuhnay]
do you take credit cards? acceptez-vous les cartes de crédit? [axeptay-voo]
fine, I'll take it d'accord, je le prends [juh luh prON]
can I take this? (leaflet etc) je peux le prendre? [puh]
how long does it take? combien de temps est-ce que ça prend? [kONb-yAN duh tON eskuh sa prON]
it takes three hours ça prend trois heures
is this seat taken? est-ce que cette place est occupée? [eskuh set plass et okOOpay]
hamburger to take away hamburger à emporter [ONportay]
can you take a little off here? (to hairdresser) pouvez-vous couper un peu par ici? [koopay AN puh]
talcum powder le talc
talk parler [parlay]

tall grand [grON]
tampons les tampons **mpl** [tONpON]
tan le bronzage [brONzahj]
to get a tan bronzer [brONzay]
tank (of car) le réservoir [rayzairvwahr]
tap le robinet [robeenay]
tape (cassette) la cassette
(sticky) le scotch®
tape measure le mètre [metr]
tape recorder le magnétophone [man-yaytofon]
taste le goût [goo]
can I taste it? est-ce que je peux goûter? [eskuh juh puh gootay]
taxi le taxi
will you get me a taxi? pouvez-vous m'appeler un taxi? [poovay-voo maplay]
where can I find a taxi? où y a-t-il des taxis? [oo yateel]

dialogue

to the airport/to Hotel ... please à l'aéroport/à l'Hôtel ..., s'il vous plaît
how much will it be? combien est-ce que ça me coûtera? [kONb-yAN eskuh sa muh kootuhra]
about 75 francs à peu près soixante-quinze francs [puh pray]
that's fine right here thanks vous pouvez me déposer ici, merci [muh daypozay]

taxi-driver le chauffeur de taxi
taxi rank la station de taxi [stass-yON]
tea (drink) le thé [tay]
tea for one/two please un thé/deux thés, s'il vous plaît [duh tay]

Ordinary tea usually comes without milk; to have milk with it ask for **'un peu de lait frais'** (some fresh milk). Herbal teas (**tisanes** or **infusions**) are very popular. The more common ones are **verveine** (verbena), **tilleul** (lime blossom), **menthe** (mint) and **camomille** (camomile).

teabags les sachets de thé **mpl** [sashay duh tay]
teach: could you teach me? est-ce que vous pouvez m'apprendre? [eskuh voo poovay maprONdr]
teacher (junior) l'instituteur **m**, l'institutrice **f** [ANsteetOOturr, -treess]
(secondary) le professeur [-urr]
team l'équipe **f** [aykeep]
teaspoon la cuillère à café [kwee-yair a kafay]
tea towel le torchon à vaisselle [torshON a vess-el]
teenager l'adolescent **m**, l'adolescente **f** [-sON, -sONt]

telegram le télégramme [taylay-]
telephone le téléphone [taylay-]
see **phone**
television la télévision [taylayveez-yON]
tell: could you tell him ...? pourriez-vous lui dire ...? [pooree-ay-voo lwee deer]
temperature (weather) la température [tONpayratOOr] (fever) la fièvre [fee-evr]
tennis le tennis [teneess]
tennis ball la balle de tennis [bal]
tennis court le court de tennis [koor]
tennis racket la raquette de tennis [raket]
tent la tente [tONt]
term (at university, school) le trimestre [treemestr]
terminus (rail) le terminus [tairmeenOOss]
terrible épouvantable [aypoovONt-abl]
terrific fantastique [fONtasteek]
than* que [kuh]
smaller than plus petit que
thanks, thank you merci [mairsee]
thank you very much merci beaucoup [bo-koo]
thanks for the help merci de m'avoir aidé
no thanks non, merci

dialogue

thanks merci
that's OK, don't mention it il n'y a pas de quoi [eel n-ya pa duh kwa]

that: that building ce bâtiment [suh]
that woman cette femme [set]
that one celui-là, **f** celle-là [suhlwee-la, sel-la]
I hope that ... j'espère que ... [kuh]
that's nice c'est joli [say]
is that ...? est-ce que c'est ...? [eskuh say]
that's it (that's right) c'est ça [say sa]
the* (singular) le, **f** la [luh] (plural) les [lay]
theatre le théâtre [tay-atr]
their* leur [lurr]
theirs* le/la leur [luh/la lurr]
them*: I know them je les connais [juh lay konay]
for them pour eux, **f** pour elles [uh, el]
with them avec eux/elles
I gave it to them je le leur ai donné [juh luh lurr ay donay]
who? – them qui? – eux/elles
then (at that time) à cette époque [set aypok] (after that) alors [alor]
there là

over there là-bas [la-ba]
up there là-haut [la-o]
is there ...? y a-t-il ...? [yateel]
are there ...? y a-t-il ...?
there is ... il y a ... [eel ya]
there are ... il y a ...
there you are (giving something) voilà [vwala]
thermometer le thermomètre [tairmometr]
Thermos flask® le thermos [tairmoss]
these*: these men ces hommes [say]
these women ces femmes
can I have these? j'aimerais ceux-ci/celles-ci, s'il vous plaît [suh-see/sel-see]
they* ils, **f** elles [eel, el]
thick épais [aypay]
(stupid) bouché [booshay]
thief le voleur, **f** la voleuse [volurr, -urz]
thigh la cuisse [kweess]
thin mince [mANss]
thing la chose [shohz]
my things mes affaires [may zafair]
think penser [pONsay]
I think so je pense que oui [juh pONss kuh wee]
I don't think so je ne crois pas [nuh krwa pa]
I'll think about it je vais y réfléchir [vay zee rayflesheer]
third party insurance l'assurance au tiers **f** [o t-yair]
thirsty: I'm thirsty j'ai soif [jay swaf]
this: this building ce bâtiment [suh]
this woman cette femme [set]
this one celui-ci, **f** celle-ci [suhlwee-see, sel-see]
this is my wife je vous présente ma femme [juh voo prayzONt ma fam]
is this ...? est-ce que c'est ...? [eskuh say]
those: those men ces hommes [say]
those women ces femmes
which ones? – those lesquel(le)s? – ceux-là/celles-là [suh-la/sel-la]
thread le fil [feel]
throat la gorge [gorj]
throat pastilles les pastilles pour la gorge **fpl** [pastee poor la gorj]
through par
does it go through ...? (train, bus) est-ce qu'il passe à ...? [eskeel pass]
throw lancer [lONsay]
throw away jeter [juhtay]
thumb le pouce [pooss]
thunderstorm l'orage **m** [orahj]
Thursday jeudi [juhdee]
ticket (for bus, train, plane) le billet [bee-yay]
(for cinema, cloakroom) le ticket [teekay]

dialogue

a return ticket to Dijon un aller-retour pour Dijon [alay-ruhtoor]
coming back when? avec retour à quelle date? [ruhtoor]
today/next Tuesday aujourd'hui/mardi prochain
that will be 300 francs trois cents francs, s'il vous plaît

ticket office (bus, rail) le guichet [geeshay]
tide la marée [maray]
tie (necktie) la cravate [kravat]
tight (clothes etc) serré [serray]
it's too tight ça me serre [sa muh sair]
tights le collant [kollON]
till (cash desk) la caisse [kess]
time* le temps [tON]
what's the time? quelle heure est-il? [kel urr eteel]
this time cette fois [set fwa]
last time la dernière fois
next time la prochaine fois
four times quatre fois
timetable l'horaire **m** [orair]
tin (can) la boîte [bwat]
tinfoil le papier d'aluminium [pap-yay]
tin opener l'ouvre-boîte **m** [oovr-bwat]
tiny minuscule [meenooskool]
tip (to waiter etc) le pourboire [poorbwahr]

Although service is included (usually 10-20 per cent of the bill), it is customary to leave a tip of about 10 per cent in restaurants when satisfied with the service. A similar tip is usual as well in bars and for taxi drivers.

tired fatigué [fateegay]
I'm tired je suis fatigué
tissues les kleenex® **mpl**
to: to Strasbourg/London à Strasbourg/Londres
to Brittany/England en Bretagne/Angleterre [ON]
to the post office à la poste
to the bar au bar [o]
toast (bread) le pain grillé [pAN gree-yay]
today aujourd'hui [ojoordwee]
toe l'orteil **m** [ortay]
together ensemble [ONsONbl]
we're together (in shop etc) nous sommes ensemble
can we pay together? pouvons-nous payer ensemble? [poovON-noo payay]
toilet les toilettes [twalet]
where is the toilet? où sont les toilettes? [oo sON lay]
I have to go to the toilet j'aimerais aller aux toilettes [jemray alay o]

Most cities now have a good number of public toilets: they are beige boxes with an automatic door that opens when you put two francs in it. The toilet itself gets cleaned automatically after each visitor. If this futuristic toilet doesn't appeal to you, you can use the toilets in restaurants and bars where you stop to eat or drink, or toilets in museums or at railway stations, where an attendant will expect you to leave a coin or two.

toilet paper le papier hygiénique [papyay eejee-ayneek]
tomato la tomate [tomat]
tomato juice le jus de tomate [joo]
tomato ketchup le ketchup
tomorrow demain [duhmAN]
 tomorrow morning demain matin
 the day after tomorrow après-demain [apray]
toner (cosmetic) la lotion tonique [lohss-yON toneek]
tongue la langue [lON-g]
tonic (water) le schweppes®
tonight ce soir [suh swahr]
tonsillitis l'angine **f** [ONjeen]
too (excessively) trop [tro]
 (also) aussi [o-see]
 too hot trop chaud
 too much trop
 me too moi aussi [mwa]
tooth la dent [dON]
toothache le mal de dents [mal duh dON]
toothbrush la brosse à dents [bross]
toothpaste le dentifrice [dONteefreess]
top: on top of ... sur ... [soor]
 at the top en haut [ON o]
top floor le dernier étage [dairn-yay aytahj]
topless seins nus [SAN noo]
torch la lampe de poche [lONp duh posh]
total le total [toh-tal]
tour l'excursion **f** [exkoors-yON]
 is there a tour of ...? y a-t-il une visite guidée de ...? [yateel oon veezeet geeday duh]
tour guide le guide [geed]
tourist le/la touriste [tooreest]
tourist information office le centre d'information touristique [sONtr dANformass-yON tooreesteek]
tour operator le voyagiste [vwy-ahjeest]
towards vers [vair]
towel la serviette [sairvee-et]
town la ville [veel]
 in town en ville [ON]
 just out of town à la sortie de la ville
town centre le centre-ville [sONtr-]
town hall la mairie [mairee]
toy le jouet [joo-ay]
track (US) le quai [kay]
 see **platform**
tracksuit le survêtement

[sOOrvetmON]
traditional traditionnel [tradeess-yonel]
traffic la circulation [seerkOOlass-yON]
traffic jam l'embouteillage **m** [ONbootay-ahj]
traffic lights les feux [fuh]
trailer (for carrying tent etc) la remorque [ruhmork]
(US) la caravane
trailer park le terrain de camping pour caravanes [terrAN duh kONpeeng poor]
train le train [trAN]
by train en train [ON]

Don't forget to validate your ticket by inserting it into the orange ticket machines in the station before you board the train. Also remember that you need to have a reservation to travel by **TGV**, and that you are required to pay a supplément for some trains and if you don't you will be fined. The French rail company, SNCF, offers a whole range of discount fares on Période Bleue (blue period) days – in effect most of the year. A leaflet showing the various discounts is given out at gares SNCF (train stations). It's worth asking, before purchasing your ticket, whether you're entitled to a tarif séjour, which means a 25 per cent reduction on the normal price if you are buying a return ticket, are willing to travel on **Période Bleue** days and will be spending Sunday at your destination.

dialogue

is this the train for ...? est-ce que ce train va bien à ...? [eskuh suh trAN va b-yAN a]
sure oui
no, you want that platform there non, il faut que vous alliez sur ce quai là-bas [eel fo kuh voo zalee-ay sOOr suh kay]

trainers (shoes) les tennis **fpl** [tenneess]
train station la gare [gar]
translate traduire [tradweer]
could you translate that? pourriez-vous me traduire cela? [pooree-ay-voo muh ... suhla]
translation la traduction [tradOOks-yON]
translator le traducteur, la traductrice [tradOOkturr, -treess]
trashcan la poubelle [poo-bel]
travel voyager [vwyahj-ay]
we're travelling around nous visitons la région [noo veezeetON la rayjeeON]
travel agent's l'agence de voyages **f** [ajONss duh vwyahj]
traveller's cheque le chèque de voyage [shek duh vwyahj]
tray le plateau [pla-toh]

tree l'arbre **m** [arbr]
tremendous fantastique [fONtasteek]
trendy à la mode
trim: just a trim please (to hairdresser) pouvez-vous me les égaliser, s'il vous plaît? [poovay-voo muh lay zaygaleezay]
trip le voyage [vwyahj]
(excursion) l'excursion **f** [exkOOrs-yON]
I'd like to go on a trip to ... j'aimerais faire une excursion à ... [jemray fair]
trolley le chariot [sharee-o]
trouble les ennuis [ON-nwee]
I'm having trouble with ... j'ai des problèmes de ... [jay day prob-lem]
sorry to trouble you désolé de vous déranger [dayzolay duh voo dayrONjay]
trousers le pantalon [pONtalON]
true vrai [vray]
that's not true ce n'est pas vrai
trunk le coffre [kofr]
trunks (swimming) le maillot de bain [my-o duh bAN]
try essayer [esay-ay]
can I have a try? (at doing something) est-ce que je peux essayer? [eskuh juh puh]
(food) est-ce que je peux goûter? [gootay]
try on essayer [essay-ay]
can I try it on? est-ce que je peux l'essayer?
T-shirt le T-shirt
Tuesday mardi [mardee]
tuna le thon [tON]
Tunisia la Tunisie [tOOneezee]
Tunisian tunisien [tOOneez-yAN]
tunnel le tunnel [tOOnel]
turn: turn left/right tournez à gauche/droite [toornay]
turn off: where do I turn off? où dois-je bifurquer? [oo dwa-juh beefOOrkay]
can you turn the heating off? pouvez-vous arrêter le chauffage? [aretay]
turn on: can you turn the heating on? pouvez-vous mettre le chauffage? [metr]
turning (in road) la bifurcation [beefOOrkass-yON]
TV la télé [taylay]
tweezers la pince à épiler [pANss a aypeelay]
twice deux fois [duh fwa]
twice as much deux fois plus [plOOss]
twin beds les lits jumeaux [lee jOOmo]
twin room la chambre à deux lits [shONbr]
twist: I've twisted my ankle je me suis tordu la cheville [juh muh swee tordOO la shuhvee]
type le type [teep]
a different type of ... une autre sorte de ... [ohtr sort duh]
typical typique [teepeek]
tyre le pneu [p-nuh]

U

ugly (person, building) laid [lay]
UK le Royaume-Uni [rwy-ohm ꝏnee]
ulcer l'ulcère **m** [ꝏlsair]
umbrella le parapluie [paraplwee]
uncle l'oncle **m** [ONkl]
unconscious sans connaissance [sON konessONss]
under (in position) sous [soo]
(less than) moins de [mwAN duh]
underdone (meat) pas assez cuit [pa zassay kwee]
underground (railway) le métro [maytro]
see **bus**
underpants le slip [sleep]
understand: I understand je comprends [juh KONprON]
I don't understand je ne comprends pas [pa]
do you understand? comprenez-vous? [KONpruhnay-voo]
unemployed au chômage [o shohmahj]
United States les États-Unis [aytazꝏnee]
university l'université **f** [ꝏneevairseetay]
unleaded petrol l'essence sans plomb **f** [essONss sON plON]
unlimited mileage le kilométrage illimité [keelomaytrahj eeleemeetay]
unlock ouvrir [oovreer]
unpack défaire sa valise [dayfair sa valeez]
until jusqu'à [jꝏska]
I'll wait until you're back j'attendrai jusqu'à ce que tu reviennes [jatONdray jꝏss-kass kuh]
unusual inhabituel [eenabeetꝏel]
up en haut [ON o]
up there là-haut [la-o]
he's not up yet (not out of bed) il n'est pas encore levé [eel nay pa zONkor luhvay]
what's up? (what's wrong?) que se passe-t-il? [kuh suh pasteel]
upmarket chic [sheek]
upset stomach l'indigestion **f** [ANdeejest-yON]
upside down à l'envers [a lONvair]
upstairs en haut [ON o]
urgent urgent [ꝏrjON]
us* nous [noo]
with us avec nous
for us pour nous
USA les USA [ꝏ-ess-a]
use utiliser [ꝏteeleezay]
may I use ...? puis-je me servir de ...? [pweej muh sairveer duh]
useful utile [ꝏteel]
usual habituel [abeetꝏel]
the usual (drink etc) comme d'habitude [kom dabeetꝏd]

V

vacancy: do you have any vacancies? (hotel) est-ce que vous avez des chambres? [eskuh voo zavay day shONbr]
vacation les vacances **fpl**
vaccination le vaccin [vaxAN]
vacuum cleaner l'aspirateur **m** [aspeeraturr]
valid (ticket etc) valable [val-abl]
how long is it valid for? jusqu'à quand est-il valable? [jooska kON eteel]
valley la vallée [valay]
valuable (adj) précieux [prayss-yuh]
can I leave my valuables here? est-ce que je peux laisser mes objets de valeur ici? [eskuh juh puh lessay may zobjay duh valurr ee-see]
value la valeur [valurr]
van la camionnette [kameeonet]
vanilla la vanille [vanee]
a vanilla ice cream une glace à la vanille [glass]
vary: it varies ça dépend [sa daypON]
vase le vase [vahz]
veal le veau [vo]
vegetables les légumes **mpl** [laygoom]
vegetarian le végétarien, la végétarienne [vayjaytaree-AN, -en]
vending machine le distributeur automatique [deestreebooturr otomateek]
very très [tray]
very little for me un tout petit peu pour moi [AN too puhtee puh]
I like it very much ça me plaît beaucoup [sa muh play bo-koo]
vest (under shirt) le maillot de corps [my-o duh kor]
via par
video (film) la vidéo [veedayo]
(recorder) le magnétoscope [man-yaytoskop]
view la vue [voo]
villa la villa [veela]
village le village [veelahj]
vinegar le vinaigre [veenegr]
vineyard le vignoble [veen-yobl]
visa le visa
visit visiter [veezeetay]
I'd like to visit ... j'aimerais visiter ... [jemray]
vital: it's vital that ... il faut absolument que ... [eel foht absoloomON kuh]
vodka la vodka
voice la voix [vwa]
voltage le voltage [volt-ahj]

The supply is 220V, though anything requiring 240V will work. Most plugs are two round pins: a travel plug is useful.

vomit vomir [vomeer]

W

waist la taille [tī]
waistcoat le gilet [jeelay]
wait attendre [atONdr]
wait for me! attendez-moi! [atONday-mwa]
don't wait for me ne m'attendez pas [nuh]
can I wait until my wife/partner gets here? est-ce que je peux attendre ma femme/mon ami(e)? [eksuh juh puh]
can you do it while I wait? pouvez-vous le faire tout de suite? [poovay-voo luh fair toot sweet]
could you wait here for me? (as said to taxi driver) est-ce que vous pouvez m'attendre ici?
waiter le serveur [sairvurr], le garçon [garsON]
waiter! garçon!
waitress la serveuse [sairvurz]
waitress! s'il vous plaît! [seel voo play]
wake: can you wake me up at 5.30? pouvez-vous me réveiller à cinq heures trente? [poovay-voo muh rayvayay]
wake-up call le réveil téléphonique [ray-vay taylayfoneek]
Wales le Pays de Galles [payee duh gal]
walk: is it a long walk? est-ce loin à pied? [es lwAN a p-yay]
it's only a short walk c'est à deux pas d'ici [set a duh pa dee-see]
I'll walk j'y vais à pied [jee vay]
I'm going for a walk je vais faire un tour [juh vay fair AN toor]
Walkman® le walkman
wall le mur [mOOr]
wallet le portefeuille [portfuh-ee]
wander: I like just wandering around j'aime bien flâner [jem b-yAN flanay]
want: I want a ... je veux un ... [juh vuh]
I don't want any ... je ne veux pas de ... [juh nuh vuh pa duh]
we want to go home nous voulons rentrer à la maison [noo voolON]
I don't want to non, je ne veux pas
he wants to ... il veut ... [eel vuh]
what do you want? que voulez-vous? [kuh voolay-voo]
ward (in hospital) la salle [sal]
warm chaud [sho]
I'm so warm j'ai tellement chaud
was*: it was ... c'était ... [saytay]
wash laver [lavay]
can you wash these?

pouvez-vous laver ceci, s'il vous plaît? [poovay-voo]
washer (for bolt etc) la rondelle [rONdel]
washhand basin le lavabo
washing (clothes) la lessive [lesseev]
washing machine la machine à laver [lavay]
washing powder la lessive [lesseev]
washing-up liquid le produit à vaisselle [prodwee a vess-el]
wasp la guêpe [gep]
watch (wristwatch) la montre [mONtr]
will you watch my things for me? pourriez-vous me garder mes affaires, s'il vous plaît? [pooree-ay-voo muh garday]
watch out! attention! [atONs-yON]
watch strap le bracelet-montre [braslay-mONtr]
water l'eau **f** [o]
may I have some water? pourriez-vous m'apporter de l'eau, s'il vous plaît? [pooree-ay-voo maportay]
waterproof (adj) imperméable [ANpairmayabl]
waterskiing le ski nautique [skee noteek]
wave (in sea) la vague [vag]
way: it's this way c'est par ici [say par ee-see]
it's that way c'est par là
is it a long way to ...? est-ce que c'est loin d'ici à ...? [eskuh say lwAN dee-see]
no way! pas question! [pa kest-yON]

dialogue

could you tell me the way to ...? pouvez-vous m'indiquer le chemin pour aller à ...?
go straight on until you reach the traffic lights continuez tout droit jusqu'aux feux [kONteenoo-ay too drwa joosko fuh]
turn left tournez à gauche [toornay]
take the first on the right prenez la première à droite [pruhnay]
see also where

we* nous [noo]
weak (person) faible [febl]
(drink) pas fort [pa for]
weather le temps [tON]

dialogue

what's the weather forecast? quelles sont les prévisions de la météo? [kels sON lay prayveez-yON duh la maytay-o]
it's going to be fine il va faire beau [eel va fair bo]
it's going to rain il va pleuvoir
it'll brighten up later ça va

s'éclaircir plus tard [sa va sayklairseer]

wedding le mariage [maree-ahj]
wedding ring l'alliance **f** [aleeONss]
Wednesday mercredi [mairkruhdee]
week la semaine [suhmen]
a week (from) today aujourd'hui en huit [ojoordwee ON weet]
a week (from) tomorrow demain en huit
weekend le week-end
at the weekend ce week-end
weight le poids [pwa]
weird bizarre
weirdo l'énergumène **mf** [aynairgOOmen]
welcome: welcome to ... bienvenue à ... [b-yAN-vuhnOO]
you're welcome (don't mention it) je vous en prie [juh voo zON pree]
well: I don't feel well je ne me sens pas bien [juh nuh muh sON pa b-yAN]
she's not well elle ne se sent pas bien [... sON ...]
you speak English very well vous parlez très bien l'anglais
well done! bravo!
this one as well celui-là aussi [o-see]
well well! (surprise) tiens! [t-yAN]

dialogue

how are you? comment vas-tu/allez-vous? [komON va-tOO/alay-voo]
very well, thanks très bien, merci [tray b-yAN]

well-done (meat) bien cuit [b-yAN kwee]
Welsh gallois [galwa]
I'm Welsh (man/woman) je suis gallois/galloise [... galwahz]
were*: we were nous étions [noo zayteeON]
you were vous étiez [voo zaytee-ay]
they were ils/elles étaient [eel/el zaytay]
west l'ouest **m** [west]
in the west à l'ouest
West Indian (adj) antillais [ONteeyay]
wet mouillé [mooyay]
what? quoi? [kwa]
what's that? qu'est-ce que c'est? [keskuh say]
what should I do? que dois-je faire? [kuh dwahj fair]
what a view! quelle vue magnifique! [kel]
what bus do I take? je prends quel bus?
wheel la roue [roo]
wheelchair le fauteuil roulant

[fotuh-ee roolON]
when? quand? [kON]
when we get back à notre retour [a notr ruhtoor]
when's the train/ferry? à quelle heure part le train/ferry? [kel urr par]
where? où? [oo]
I don't know where it is je ne sais pas où il est

dialogue

where is the cathedral? où est la cathédrale? [oo ay]
it's over there c'est par là [say]
could you show me where it is on the map? pouvez-vous me montrer où ça se trouve sur la carte?
it's just here c'est ici

which: which train? quel train? [kel]

dialogue

which one? lequel (laquelle)? [luhkel, lakel]
that one celui-là (celle-là) [suhlwee-la, sel-la]
this one? celui-ci (celle-ci)? [suhlwee-see]
no, that one non, celui-là (celle-là)

while: while I'm here pendant que je suis ici [pondON kuh]
whisky le whisky
white blanc, **f** blanche [blON, blONsh]
white wine le vin blanc [VAN blON]
who? qui? [kee]
who is it? qui est-ce? [ess]
the man who ... l'homme qui ...
whole: the whole week toute la semaine [toot]
the whole lot le tout [luh too]
whose: whose is this? à qui est ceci? [a kee ay suhsee]
why? pourquoi? [poorkwa]
why not? pourquoi pas? [pa]
wide large [larj]
wife: my wife ma femme [fam]
will*: will you do it for me? pouvez-vous faire ça pour moi? [poovay-voo]
wind le vent [vON]
window la fenêtre [fuhnetr]
near the window près de la fenêtre
in the window (of shop) en vitrine [ON veetreen]
window seat le siège près de la fenêtre [pray duh la fuhnetr]
windscreen le pare-brise [par-breez]
windscreen wiper l'essuie-glace **m** [eswee-glass]
windsurfing la planche à voile [plONsh a vwal]
windy: it's so windy il y a beaucoup de vent [eelya bo-

koo duh vON]
wine le vin [VAN]
can we have some more wine? encore un peu de vin, s'il vous plaît [ONkor AN puh]
wine list la carte des vins [kart day VAN]
wine merchant le marchand de vins [marshON duh VAN]
wine-tasting la dégustation [daygOOstass-yON]
winter l'hiver **m** [eevair]
in the winter en hiver [ON]
winter holiday les vacances d'hiver [vakONss deevair]
wire le fil de fer [feel duh fair]
(electric) le fil (électrique) [aylektreek]
wish: best wishes meilleurs vœux [mayurr vuh]
with avec [avek]
I'm staying with ... j'habite chez ... [jabeet shay]
without sans [sON]
witness le témoin [taymwAN]
will you be a witness for me? voulez-vous me servir de témoin? [voolay-voo muh sairveer duh]
woman la femme [fam]

women
Women are bound to experience sexual harassment in France, where many men make a habit of looking you up and down, and more often than not, passing comment. A '**bonjour**' or '**bonsoir**' on the street is almost always a pick-up line. If you so much as return the greeting, you've left yourself open to a persistent monologue and a difficult brush-off job.

wonderful merveilleux [mairvayuh]
won't*: the car won't start la voiture ne veut pas démarrer [nuh vuh pa]
wood (material) le bois [bwa]
woods (forest) la forêt [foray]
wool la laine [len]
word le mot [mo]
work le travail [trav-ī]
I work in ... je travaille dans ... [juh trav-ī]
it's not working ça ne marche pas [sa nuh marsh pa]
world le monde [mONd]
worried inquiet, **f** inquiète [ANkee-ay, -et]
worse: it's worse c'est pire [say peer]
worst le pire [luh peer]
worth: is it worth a visit? est-ce que ça vaut le détour? [eskuh sa vo luh daytoor]
would: would you give this to ...? pourriez-vous donner ceci à ...? [pooree-ay-voo donay suhsee]
wrap: could you wrap it up? pourriez-vous me l'emballer? [pooree-ay-voo muh lONbalay]
wrapping paper le papier

d'emballage [pap-yay dONbalahj]
wrist le poignet [pwAN-yay]
write écrire [aykreer]
could you write it down? pouvez-vous me l'écrire? [poovay-voo muh laykreer]
how do you write it? comment est-ce que ça s'écrit? [komON teskuh sa saykree]
writing paper le papier à lettres [pap-yay a letr]
wrong: it's the wrong key ce n'est pas la bonne clef [suh nuh pa la bon klay]
this is the wrong train ce n'est pas le bon train
the bill's wrong il y a une erreur dans la facture [eelya oon air-rurr dON la faktoor]
sorry, wrong number excusez-moi, j'ai fait un mauvais numéro [exkoozay-mwa jay fay AN movay noomayro]
sorry, wrong room excusez-moi, je me suis trompé de chambre [juh muh swee trONpay]
there's something wrong with ... ... ne marche pas bien [nuh marsh pa b-yAN]
what's wrong? qu'y a-t-il? [k-yateel]

X

X-ray les rayons X **mpl** [rayON eex]

Y

yacht le voilier [vwal-yay]
yard* le jardin [jardAN]
year l'année **f** [anay]
yellow jaune [jo-n]
yes oui [wee]
you're not going already, are you? – yes tu ne t'en vas pas déjà, hein? – si [too nuh tON va pa day-ja AN – see]
yesterday hier [yair]
yesterday morning hier matin
the day before yesterday avant-hier [avONt-yair]
yet encore [ONkor]
have you heard from him yet? est-ce que vous avez déjà eu de ses nouvelles? [eskuh voo zavay day-ja oo duh say noovel]

dialogue

is it here yet? est-ce que c'est arrivé? [eskuh say]
no, not yet non, pas encore [pa zONkor]
you'll have to wait a little longer yet il vous faudra attendre encore un peu

yoghurt le yaourt [ya-oor]
you* (polite or plural) vous [voo] (singular, familiar) tu [too]
this is for you c'est pour toi/vous [twa]
with you avec toi/vous

In French, when you address strangers or people with whom you have a semi-formal relationship (e.g. shopkeepers, hotel staff), and when you are speaking to more than one person, you should use the **vous** form of 'you', which takes the second person plural of the verb. The familiar **tu** form, which takes the second person singular of the verb, is used to address family, friends, children and informal acquaintances.

young jeune [jurn]
your* votre, pl vos [votr, vo]
(singular, familiar) ton, **f** ta, pl tes [tON, ta, tay]
yours* le/la vôtre [luh/la vohtr], pl les vôtres
(singular, familiar) le tien, **f** la tienne [t-yAN, t-yen], pl les tiens/tiennes
youth hostel l'auberge de jeunesse **f** [obairj duh jur-ness]

Z

zero zéro [zayro]
zip la fermeture éclair [fairmtOOr ayklair]
could you put a new zip on? pourriez-vous mettre une nouvelle fermeture éclair? [pooree-ay-voo metr OOn noovel]
zoo le zoo [zo]

French → English

A

a: il/elle a he/she/it has
à [a] to; at; in; by.
à la gare at the station
abcès **m** [absay] abscess
abeille **f** [abay] bee
abonnements **mpl** [abonnuh-mON] season tickets
abord: d'abord [dabor] first
absolument [absoloomON] absolutely
accélérateur **m** [axaylayraturr] accelerator
accélérer [axaylayray] to accelerate
accepter [axeptay] to accept
accès autorisé pour livraisons deliveries only
accès aux quais to the platforms
accès aux trains to the trains
accès interdit no entry
accès réservé au personnel staff entrance only
accès réservé aux riverains no entry except for access
accès réservé aux voyageurs munis de billets ticket holders only
accompagner [akONpan-yay] to accompany
accord: d'accord [dakor] OK
je suis d'accord I agree
accotement non stabilisé soft verge
accueil **m** [akuh-ee] reception
accusé de réception **m** [akoozay duh rayseps-yON] acknowledgement of receipt
achat **m** [a-sha] purchase
faire des achats to go shopping
acheter [ashtay] to buy
acide [a-seed] sour
acteur **m** [akturr] actor
actrice **f** [aktreess] actress
adaptateur **m** [adaptaturr] adaptor
addition **f** [adeess-yON] bill
adolescent **m** [adolessON] teenager
s'**adresser à ...** [sadressay] ask ...
adressez-vous à la réception ask at reception
aérogare **f** [a-airogar] air terminal
aéroglisseur **m** [a-airogleessurr] hovercraft
aéroport **m** [a-airopor] airport
affaires **fpl** [affair] things, belongings; business
affichage **m** [affeeshahj] display
affiche **f** [affeesh] poster
afficher [affeeshay] to display
affranchir [affrONsheer] to stamp
affranchissement **m** [affrONsheess-mON] postage
affreux [affruh] awful
afin que [afAN kuh] so that
âge **m** [ahj] age
agence **f** [ajONss] agency
agence de voyages **f** [duh vwyahj] travel agent's

agenda m [ajANda] diary
agent conservateur [ajON kONsairvaturr] preservative
agent de police m [duh poleess] policeman
agiter avant l'emploi shake before use
agrandissement m [agrONdeess-mON] enlargement
agréable [agray-abl] pleasant
agriculteur m [agreekoolturr] farmer
ai: j'ai [jay] I have
aide f [ed] help
aider [ayday] to help
aiguille f [aygwee] needle
aile f [el] wing
ailleurs [ī-yur] elsewhere
aimable [aymabl] kind
aimer [aymay] to like; to love
ne pas aimer to dislike
aimerais: j'aimerais [jemray] I would like
ainsi [ANsee] so; like this
ainsi que (just) as
air m [air] air
avoir l'air [avwahr] to look
air conditionné [kondeess-yonay] air conditioning
aire de croisement f [air duh krwaz-mON] passing place
aire de repos [ruhpo] rest area
aire de service [sairveess] service area
aire de stationnement [stass-yonuh-mON] parking area
ajouter [ajootay] to add
alimentation f [aleemONtass-yon] food; grocer
alimentation générale [jaynayral] grocer
allaiter [alaytay] to breastfeed
Allemagne f [almañ] Germany
allemand [almON] German
aller [alay] to go
comment allez-vous? [komON talay voo] how are you?
s'en aller [sON] to go away
allez-vous-en! [alay-voo zON] go away!
aller chercher [shairshay] to go and get, to fetch
aller-retour m [alay ruhtoor] return/round trip ticket
aller simple m [sANpl] single ticket
aller voir [vwahr] to go and see, to go and visit
allumage m [aloomahj] ignition
allumer [aloomay] to light; to switch on
allumette f [aloomet] match
allumez vos phares switch on your lights
allumez vos veilleuses switch on your sidelights/parking lights
alors [alor] then; well
alpinisme m [alpeeneess-muh] mountaineering
ambassade f [ONbasad] embassy
améliorer [amayleeoray] to improve
amende f [amONd] fine
amener [amuhnay] to bring
amer [amair] bitter
américain [amayreekAN]

American
Amérique **f** [amayreek] America
ameublement **m** [amurbluhmON] furniture
ami **m**, **amie** **f** [amee] friend
amortisseur **m** [amorteessurr] shock-absorber
amour **m** [amoor] love
faire l'amour [fair] to make love
ampoule **f** [ONpool] light bulb; blister
s'**amuser** [samOOzay] to have fun
an **m** [ON] year
analgésique **m** [an-aljayzeek] painkiller
ancien [ONss-yAN] ancient; old, former
ancien franc [frAN] old French franc (= 1 centime)
ancre **f** [ONkr] anchor
anémique [anaymeek] anaemic
anesthésie générale **f** [anestayzee jaynayral] general anaesthetic
anesthésie locale [lo-kal] local anaesthetic
angine **f** [ONjeen] tonsillitis
angine de poitrine [pwatreen] angina
anglais [ONglay] English
Anglais **m** Englishman
les Anglais the English
Anglaise **f** [ONglez] Englishwoman
Angleterre **f** [ONgluhtair] England
année **f** [anay] year
anniversaire **m** [aneevairsair] birthday
anniversaire de mariage [maree-ahj] wedding anniversary
annuaire **m** [anOO-air] phone book
annulé [anOOlay] cancelled
annuler [anOOlay] to cancel
antigel **m** [ONtee-jel] antifreeze
antihistaminique **m** [ONteeheestameeneek] antihistamine
anti-insecte: la crème anti-insecte [krem ONtee-ANsekt] insect repellent
antiquaire **m** [ONteekair] antique shop
août [oo] August
apparaître [aparetr] to appear
appareil **m** [aparay] device; camera
qui est à l'appareil? who's speaking?
Madame ... à l'appareil Madame ... speaking
cet appareil ne rend pas la monnaie this machine does not give change
cet appareil rend la monnaie this machine gives change
appareil acoustique **m** hearing aid
appareil-photo **m** camera
appartement **m** [apartmON] flat, apartment
appartenir [apartuhneer] to belong

appeler [aplay] to call
comment vous appelez-vous? [komON voo zaplay-voo] what's your name?
je m'appelle ... [juh mapel] my name is ...
appendicite f [apANdeesseet] appendicitis
apporter [aportay] to bring
on peut apporter son repas you may eat your own food here
apprendre [aprONdr] to learn
s'**approcher (de)** [saproshay] to go/come near
appuyer [apwee-yay] to lean, to push
appuyer ici press here
appuyez pour ouvrir press to open
après [apray] after
après-demain [-duhmAN] the day after tomorrow
après-midi m afternoon
arabe (m/f) [a-rab] Arabic; Arab
araignée f [aren-yay] spider
arbre m [arbr] tree
arc-en-ciel m [arkONss-yel] rainbow
argent m [arjON] money; silver
argent massif solid silver
armoire f [armwahr] cupboard
arnaque f [arnak] rip-off, swindle
arôme m [arohm] flavour
arôme naturel/artificiel natural/artificial flavouring
arrêt m [aray] stop
arrêt d'autobus bus stop
arrêt de bus bus stop
arrêté: par arrêté préfectoral by order
arrêter [aretay] to stop; to arrest
s'**arrêter** to stop
arrêtez! stop!
arrêtez votre moteur switch off your engine
arrêt facultatif request stop
arrêt interdit no stopping
arrière m [aree-air] back
la roue arrière the back wheel
le siège arrière the back seat
arrivée(s) f(pl) [areevay] arrival(s)
arriver [areevay] to arrive; to happen
arrondissement m [arONdeess-mON] administrative district of Paris
arthrite f [artreet] arthritis
articles mpl [arteekl]**: les articles soldés ne sont ni repris ni échangés** no refund or exchange of reduced price goods
articles de camping camping accessories
articles de sport sports goods
articles de voyage travel accessories
articles ménagers [mayna-jay] household goods
artisanat m [arteezana] crafts
arts ménagers mpl [ar mayna-jay] household goods

as: tu as [a] you have
as-tu ...? do you have ...?
ascenseur m [asONsurr] lift, elevator
aspirateur m [aspeeraturr] hoover®
s'asseoir [sasswahr] to sit down
asseyez-vous [asay-ay-voo] sit down
assez (de) [assay] enough; quite
j'en ai assez [jON ay assay] I have enough; I'm fed up
assieds-toi [ass-yay-twa] sit down
assiette f [ass-yet] plate
assurance f [assOOrONss] insurance
assure la correspondance avec ... connects with ...
asthme m [ass-muh] asthma
astucieux [astOOss-yuh] clever
athée m/f [atay] atheist
athlétisme m [atlayteess-muh] athletics
Atlantique m [atlONteek] Atlantic
attachez vos ceintures fasten your seat belt
attaque f [atak] attack; stroke
atteindre [atANdr] to reach
attendez ici wait here
attendez-moi! wait for me!
attendez votre ticket wait for your ticket
attendre [atONdr] to wait
attendre la sonorité wait for the dialling tone
attention! [atONss-yON] look out!; caution!
attention à la marche mind the step
attention, chien méchant beware of the dog
attention, enfants caution, children
attention, fermeture automatique des portes caution, doors close automatically
attention, peinture fraîche wet paint
atterrir [ataireer] to land
attraper [atrapay] to catch
au [o] to the; at the; in the; by the; with
auberge f [obairj] inn
auberge de jeunesse [jur-ness] youth hostel
aucun [oKAN] none, not any
au-dessous de [o-duhsoo duh] below
au-dessus de [o-duhsOO duh] above
audiophone m [odeeo-fon] hearing aid
aujourd'hui [ojoordwee] today
aujourd'hui en huit a week today
auprès de [opray duh] near
auquel [okel] to which; at which
aurai: j'aurai [joray] I will have
aura: il/elle aura [ora] he/she/it will have
aurais: j'aurais/tu aurais [oray] I/you would have

auras: tu auras [ora] you will have
au revoir goodbye
aurez: vous aurez [oray] you will have
auriez: vous auriez [oree-ay] you would have
aurions: nous aurions [oree-ON] we would have
aurons: nous aurons [orON] we will have
auront: ils/elles auront [orON] they will have
aussi [o-see] also
aussi grand que as big as
moi aussi me too
aussi ... que possible as ... as possible
aussitôt [o-seeto] at once
aussitôt que as soon as
Australie f [ostralee] Australia
australien [ostralee-AN] Australian
autant (de) [otON duh] as much; as many
autobus m [otoboss] bus
autocar m coach, bus
automne m [otON] autumn
automobiliste m/f [otomobeeleest] car driver; motorist
autoradio m [otorad-yo] car radio
autoroute f [otoroot] motorway, highway
autoroute à péage toll motorway/highway
auto-stop m [otostop] hitch-hiking
faire de l'autostop to hitchhike
autre [ohtr] other
un/une autre another
autre chose [shohz] something else
autres destinations other destinations
autres directions other destinations
Autriche f [otreesh] Austria
autrichien [otreeshee-AN] Austrian
aux [o] to the; at the; in the; by the; with
auxquel(le)s [okel] to which; at which; in which; by which
avaler [avalay] to swallow
avance: d'avance [davONss] in advance
en avance early
avancer [avONsay] to move forward, to advance
avant m [avON] front
avant before
avant JC BC
avant-hier [avON-tee-air] the day before yesterday
avec [avek] with
averse f [avairss] shower
aveugle [avurgl] blind
avez: vous avez [voo zavay] you have
avez-vous ...? do you have ...?
avion m [av-yON] plane
par avion by airmail
avis m [avee] notice

avocat **m** [avoka] lawyer
avoir* [avwahr] to have
avons: nous avons [noo zavON] we have
avril [avreel] April
ayant [ay-yON] having

B

bac **m** ferry
bagages **mpl** [bagahj] luggage
 faire ses bagages to pack
bagages à main [MAN] hand luggage
bagarre **f** [ba-gar] fight
bagnole **f** [ban-yol] car (familiar word)
bague **f** [bag] ring
baignade dangereuse danger, do not swim here
baignade interdite no swimming
se baigner [suh ben-yay] to go swimming
baignoire **f** [beñ-wahr] bathtub
bain **m** [bAN] bath
bains douches municipaux public baths
baiser **m** [bezzay] kiss
baiser to screw
bal **m** dance
 bal du 14 juillet open air dance on the French national holiday
balade **f** [bal-ad] walk, stroll
se balader [suh baladay] to go for a stroll
baladeur **m** [baladurr] personal stereo
balcon **m** [balkON] balcony
balle **f** [bal] ball
balles [bal] francs (familiar word)
ballon **m** [balON] ball; balloon
bande d'arrêt d'urgence hard shoulder
bande magnétique **f** [man-yayteek] tape
bande médiane [mayd-yan] central reservation
banlieue **f** [bON-l-yuh] suburbs
banque **f** [bONK] bank
barbe **f** [barb] beard
barque **f** [bark] small boat
barrière **f** [baree-air] fence
barrière de dégel road closed to heavy vehicles during thaw
bas **mpl** [ba] stockings
bas low
 en bas [ON] downstairs
baskets **fpl** [bass-ket] trainers
bateau **m** [bato] boat
bateau à rames [ram] rowing boat
bateau à vapeur [vapurr] steamer
bateau à voile [vwahl] sailing boat
bateau-mouche [-moosh] pleasure boat on the Seine
bâtiment **m** [bateemON] building
batterie **f** [batree] battery
se battre [suh batr] to fight
baume après-shampoing **m** [bohm apray-shONpwAN] conditioner

bd boulevard
BD (bande dessinée) f [bay-day (bONd desseenay)] comic strip
beaucoup [bo-koo] a lot; much
beaucoup de ... a lot of ...
beau, f belle [bo, bel] beautiful; fine
il fait beau the weather is good
beau-fils m [-feess] son-in-law
beau-père m [-pair] father-in-law
bébé m [bay-bay] baby
belge [belj] Belgian
Belgique f [beljeek] Belgium
belle [bel] beautiful
belle-fille f [-fee] daughter-in-law
belle-mère f [-mair] mother-in-law
béquilles fpl [baykee] crutches
besoin: j'ai besoin de ... [jay buhzwAN duh] I need ...
bibliothèque f [beebleeo-tek] library
bibliothèque municipale public library
bicyclette f [beesseeklet] bicycle
bien [b-yAN] well, fine
bien du/de la/des many, a lot of
bien portant [portON] in good health
bien que [kuh] although
bien sûr [sOOr] of course
bientôt [b-yanto] soon
à bientôt see you later
bienvenue! [b-yAN-vuhnOO] welcome!
bienvenue sur notre réseau welcome to our network
bijouterie f [beejootuhree] jeweller's
bijoux mpl [beejoo] jewellery
billet m [bee-yay] ticket
billet de banque [bONk] banknote, bill
billets tickets; (bank)notes, bills
billet Section Urbaine ticket valid for suburban train and métro and all RER
billets internationaux international tickets
billets périmés used tickets
blaireau m [blairo] shaving brush
blanc, f blanche [blON, blONsh] white
blanchisserie f [blONsheesree] laundry
blessé [blessay] injured; hurt
blessure f [blessOOr] wound
bleu [bluh] blue
bleu m bruise
boire [bwahr] to drink
bois m [bwa] wood
boîte f [bwat] box; can; nightclub
boîte à/aux lettres [letr] letterbox
boîte de nuit [nwee] nightclub
boîte de vitesses [veetess] gearbox
bol m bowl

bombe f [bONb] bomb
bon [bON] good
bon! right!, OK!
bon anniversaire! happy birthday!
bon appétit! enjoy your meal!
bon après-midi! have a good afternoon!
bonbon m [bON-bON] sweet, candy
bondé [bONday] crowded
bonde f [bONd] plug
bonjour [bONjoor] hello; good morning
bon marché [bON marshay] cheap
bonne année! [bon anay] happy New Year!
bonne chance! [shONss] good luck!
bonne journée! [joornay] have a good day!
bonne nuit [nwee] good night
bonne route! [root] safe journey!
bonnet de bain m [bonay duh bAN] bathing cap
bonsoir [bONswahr] good evening
bon voyage! have a good trip!
bord m [bor] edge
au bord de la mer [o] at the seaside
borne f [born] kilometre (familiar word)
botte f [bot] boot
bottin m [botAN] telephone directory
bouche f [boosh] mouth
bouché [booshay] blocked
boucherie f [booshree] butcher's
boucherie-charcuterie [-sharkOOtree] butcher's (also selling pâté and sausages)
boucherie chevaline horsemeat butcher
bouchon m [booshON] cork; stopper; traffic jam
bouclé [booklay] curly
boucles d'oreille fpl [bookl doray] earrings
bouée f [boo-ay] buoy
bouffe f [boof] grub, food
bouger [boojay] to move
bougie f [boojee] candle; spark plug
bouillotte f [boo-ee-yot] hot-water bottle
boulangerie f [boolONjree] baker's
boulangerie-pâtisserie baker's and cake shop
boules fpl [bool] (French-style) bowling
boules Quiès® [kee-ess] earplugs
boulevard périphérique m ring road
bourré [booray] pissed
boussole f [boossol] compass
bouteille f [bootay] bottle
boutique f small shop
boutique de mode clothes boutique
boutique hors-taxe [or tax]

duty free shop
bouton m [bootON] button; spot
boxe f [box] boxing
BP (boîte postale) PO Box
bras m [bra] arm
brasserie f pub/bar/café serving food
brave [brahv] good; brave
bref brief
Bretagne f [bruhtañ] Brittany
bricolage m [breekolahj] do-it-yourself, DIY (supplies)
bricoler [breekolay] to do DIY
briller [bree-yay] to shine
briquet m [breekay] lighter
brise f [breez] breeze
britannique British
brocante secondhand goods
broche f [brosh] brooch
bronchite f [brONsheet] bronchitis
bronzage m [brONzahj] suntan
bronzer [bronzay] to tan
se bronzer to sunbathe
brosse f [bross] brush
brosse à cheveux [shuhvuh] hairbrush
brosse à dents [dON] toothbrush
brosser [brossay] to brush
brouillard m [broo-ee-yar] fog
brouillard fréquent risk of fog
bruit m [brwee] noise
brûler [brOOlay] to burn
brûlure f [brOOlOOr] burn
brume f [brOOm] mist
brun [brAN] brown
brushing m blow-dry
bruyant [brwee-yON] noisy
bu [bOO] drunk
buffet à volonté unlimited buffet
bureau m office
bureau d'accueil [dakuh-ee] reception centre
bureau de poste [posst] post office
bureau des objets trouvés [objay troovay] lost property office
bureautique f office automation
butagaz m camping gas
buvette f [bOOvet] refreshment room; refreshment stall
buvez: vous buvez [bOOvay] you drink
buvons: nous buvons [bOOvON] we drink

C

ça* [sa] it; that
ça alors! well really!; I don't believe it!
ça va? how's things?
ça va it's OK, I'm OK; that's fine
ça va mieux I'm feeling better; things are better
cabas m [kaba] shopping bag
cabine f [kabeen] cabin
cette cabine peut être appelée au numéro: ... incoming calls can be made to this phonebox using the

following number: ...
cabine téléphonique phone box
cabines d'essayage fitting rooms
cabinet dentaire m dentist's surgery
cabinet médical doctor's surgery
cacher [kashay] to hide
cacher [kashair] kosher
cachet m [kashay] tablet
caddie m (supermarket) trolley
cadeau m [kado] present, gift
cadeaux-souvenirs gift shop
cafard m [kafar] cockroach
j'ai le cafard I feel a bit down
café m [kafay] coffee, black coffee; café, bar
café complet [kONplay] continental breakfast
cahier m [ky-yay] notebook; exercise book
caisse f [kess] till, cash desk
caisse d'épargne [dayparñ] savings bank
caissier m cashier
calculette f [kalœlet] calculator
calendrier m [kalONdree-ay] calendar
calmant m [kalmON] tranquillizer
caméra f [kamayra] cine-camera; (TV) camera
camion m [kam-yON] lorry
camionnette f [kam-yonet] van
campagne f [kONpañ] countryside
à la campagne in the country
camping m [kONpeeng] camping; campsite
camping-car m mobile home
camping-caravaning site for camping and caravans
camping interdit no camping
canadien [kanadee-AN] Canadian
canif m [kaneef] penknife
canne à pêche f [kan a pesh] fishing rod
canoë m [kano-ay] canoe; canoeing
canton m [kONtON] administrative district of Switzerland
caoutchouc m [ka-oochoo] rubber
capitaine m [kapeeten] captain
capot m [kapo] bonnet, (US) hood
car m coach, bus
car for, because
caravane f caravan
carburateur m carburettor
cardiaque: être cardiaque to have a heart condition
carie f [karee] caries
carnet m [karnay] book (of tickets)
carnet d'adresses [dadress] address book
carnet de tickets [teekay] book of tickets
carnet de timbres [tANbr] book of stamps

carrefour **m** **[karfoor]** crossroads, intersection
carrefour dangereux dangerous crossroads/intersection
carrosserie **f** garage that does bodywork repairs
carte **f** **[kart]** card; map; pass
carte d'anniversaire birthday card
carte de crédit **[kraydee]** credit card
carte d'embarquement **[ONbarkmON]** boarding pass
carte de réduction **[raydOOx-yON]** card entitling the holder to price reductions
carte de visite **[veezeet]** (business) card
carte d'identité **[eedONteetay]** ID card
carte grise **[greez]** car registration book
carte orange **[orONj]** season ticket for transport in Paris and its suburbs
carte postale **[poss-tal]** postcard
carte refusée card rejected
carte routière **[root-yair]** road map
carte verte **[vairt]** green card
carton **m** **[kartON]** box; cardboard
cascade **f** **[kaskad]** waterfall
casquette **f** **[kasket]** cap
cassé **[kassay]** broken
casser **[kassay]** to break
casserole **f** saucepan
cauchemar **m** **[kohsh-mar]** nightmare
cause **f** **[kohz]** cause
à cause de because of
CCP (compte de chèques postaux) giro account
ce* **[suh]** this; that; it
ce serait **[suhray]** it would be
ceci **[suhsee]** this
cédez le passage give way, yield
ceinture **f** **[sANtOOr]** belt
ceinture de sécurité **[saykOOreetay]** seat belt
cela **[suhla]** that
célèbre **[saylebr]** famous
célibataire **m** **[sayleebatair]** bachelor
célibataire single
celle-ci **[sel-see]** this one
celle-là **[-la]** that one
celles-ci **[sel-see]** these
celles-là those
celui-ci **[suhlwee-see]** this one
celui-là that one
cendrier **m** **[sONdree-ay]** ashtray
cent **[sON]** hundred
centime **m** **[sONteem]** centime (1/100 franc)
centre **m** **[sONtr]** centre
centre commercial shopping centre
centre culturel arts centre
centre sportif sports centre
centre-ville city centre
cependant **[suhpONdON]** however
ce que **[suh kuh]** what
ce qui **[kee]** what

certain [sairtAN] sure, certain; some
ces* [say] these
c'est [say] it is; that's
c'est ça that's it
c'est-à-dire [setadeer] that is to say
cet [set] this; that
c'était [saytay] it was
cette* [set] this; that
ceux-ci* [suh-see] these
ceux-là* those
CFF (Chemins de fer fédéraux) Swiss railways
chacun [shakAN] each one; everyone
chaîne f [shen] chain; channel; stereo
chaise f [shez] chair
chaise longue deck chair
chaleur f [shalurr] heat
chambre f [shONbr] room; bedroom
chambre à air inner tube
chambre à coucher [kooshay] bedroom
chambre à deux lits [duh lee] twin room
chambre pour deux personnes [pairson] double room
chambre pour une personne [oon] single room
chambres à louer rooms to let
champ m [shON] field
chance f [shONss] luck; chance
change m [shONj] change; exchange; currency exchange
change de devises currency exchange
changement à ... change at ...
changer [shonjay] to change
se **changer** to change
changer de train to change trains
changer de vitesse to change gear
changeur de monnaie m change machine
chanson f [shONsON] song
chanter [shONtay] to sing
chantier m roadworks; building site
chantilly f [shontee-yee] whipped cream
chapeau m [shapo] hat
chapeau de soleil [solay] sun hat
chapellerie f hat shop
chaque [shak] each, every
charcuterie f [sharkootree] delicatessen; cold meat, sausages, salami, pâtés etc
chariot m [sharee-o] trolley
chariot obligatoire you must take a trolley
charter m charter flight
chasse gardée hunting preserve
chat m [sha] cat
châtain [shatAN] chestnut, brown
château m [shato] castle; mansion
château fort fortified castle
chaud [sho] warm, hot
chauffage m [shofahj] heating

chauffage central [sON-tral] central heating
chauffard! [shofar] learn to drive!
chauffe-eau m [shohf-o] water heater
chaussée déformée uneven road surface
chaussée glissante slippery road surface
chaussée rétrécie road narrows
chaussée verglacée icy road
chaussettes fpl [sho-set] socks
chaussures fpl [sho-sOOr] shoes
chaussures de ski ski boots
chaussures de tennis gym shoes
chauve [shohv] bald
CH (Confédération Helvétique) Switzerland
chemin m [shuhmAN] path
chemin de fer [duh fair] railway
chemise f [shuhmeez] shirt
chemise de nuit [duh nwee] nightdress
chemiserie menswear
chemisier m [shuhmeez-yay] blouse
chèque m [shek] cheque, (US) check
les chèques ne sont acceptés qu'à partir de 100 F cheques accepted for amounts over 100F only
les chèques ne sont pas acceptés we do not accept cheques
chèque de voyage [duh vwyahj] traveller's cheque
chéquier m [shaykee-ay] cheque book
cher [shair] expensive; dear
chercher [shairshay] to look for
cheveux mpl [shuhvuh] hair
cheville f [shuhvee] ankle
chez [shay] at; among
chez Nadine at Nadine's
faites comme chez vous make yourself at home
chez Marcel/Mimi (name of bar etc) Marcel's/Mimi's
chien m [shee-AN] dog
les chiens doivent être tenus en laisse dogs must be kept on a leash
choc m [shok] shock
chocolat à croquer m [shokola a krokay] plain chocolate
chocolat au lait [o lay] milk chocolate
chocolatier m chocolate shop
choisir [shwazeer] to choose
choix m [shwa] choice
chômage: au chômage [o shohmahj] unemployed
chose f [shohz] thing
Chronopost® express mail
chute de neige f [shOOt duh nej] snowfall
chute de pierres falling rocks
ciel m [see-el] sky; heaven
cigare m [seegar] cigar
cimetière m [seemt-yair] cemetery
cinémathèque f film theatre, movie theater

cinglé m [sANglay] nutter, nutcase
cinq [sANK] five
cinquante [sANKONt] fifty
cinquième [sANK-yem] fifth
cintre m [sANtr] coathanger
cirage m [seerahj] shoe polish
circuit touristique tourist route
circulation f [seerkOOlass-yON] traffic
circulation alternée single line traffic
circuler [seerkOOlay] to run
circule le ... runs on ...
ne circule pas le samedi/dimanche does not run on Saturdays/Sundays
circulez! move along!
circulez sur une file single line traffic
cire pour voiture f [seer poor vwatOOr] car wax
cirque m [seerk] circus
ciseaux mpl [seezo] scissors
cité universitaire f university halls of residence
clair clear
bleu clair light blue
classe f [klass] class
clé f [klay] key
clé anglaise [ONglez] wrench
clignotant m [kleen-yotON] indicator
climat m [kleema] climate
climatisation f [kleemateezass-yON] air-conditioning
climatisé air-conditioned
clinique f clinic
cloche f bell
clôture électrifiée electric fence
clou m [kloo] nail
cochon m [koshON] pig
code de la route m [kod duh la root] highway code
code postal [poss-tal] postcode, zip code
coffre m [kofr] boot, (US) trunk
coiffer [kwafay] to comb
se coiffer to do one's hair
coiffeur m, coiffeuse f [kwafurr, -urz] hairdresser
coiffeur pour dames [poor dam] ladies' hairdresser
coiffeur pour hommes [om] men's hairdresser, barber's
coiffure f [kwafOOr] hairstyle; hairdresser's
coin m [kwAN] corner
coincé [kwANsay] stuck
col m collar; (mountain) pass
col fermé pass closed
col ouvert pass open
col roulé [roolay] polo neck (jumper)
colis m [kolee] parcel, package
colis France parcels for France only
collant m [kolON] tights
colle f [kol] glue
collectionner [kolex-yonay] to collect
collier m [kol-yay] necklace
colline f [koleen] hill
combien? [kONb-yAN] how many?, how much?

commander [komONday] to order
comme [kom] like; as; how
commencer [komONsay] to begin
comment? [komON] how?; pardon?; sorry?
comment allez-vous? [talay-voo] how are you?
comment ça va? [sa] how are things?
comment vas-tu? [va-too] how are you?
commerçant m [komairsON] shopkeeper
commissariat m [komeessaree-a] police station
commissariat de police police station
commotion cérébrale f [komoss-yON sayray-bral] concussion
communication f [komooneekass-yON] call
communication internationale international call
communication interurbaine long-distance call
communication locale local call
communication urbaine local call
compagnie aérienne f [kompan-yee a-ayree-en] airline
comparer [kONparay] to compare
compartiment fumeurs smoking compartment
compartiment non-fumeurs non-smoking compartment
complet m [kONplay] suit
complet full, no vacancies
complètement [kONpletmON] totally
compliqué [kONpleekay] complicated
composer le numéro dial the number
composez sur le clavier numérique le montant choisi pour la vignette enter selected value of postage label on numerical keyboard (francs, comma, centimes)
composez votre code confidentiel à l'abri des regards indiscrets enter your PIN without letting anybody see it
composition contents
composition du train order of cars
compostage: le compostage des billets est obligatoire tickets are valid only if punched
compostez votre billet validate/punch your ticket in the machine
comprendre [kONprONdr] to understand; to include
comprimé m [kONpreemay] tablet
comprimé effervescent effervescent tablet
compris [kONpree] included
comptable m [kONtabl]

accountant
comptant: payer comptant [kONtON] pay cash
compteur m [kONturr] speedometer
con m [kON] stupid idiot; stupid bastard
concessionnaire m agent
concierge m/f caretaker
conditions d'enneigement snow conditions
conditions pour skier skiing conditions
conducteur m [kONdOOkturr] driver
conductrice f [kONdOOktreess] driver
conduire [kONdweer] to drive
confirmer [kONfeermay] to confirm
confiserie f confectioner, sweet shop
congé annuel m annual holiday
congélateur m [kONjaylaturr] freezer
connaître [konetr] to know
conseiller [kONsay-yay] to advise
conserver: se conserve au moins ... après la date-limite de vente keeps for at least ... after the sell-by date
conserver au frais (et au sec) keep in a cool (dry) place
conservez votre ticket sur vous keep your ticket with you
conservez votre titre de transport jusqu'à la sortie keep your ticket till you leave the station
consigne f [kONseeñ] left luggage, baggage checkroom
consigne automatique left luggage lockers
consommation f [kONsomass-yON] drink
consommation au comptoir drink at the bar
consommation en salle drink in the lounge
consommer avant le ... eat by ..., best before ...
constipé [kONsteepay] constipated
consulat m [kONsOOla] consulate
contacter [kONtaktay] to contact
contagieux [kONtah-jyuh] contagious
contenir [kONtuhneer] to contain
ne contient pas de ... contains no ...
content [kONtON] pleased
contenu contents
continuer [kONteenOO-ay] to continue, to go on
contraceptif m contraceptive
contractuel m traffic warden
contraire m [kONtrair] opposite
contre [kONtr] against
contre les ... for ...
contre-indications contra-indications

contrôle des bagages m baggage security check
contrôle des passeports passport control
contrôles radar radar speed checks
convoi exceptionnel long vehicle
copain m [kopAN] pal, mate; boyfriend
copine f [kopeen] friend; girlfriend
coquillage m [kokee-ahj] shell
Corail m intercity train
cor au pied m [o p-yay] corn
corde f rope
cordonnerie f cobbler's
cordonnier m cobbler, shoe repairs
corps m [kor] body
correspondance f [koresspONdONss] connection
correspondance Porte d'Orléans all stops on the line to Porte d'Orléans
Corse f [korss] Corsica
costume m suit
côté m [kotay] side
à côté de next to
mettre de côté to put aside
côte f [koht] coast; rib
Côte d'Azur French Riviera
côté non stabilisé soft verge
coton m [kotON] cotton
coton hydrophile [eedrofeel] cotton wool, absorbent cotton
cou m [koo] neck
couche f [koosh] nappy
coucher: aller se coucher [alay suh kooshay] to go to bed
au coucher seulement only when you go to bed
couchette f couchette; reclining seat; bunk bed
coude m [kood] elbow
coudre [koodr] to sew
couette f [kwet] continental quilt; bunch (in hair)
couler [koolay] to sink; to run
couleur f [koolurr] colour
couloir bus et taxis bus and taxi lane
coup m [koo] blow, knock; stroke
tout d'un coup suddenly
coup de fil phonecall
coup de soleil [solay] sunburn
coupe f [koop] haircut
coupe de cheveux [duh shuhvuh] haircut
couper [koopay] to cut
coupure f [koopoor] cut
coupure de courant [duh koorON] power cut
cour court; courtyard
courageux [koorahj-uh] brave
courant d'air m [koorON dair] draught
courant dangereux dangerous current
courir [kooreer] to run
courrier m [kooree-ay] mail; letters and postcards
courrier recommandé registered mail
courroie du ventilateur f [koorwa doo vONteelaturr] fan

belt
cours du change m [koor doo shONj] exchange rate
course f [koorss] race
faire des courses to go shopping
course automobile racing track
court [koor] short
court de tennis m tennis court
cousin m, cousine f [koozAN, -een] cousin
couteau m [kooto] knife
coûter [kootay] to cost
coutume f [kootoom] custom
couture f dressmaking; couture
couvent m [koovON] convent
couvercle m [koovairkl] lid
couvert [koovair] covered; overcast
couverts mpl [koovair] cutlery
couverts à poisson fish cutlery
couverture f [koovairtoor] blanket
couverture chauffante [shohfONt] electric blanket
couvre-lit m [koovr-lee] bedspread
cracher [krashay] to spit
crachin m [krashAN] drizzle
craindre [krANdr] to fear
crampe f [krONp] cramp
crâne m [krahn] skull
cravate f tie
crayon m pencil
crédit ... unités ... units remaining, credit ...
crème de beauté f [botay] cold cream
crème démaquillante [daymakee-yONt] cleansing cream
crème hydratante [eedratONt] moisturizer
crémerie f dairy
crêperie f [krepuhree] pancake restaurant
crevaison f [kruhvezzON] puncture
crevé [kruhvay] knackered; punctured
cric m jack
crier [kree-ay] to shout
crise f [kreez] fit, attack; crisis
crise cardiaque heart attack
crise de foie [duh fwa] upset stomach
crise d'épilepsie epileptic fit
croire [krwahr] to believe
croisement m [krwazmON] junction, intersection
croisière f [krwaz-yair] cruise
crosse de golf f golf club
CRS (Compagnie républicaine de sécurité) **f** [say-air-ess] riot police; **m** riot policeman
cuiller f, cuillère f [kwee-yair] spoon
cuillère à café teaspoon
cuillère à dessert dessert spoon
cuillère à soupe soup spoon
cuillerée f spoonful
cuir m [kweer] leather
cuisine f kitchen; cooking

cuisiner [kweezeenay] to cook
cuisinier m [kweezeen-yay] cook
cuisinière f [kweezeen-yair] cooker; cook
cuisse f [kweess] thigh; leg (of chicken)
cycles cycle shop
cyclisme m [seekleess-muh] cycling
cycliste m/f [seekleest] cyclist
cyclotourisme m cycle touring
cystite f [seess-teet] cystitis

D

daim m [dAN] suede
dame f [dam] lady
dames ladies' (toilets); draughts, checkers
dancing m [dONseeng] dance hall, night club
danger m [dONjay] danger
danger de mort danger of death
dangereux [dONjuhruh] dangerous
dans [dON] in; into
danse f [dONss] dance; dancing
danser [dONsay] to dance
date f [dat] date
date de naissance [nessONss] date of birth
date limite de vente sell-by date
de [duh] of; from
debout [duhboo] standing
début m beginning
débutant m beginner
décembre [daysONbr] December
décider [dayseeday] to decide
déclarer [dayklaray] to declare, to state
décoller [daykolay] to take off
déconseillé aux personnes sensibles unsuitable for people of a nervous disposition
décontracté [dayKONtraktay] casual; laid-back
découpez suivant le pointillé cut along the dotted line
découvrir [daykoovreer] to discover
décrire [daykreer] to describe
décrochez lift the receiver
déçu [daysoo] disappointed
dedans [duhdON] inside
défaire sa valise [dayfair] to unpack
défectueux [dayfektoo-uh] faulty
défendu [dayfONdoo] forbidden
défense de ... [dayfONss] ... forbidden, no ..., do not ...
défense d'afficher stick no bills
défense de déposer des ordures no litter, no dumping
défense d'entrer no entry
défense de fumer no smoking
défense de laisser des

bagages dans le couloir bags must not be left in the corridor
défense de marcher sur la pelouse keep off the grass
défense de parler au conducteur do not talk to the driver
défense de ... sous peine d'amende ... will be fined
défense de stationner no parking
défense de traverser les voies it is forbidden to cross the railway/railroad lines
dégagé clear
dégoûtant [daygootON] disgusting
degré **m** [duhgray] degree
dégueulasse [daygurlass] disgusting
dégustation (de vin) **f** [dayg00stass-yON] wine tasting
dégustation gratuite free wine-tasting
dehors [duh-or] outside
dehors! get out!
déjà [dayja] already
déjeuner **m** [dayjuhnay] lunch; breakfast
delco **m** distributor
délicieux [dayleess-yuh] delicious
deltaplane **m** [-plan] hang-gliding
demain [duhmAN] tomorrow
à demain see you tomorrow
demander [duhmONday] to ask
demandez à la caisse ask at the cash desk
démangeaison **f** [daymONjezzON] itch
démaquillant **m** [daymakee-yON] skin cleanser
se **démaquiller** [daymakee-yay] to remove one's make-up
démarrer [daymaray] to start up
demi [duhmee] half
demi-litre **m** half a litre
demi-heure **f** [-urr] half an hour
demi-journée **f** [-joornay] half a day
demi-pension **f** [-pONss-yON] half board, American plan
demi-tour **m** U-turn
dent **f** [dON] tooth
dentier **m** [dONt-yay] dentures, false teeth
dentifrice **m** [dONteefreess] toothpaste
dentiste **m/f** [dONteest] dentist
dépanneuse **f** [daypanurz] breakdown lorry
département **m** [daypartmON] administrative district of France
départementale **f** [daypartmONtal] B road
départ(s) departure(s)
dépasser [daypassay] to pass
se **dépêcher** [suh daypeshay] to hurry
dépêchez-vous! hurry up!
dépendre: ça dépend [sa daypON] it depends
dépenser [daypONsay] to spend

dépliant **m** [dayplee-ON] leaflet
dépression (nerveuse) **f** [daypress-yON nairvurz] nervous breakdown
déprimé [daypreemay] depressed
depuis (que) [duhpwee (kuh)] since
dérangement: en dérangement out of order
déranger [dayrONjay] to disturb
ça vous dérange si ...? [sa voo dayrONj] do you mind if ...?
déraper [dayrapay] to skid
dermatologue **m/f** [dairmatolog] dermatologist
dernier [dairn-yay] last
l'année dernière last year
derrière [dairyair] behind
derrière **m** bottom
des* [day] of the; from the; some
des biscuits some biscuits
dès [day] from
dès que as soon as
désagréable [dayzagray-abl] unpleasant
désastre **m** [dayzastr] disaster
descendre [duhsONdr] to go down; to get off
se **déshabiller** [suh dayzabee-yay] to undress
désinfectant **m** [dayzANfektON] disinfectant; antiseptic
désirer [dayzeeray] to want, to wish for
désolé: je suis désolé [dayzolay] I'**m** sorry
desquels [daykel] of which; from which
dessert **m** [desair] dessert
dessert ... stops at ...
dessin **m** [duhsAN] drawing
dessiner [duhseenay] to draw
dessous [duhsoo] underneath; under it
dessus [duhsoo] above; on top; on it
destinataire **m/f** addressee; consignee
détaxe à l'exportation **f** tax refund on export goods
détendre: se détendre [suh daytONdr] to relax
détester [daytestay] to hate
deux [duh] two
deuxième étage **m** [duhz-yem aytahj] second floor, (US) third floor
devant [duhvON] in front of; in front
développement de pellicules/photos film processing
développer [dayvlopay] to develop
devenir [duhvuhneer] to become
déviation **f** diversion
devises étrangères **fpl** [duhveez aytrONjair] foreign currency
devoir **m** [duhvwahr] duty
devoir to have to
devrai: je devrai [duhvray] I will have to
devrais: je/tu devrais [duhvray] I/you should
devras: tu devras [duhvra] you

will have to
devrez: vous devrez [duhvray] you will have to
devriez: vous devriez [duhvree-ay] you should
diabétique diabetic
diamant m [dee-amON] diamond
diapositive f [dee-apozeeteev] slide
diarrhée f [dee-aray] diarrhoea
dictionnaire m [deex-yonair] dictionary
diététique health food
Dieu m [d-yuh] God
différent [deefayrON] different
difficile [deefeesseel] difficult
Diligo® pre-stamped parcel, for France only
diluer [deeloo-ay] to dissolve
diluer dans un peu d'eau dissolve in water
dimanche [deemONsh] Sunday
dimanches et jours fériés Sundays and public holidays
dîner m [deenay] dinner
dîner to have dinner
dîner-spectacle dinner during the show (in cabaret)
dingue [dAN-g] crazy
dire [deer] to say; to tell
directeur m [deerekturr] manager; director; headteacher
direction f [deerex-yON] steering; direction
dis: je/tu dis [dee] I/you say
disent: il/elles disent [deez] they say
disons: nous disons [deezON] we say
disparaître [deesparetr] to disappear
disquaire m [deeskair] record shop
disque m [deesk] record
disque compact compact disc
disque obligatoire parking disk compulsory
dissolvant m [deessolvON] nail-polish remover
Distingo® envelope with pre-printed address box
distributeur automatique de billets m ticket machine
distributeur (automatique) de billets (de banque) cash machine, ATM
distributeur de boissons drinks vending machine
dit [dee] says; said
dites: vous dites [deet] you say
divorcé [deevorsay] divorced
divorcer [deevorsay] to get a divorce
dix [deess] ten
dix-huit [deez-weet] eighteen
dixième [deez-yem] tenth
dix-neuf [deez-nuhf] nineteen
dix-sept [deesset] seventeen
d'occasion [dokaz-yON] second-hand
docteur m [dokturr] doctor
doigt m [dwa] finger

dois: je/tu dois [dwa] I/you must
doit: il/elle doit [dwa] he/she/it must
doivent: ils/elles doivent [dwav] they must
dolmen m megalithic tomb
domicile m home address
dommage: c'est dommage [domahj] it's a pity
donc [dONk] then, therefore
donner [donay] to give
dont [dON] of which; whose
dormir [dormeer] to sleep
dos m [doh] back
dose pour adultes/enfants dose for adults/children
douane f [dwan] Customs
doubler [dooblay] to overtake
douce [dooss] soft; sweet
douche f [doosh] shower
douleur f [doolurr] pain
douloureux [doolooruh] painful
douter [dootay] to doubt
doux, f douce [doo, dooss] soft; sweet
douzaine f [doozen] dozen
douze [dooz] twelve
drap m [dra] sheet
drapeau m [drapo] flag
draps de lit mpl [dra duh lee] bed linen
drogue f [drog] drug
droguerie f [drogree] shop selling selling non-prescription medicines, toiletries and household goods
droit [drwa] straight
droit m right
droite f [drwat] right
à droite (de) on the right (of)
drôle funny
du* [doo] of the; from the; some
du vin some wine
dû: j'ai dû [doo] I had to; I must have
duquel [dookel] of which; from which
dur [door] hard
durer [dooray] to last; to keep
durée de conservation ... keeps for ...

E

eau f [o] water
eau de Javel [duh javel] bleach
eau non potable not drinking water
eau potable drinking water
échanger [ayshONjay] to exchange
échange/remboursement exchange/refund
échantillon gratuit – ne peut être vendu free sample – not for sale
échecs mpl [ayshek] chess
écharpe f [aysharp] scarf
échelle f [ayshel] ladder
école f [aykol] school
école de langues [duh lON-g] language school
économique [aykonomeek]

economy; economy-rate
Écopli® m [aykoplee] economy-rate letter for France
écossais [aykossay] Scottish
Écosse f [aykoss] Scotland
écouter [aykootay] to listen (to)
écrire [aykreer] to write
écrou m [aykroo] nut
édifice public m [aydeefeess pOObleek] public building
édredon m [aydruhdON] duvet
égal [aygal] equal
ça m'est égal I don't mind
égaliser [aygaleezay] to equalize; to trim
église f [aygleez] church
élastique m [aylasteek] rubber band
électricité f [aylektreesseetay] electricity
électroménager m household appliances
électrophone m [aylektrofon] record player
élever [ayluhvay] to raise; to lift up
elle* [el] she; her; it
elle-même [el-mem] herself; speaking
elles* [el] they; them
emballer [ONbalay] to wrap
embarquement (immédiat) boarding (now)
embouteillage m [ONbootay-ahj] traffic jam
embranchement m [ONbrONshmON] fork
embranchement d'autoroutes motorway junction
embrasser [ONbrassay] to kiss
embrayage m [ONbray-ahj] clutch
émission f [aymeess-yON] programme
emmener [ONmuhnay] to give a lift to; to take away
Empire [ONpeer] Napoleon's reign (1804-14)
emplacement m [ONplassmON] site
emplacement réservé no parking
employer [ONplwy-yay] to use; to employ
emporter [ONportay] to take away
emprunter [ONprANtay] to borrow
empruntez le passage souterrain use the underpass
en [ON] in; to; by
en 1945 in 1945
en France in France
en bas [ba] downstairs
en haut [o] upstairs
en cas d'incendie in the event of fire
en cas d'urgence in an emergency
en cas d'affluence ne pas utiliser les strapontins do not use fold-down seats when the train is crowded
en face de opposite
enceinte [ONSANT] pregnant
enchanté [ONshONtay] pleased

to meet you
encolure f [ONkolOOr] collar size
encore [ONkor] again; still
encore plus beau even more beautiful
encore une bière another beer
endommager [ONdoma-jay] to damage
endormi [ONdormee] asleep
enfant m/f [ONfON] child
enfin [ONfAN] at last
enflé [ONflay] swollen
enjoliveur m [ONjoleevurr] hub cap
enlever [ONluhvay] to take away; to remove
ennuyer [ON-nwee-yay] to bother; to bore
s'ennuyer to be bored
ennuyeux [ON-nwee-yuh] annoying; boring
énorme [aynorm] enormous
énormément [aynormaymON] enormously
enregistrement des bagages m check-in
enrhumé: je suis enrhumé [ONrOOmay] I've got a cold
enseignant m [ONsen-yON] teacher
enseigner [ONsen-yay] to teach
ensemble [ONsONbl] together
ensoleillé [ONsolay-yay] sunny
ensuite [ONsweet] afterwards
entendre [ONtONdr] to hear
enterrement m [ONtairmON] funeral
entier [ONteeyay] whole
entièrement [ONtee-yairmON] entirely
entorse f [ONtorss] sprain
entracte m interval
entraînement m [ONtrenmON] training
entre [ONtr] between; among
entrée f [ONtray] entrance, way in; entrée
entrée à l'avant entry at the front
entrée des artistes stage door
entrée de service tradesman's entrance
entrée gratuite admission free
entrée interdite no admittance, no entry
entrée libre admission free
entrejambe m inside leg measurement; crutch
entrer [ONtray] to go in; to come in; to enter
vous entrez dans un espace non fumeur you are entering a no smoking area
entrez! [ONtray] come in!
entrez sans frapper enter without knocking
entrez sans sonner enter without ringing the bell
envers [ONvair] to, towards
envie: j'ai envie de [ONvee] I feel like
environ [ONveerON] about
envoi d'un objet recommandé avec/sans avis de réception mailing of a registered item with/without receipt note
envoi recommandé m

recorded delivery
envoyer [ONvwy-ay] to send
épais [aypay] thick
épaule f [aypol] shoulder
épeler [ayplay] to spell
épicerie f [aypeesree] grocer's
épicerie fine delicatessen
épingle f [aypANgl] pin
épingle de nourrice [duh nooreess] safety pin
épouse f [aypooz] wife
épouser [aypoozay] to marry
épouvantable [aypoovONtabl] terrible
épuisé [aypweezay] exhausted
équipage m [aykeepahj] crew
équipe f [aykeep] team
équipements sportifs sporting facilities
équitation f [aykeetass-yON] horse riding
erreur f [air-rurr] mistake
éruption f [ayrOOps-yON] rash
es: tu es [ay] you are
escale f [eskal] stop-over
escalier m [eskal-yay] stairs
escalier roulant [roolON] escalator
Espagne f [españ] Spain
espagnol [espan-yol] Spanish
espèce de con! [espess duh kON] you stupid bastard!
espérer [espayray] to hope
espoir m [espwahr] hope
esquimau m [eskeemo] ice cream on a stick, ice lolly
essayer [essay-ay] to try; to try on
essence f [essONss] petrol, gas
essieu m [ess-yuh] axle
essuie-glace m [ess-wee-glass] windscreen wiper
est: il/elle est [ay] he/she/it is
est m east
à l'est de east of
est-ce que ...? [eskuh] to form questions
est-ce que vous pensez ...? do you think ...?
est-ce qu'il y a ...? [eskeel ya] is there ...?; are there ...?
estomac m [estoma] stomach
et [ay] and
et ... et both ... and
étage m [aytahj] floor
1er étage first floor, (US) second floor
étage inférieur lower floor
étage supérieur upper floor
étang m [aytON] pond
étant [aytON] being
état m [ayta] state
États-Unis mpl [ayta zOOnee] United States
été m [aytay] summer
été been
éteignez vos phares switch off your lights
éteignez vos veilleuses switch off your sidelights/parking lights
éteindre [aytANdr] to switch off
éteint [aytAN] switched off; out
s'étendre [saytONdr] to lie down; to extend
éternuer [aytairnOO-ay] to

sneeze
êtes: vous êtes [et] you are
étiquette f label
étoile f [aytwal] star
étonnant [aytonON] astonishing
étranger m [aytrONjay] foreigner
à l'étranger abroad
étranger foreign
étranger service prioritaire overseas priority mail
être* [etr] to be
étroit [aytrwa] narrow; tight
études fpl [aytood] studies
étudiant m, étudiante f [aytood-yON, -yONt] student
étudier [aytood-yay] to study
eu [oo] had
européen [urropay-AN] European
eux* [uh] them
s'**évanouir** [sayvanweer] to faint
évidemment [ayveedamON] obviously
évident [ayveedON] obvious
évier m [ayv-yay] sink
exagérer [exajayray] to exaggerate
examiner [exameenay] to examine
excédent de bagages m excess baggage
excès de vitesse m speeding
s'**excuser** [sexkoozay] to apologize
excusez-moi [exkoozay mwa] sorry; excuse me
exemple m [exONpl] example
par exemple for example
exiger [exeejay] to demand
exigez votre reçu ask for a receipt
expliquer [expleekay] to explain
exposition f exhibition; exposure
exprès [expray] deliberately
par exprès [express] special delivery
express m ordinary fast train
extincteur m [extANkturr] fire extinguisher

F

fabriqué en/au ... made in ...
fâché [fashay] angry
facile [fasseel] easy
façon f [fassON] way
de façon que so that
facteur m postman
facultatif optional; request
faible [febl] weak
faim: j'ai faim [fAN] I'm hungry
faire* [fair] to do; to make
ça ne fait rien [san fay ree-AN] it doesn't matter
faisons: nous faisons [fuhzON] we do; we make
fait: il/elle fait [fay] he/she/it does; he/she/it makes
fait did; made
faites: vous faites [fet] you do; you make
faites attention! be careful!
faites l'appoint have the right

change ready
faites vérifier votre niveau d'huile have your oil checked
fait main hand-made
falaise f [falez] cliff
falloir [falwahr] to be necessary
il va falloir ... it will be necessary to ...
famille f [fameel] family
fard à paupières m [far a pohp-yair] eye-shadow
fatigué [fateegay] tired
fauché [fohshay] broke
fausse [fohss] wrong
faut: il faut que je/vous ... [eel fo kuh] I/you must ...
faute f [foht] mistake; fault
fauteuil roulant m [fotuh-ee roolON] wheelchair
faux, f fausse [fo, fohss] wrong
faux numéro wrong number
favori favourite
FB (franc belge) Belgian franc
félicitations! [fayleesseetass-yON] congratulations!
femelle [fuhmel] female
femme f [fam] woman; wife
femme d'affaires [dafair] businesswoman
femme de chambre [duh shONbr] chambermaid
fenêtre f [fuhnetr] window
fer m [fair] iron
fer à repasser [ruhpassay] iron
ferai: je ferai [fuhray] I will do; I will make
fera: il/elle fera [fuhra] he/she/it will do; he/she/it will make
feras: tu feras [fuhra] you will do; you will make
ferez: vous ferez [fuhray] you will do; you will make
fermé [fairmay] closed
fermé jusqu'au ... closed until ...
fermé le ... closed on ...
ferme f [fairm] farm
fermer [fairmay] to close
fermer à clé [klay] to lock
fermer la grille [gree] close the outside door
fermeture annuelle f annual holiday, annual closure
fermeture automatique des portes doors close automatically
fermeture éclair f [fairmuhtoor ayklair] zip
fermeture hebdomadaire le lundi closed on Mondays
fermez le volet svp please close the flap
ferons: nous ferons [fuhrON] we will do; we will make
feront: ils/elles feront [fuhrON] they will do; they will make
fête f [fet] party; feast day
fête des vendanges [vONdONj] grape harvest festival
fête de village [veelajh] village fair
fête nationale 14 July (national holiday)
feu m [fuh] fire

vous avez du feu? [voo zavay doo] have you got a light?
feuille f [fuh-ee] leaf
feux arrière mpl [fuh aree-yair] rear lights
feux d'artifice fireworks
feux de camp interdits no campfires
feux de position sidelights
feux de signalisation traffic lights
février [fayvree-ay] February
FF (franc français) French franc
fiancé engaged
se **fiancer** [suh fee-ONsay] to get engaged
fibres naturelles natural fibres
ficelle f [feessel] string
fier [fee-air] proud
fièvre f [fee-evr] fever
avoir de la fièvre to have a temperature
fil m [feel] thread
fil de fer [duh fair] wire
file f [feel] lane
fille f [fee] girl; daughter
film en VO m film in the original language
fils m [feess] son
filtre m [feeltr] filter
fin f [fAN] end
fin fine
fin d'autoroute end of motorway
fin de ... end of ...
fin de série oddment
finir [feeneer] to finish
fleur f [flurr] flower
fleuriste m [flurreest] florist's
foire f [fwahr] fair
foire à la brocante [brokONt] street market for antiques and bric-à-brac
fois f [fwa] time
une fois once
folle [fol] mad
fonctionnaire m/f [fONks-yonair] civil servant
fond m [fON] bottom
au fond de at the bottom of
fond de teint [duh tAN] foundation cream
fontaine f [fONten] fountain
font: ils/elles font [fON] they do; they make
footing m jogging
forêt f [foray] forest
forme: en forme [form] fit
formellement interdit strictly prohibited
formez le ... dial ...
formidable [formeedabl] great
formulaire m [formoolair] form
fort [for] strong; loud; loudly
fou, f folle [foo, fol] mad
foulard m [foolar] scarf
foule f [fool] crowd
foulure f [fooloor] sprain
four m [foor] oven
fourchette f [foorshet] fork
fournitures de bureau office supplies
fourreur m furrier
fous: je m'en fous [juh mON foo] I don't give a damn
fous le camp! [kON] get lost!
foutre [footr] to put; to do

allez vous faire foutre! [alay voo fair] go to hell!
fraîche [fresh] fresh
frais mpl [fray] charges
frais, f fraîche [fray, fresh] fresh
franc m [frON] franc
français [frONsay] French
Français m Frenchman
Française f [frONsez] French woman
franc belge [belj] Belgian franc
franc français [frONsay] French franc
franc suisse [sweess] Swiss franc
frapper [frapay] to hit
frappez avant d'entrer knock before entering
frein m [frAN] brake
frein à main [mAN] handbrake
freiner [frenay] to brake
frein moteur: utilisez votre frein moteur engage lower gear
frère m [frair] brother
fr (franc) franc
frigo m fridge
frisé [freezay] curly
froid [frwa] cold
fromager m [fromajay], **fromages** [fromahj] cheese shop
front m [frON] forehead
frontière f [frONt-yair] border
FrS (franc suisse) Swiss franc
fuite f [fweet] leak
fumée f [fomay] smoke
fumer [fomay] to smoke
fumeurs [fomurr] smokers
fusible m [foozeebl] fuse
fusil m [foozee] gun

G

gagner [gan-yay] to win; to earn
galerie f gallery; roof rack; circle
galerie d'art [dar] art gallery
gallois [galwa] Welsh
gallo-romain civilization following Roman conquest of Gaul
ganterie f glove shop
gants mpl [gON] gloves
garçon m [garson] boy; waiter
garder [garday] to keep
gare f [gar] train station
gare routière [root-yair] bus station
se **garer** [suh garay] to park
gare SNCF [ess-en-say-ef] French train station
gas-oil m diesel
gauche f [gohsh] left
à gauche (de) on the left (of)
gaucher [gohshay] left-handed
Gaulois Gauls (original inhabitants of France)
gazole m diesel
gel m [jel] frost; gel
gelé [juhlay] frozen
gelée f [juhlay] frost
geler [juhlay] to be freezing
gélule f [jayloOl] capsule

gênant [jenON] embarrassing
gendarme m policeman
gendarmerie f police station
gendre m [jONdr] son-in-law
gêner [jenay] to embarrass; to hinder
généralement [jaynayralmON] generally
généraliste m/f [jaynayraleest] GP, family doctor
génial! [jayn-yal] great!, fantastic!
genou m [juhnoo] knee
gens mpl [jON] people
gentil [jONtee] kind; nice
gérant m [jayrON] manager
gilet m [jeelay] cardigan
gilet de corps [duh kor] vest
gîte m rural holiday accommodation
gîte et petit déjeuner [jeet ay puhtee dayjuhnay] bed and breakfast
glacier m [glassee-ay] ice cream shop; glacier
glissant [gleessON] slippery
Golfe de Gascogne m Bay of Biscay
gomme f [gom] rubber, eraser
gorge f [gorj] throat
goût m [goo] taste
goûter [gootay] to taste
goûter m tea (meal)
gouttes fpl [goot] drops
grâce à [grass] thanks to
grand [grON] large; tall; great
Grande-Bretagne f [grONd-bruhtañ] Great Britain
grandes lignes main lines
grande surface f [sOOrfass] superstore
grandes vacances fpl [grONd vakONss] summer holidays
grand magasin m [magazAN] department store
grand-mère f [grON-mair] grandmother
grand-père m [-pair] grandfather
gras m [gra] fat
gras, f grasse [gra, grass] greasy
gratuit [gratwee] free
grave [grahv] serious; deep
gravillons loose chippings
grec, f grecque [grek] Greek
grêle f [grel] hail
grippe f [greep] flu
gris [gree] grey
gros [gro] big; fat
grossier [gross-yay] rude
grotte f [grot] cave
groupe sanguin m [groop sONgAN] blood group
guêpe f [gep] wasp
guère [gair] hardly
guérir [gay-reer] to heal, to cure; to recover
guerre f [gair] war
gueule de bois f [gurl duh bwa] hangover
guichet m [geeshay] ticket office; box office; counter
guichet automatique cash dispenser, ATM
guichet fermé position closed
guide touristique m/f [geed tooreesteek] tourist guide

gymnase **m** [jeemnaz] gymnasium
gynécologue **m/f** [jeenaykolog] gynaecologist

H

habillé [abeeyay] formal; dressed
habiller [abeeyay] to dress
s'habiller to get dressed
habiter [abeetay] to live
habitude **f** [abeetOOd] habit
d'habitude usually
habituel [abeetOOel] usual
s'**habituer à** [sabeetOO-ay] to get used to
haïr [a-eer] to hate
hall d'arrivée **m** arrival hall, arrivals
hall (de) départ departures, departure hall
hall de gare station concourse
halte stop
hameau **m** [amo] hamlet
hanche **f** [ONsh] hip
handicapé [ONdeekapay] disabled
hasard: par hasard [azar] by chance
haut [o] high
en haut upstairs
hauteur limitée à ... maximum height ...
herbe **f** [airb] grass
heure **f** [urr] hour; time
quelle heure est-il? [kel urr ayteel] what time is it?
à l'heure on time
3 heures de l'après-midi 3 p.m.
5 heures du matin 5 a.m.
11 heures du soir 11 p.m.
heure limite d'enregistrement check-in deadline
heures d'affluence rush hour
heures des levées collection times
heures de visite visiting hours
heures d'ouverture opening times
heureusement [urrurzmON] fortunately
heureux [ur-ruh] happy
hexagone: l'hexagone **m** France (colloquial name)
hier [yair] yesterday
hippisme **m** [eepeess-muh] horse-riding
histoire **f** [eestwahr] history; story
hiver **m** [eevair] winter
HLM (habitation à loyer modéré) **f** [ash-el-em] council flat, public housing unit
hollandais [olONday] Dutch
homme **m** [om] man
homme d'affaires [dafair] businessman
hommes [om] gents, men's room
honnête [onet] honest
honteux [ONtuh] ashamed
hôpital **m** [opeetal] hospital
hoquet **m** [okay] hiccups

horaire m [orair] timetable, schedule
horaire d'ouverture opening times
horloge f [orloj] clock
horlogerie f watchmaker's
horlogerie-bijouterie watchmaker and jeweller's
horodateur m parking meter, pay and display
hors-bord m [or-bor] outboard motorboat
hors de [or duh] out of
hors saison off season
hors service out of order
hors taxes [tax] duty-free
hôtel m [otel] hotel
hôtel de ville [duh veel] town hall, city hall
hôtesse de l'air f [otess] air hostess
huile f [weel] oil
huile solaire suntan oil
huit [weet] eight
huitième [weet-yem] eighth
humeur f [oomurr] mood
humide [oomeed] damp
humidité f [oomeedeetay] dampness
hypermarché m [eepairmarshay] supermarket; hypermarket

I

I tourist information
ici [ee-see] here
idée f [eeday] idea
il* [eel] he; it
île f [eel] island
il est interdit de ... ... is prohibited
il est interdit de déposer des ordures no litter, no tipping
il est interdit de donner à manger aux animaux do not feed the animals
il est interdit de marcher sur les pelouses keep off the grass
il n'y a pas ... [eel nya pa] there isn't ...; there aren't ...
il n'y a pas de quoi! [duh kwa] don't mention it!
ils* [eel] they
il y a ... [eelya] there is ...; there are ...
il y a trois jours three days ago
est-ce qu'il y a ...? [eskeel ya] is there ...?; are there ...?
imbécile! [ANbayseel] idiot!
immédiatement [eemaydee-atmON] immediately
immeuble m [eemurbl] block (of flats); building
impasse dead end
imperméable m [ANpairmay-abl] raincoat
imprimé printed matter
incroyable [ANkrwyabl] incredible
indicatif m [ANdeekateef] dialling code, area code; country code
indiquer [ANdeekay] to indicate, to point out
s'infecter [sANfektay] to

become infected
infirmerie f [ANfeermuhree] infirmary
infirmière f [ANfeerm-yair] nurse
informations fpl [ANformass-yON] news; information
informatique f [ANformateek] information technology; computing
informer [ANformay] to inform
infraction f [ANfrax-yON] offence
insérer le jeton insert token
insérez votre carte insert your card
insolation f [ANsolass-yON] sunstroke
insomnie f [ANsomnee] insomnia
institut de beauté m [ANsteetOO duh botay] beauty salon
instrument de musique m [ANstrOOmON duh mOOzeek] musical instrument
insupportable [ANsOOportabl] obnoxious
interdiction de ... [ANtairdeex-yON] no ...
interdiction de fumer no smoking
interdiction de marcher sur la voie do not walk on the track
interdiction de parler au conducteur do not speak to the driver
interdiction de stationner no parking
interdit [ANtairdee] forbidden, prohibited
interdit à tous véhicules no access to any vehicle
interdit aux forains et aux nomades no gypsies
interdit aux mineurs no admittance to minors
interdit aux moins de ... ans children under ... not admitted
interdit aux voyageurs no access for passengers; staff only
intéressant [ANtayressON] interesting
s'**intéresser à** [sANtayressay] to be interested in
intérieur: à l'intérieur [ANtayree-urr] inside
interrupteur m [ANtairOOpturr] switch
intoxication alimentaire f [ANtoxeekass-yON aleemONtair] food poisoning
introduire [ANtrodweer] to introduce; to insert
introduire carte ou composer numéro libre insert card or dial freephone number
introduire les pièces ici insert coins here
introduisez une pièce de 2 francs et tournez la poignée insert a 2 franc coin and turn the handle
introduisez votre pièce ici insert coin here
invité m [ANveetay] guest
inviter [ANveetay] to invite
irai: j'irai [eeray] I will go

ira: il/elle ira [eera] he/she/it will go
iras: tu iras [eera] you will go
irez: vous irez [eeray] you will go
irlandais [eerlONday] Irish
Irlande du Nord f [eerlONd doo nor] Northern Ireland
irons: nous irons [eerON] we will go
iront: ils/elles iront [eerON] they will go
issue de secours emergency exit, fire escape
italien [eetalyAN] Italian
itinéraire m [eeteenayrair] route
itinéraire bis alternative route
itinéraire conseillé recommended route
itinéraire de délestage alternative route
itinéraire obligatoire compulsory route (for heavy vehicles etc)
ivre [eevr] drunk
ivresse f [eevress] drunkenness

J

jaloux [jaloo] jealous
jamais [jamay] never; ever
jambe f [jONb] leg
janvier [jONvee-ay] January
jardin m [jardAN] garden
jardin public public gardens, park
jardin zoologique zoo
jauge f [johj] gauge
jaune [jo-n] yellow
je* [juh] I
jean m jeans
j'écoute [jaykoot] speaking
jetable [juhtahbl] disposable
jeter [juhtay] to throw (away)
jeton m [juhtON] token
jeu m [juh] game
jeu de société board game
jeudi [juhdee] Thursday
jeun: le matin à jeun first thing in the morning on an empty stomach
jeune [jurn] young
jeune femme f [fam] young woman
jeune fille f [fee] girl
jeune homme m [om] young man
jeux mpl [juh] games
jeux électroniques computer games
jeux interdits aux moins de 16 ans use of gaming machines forbidden for those under 16
joindre [jwANdr] to join
joli [jolee] pretty
jouer [joo-ay] to play
jouet m [joo-ay] toy
jour m [joor] day
jour férié [fayree-ay] public holiday
journal m [joornal] newspaper
journaux newspapers, stationer
journée f [joornay] day
journée continue open all day

journées à tarif réduit cheap travel days
jours de semaine uniquement weekdays only
jours impairs odd dates of the month (parking allowed)
jours ouvrables weekdays
jours pairs/impairs parking allowed only on even/odd days of the month
joyeuses Pâques! [jwy-urz pak] happy Easter!
juif, f juive [jweef, jweev] Jewish
juillet [jwee-yay] July
juin [jWAN] June
juive [jweev] Jewish
jumeaux mpl [jOOmo] twins
jumelé [jOOmuhlay] twinned
jumelles fpl [jOOmel] binoculars; twins
jupe f [jOOp] skirt
jupon m [jOOpON] petticoat
jusqu'à (ce que) [jOOska(ss kuh)] until
jusque [jOOsk] up to, as far as; till
juste [jOOst] fair; right

K

kermesse f [kairmess] fair
kiosque à journaux m newspaper stand
klaxon m horn
klaxonner [klaxonay] to hoot
K-way® m [ka-way] cagoule

L

l'* the; him; her; it
la* the; her; it
là [la] there
là-bas [laba] over there
lac m lake
lacets mpl [lassay] shoe laces
laid [lay] ugly
laine f [len] wool
laisser [lessay] to let; to leave
lait m [lay] milk
laiterie dairy (Switzerland)
lait solaire [solair] suntan lotion
lame de rasoir f [lahm duh razwahr] razor blade
lampe de poche f [lONp duh posh] torch
lancer [lONsay] to throw
landau m [lONdo] pram
langue f [lON-g] tongue; language
laque f [lak] hair spray
laquelle [lakel] which one
large [larj] wide
lavabo m washbasin
lavage à la main hand wash
lavage du pare-brise screen wash
lave-auto m [lav-oto] car wash
laver [lavay] to wash
se laver to wash, to have a wash
laverie automatique f [lavree otomateek] launderette, laundromat
laver séparément wash

separately
lave-vaisselle m [lav-vess-el] dish washer
lavoir m [lavwahr] wash house
lavomatic m launderette, laundromat
layette f babywear
le* [luh] the; him; it
leçon f [luhsON] lesson
lecteur de cassettes m [lekturr] cassette player
lendemain m [lONduhmAN] the next day
lent [lON] slow
lentement [lONtuhmON] slowly
lentilles de contact fpl [lONtee duh] contact lenses
lentilles dures [door] hard lenses
lentilles semi-rigides [-reejeed] gas-permeable lenses
lentilles souples [soopl] soft lenses
lequel [luhkel] which one
les* [lay] the; them
lesquel(le)s [laykel] which ones
lessive f [lesseev] washing powder; washing
faire la lessive do the washing
lettre f [letr] letter
leur* [lurr] their; (to) them
le/la leur theirs
leurs* [lurr] their
les leurs theirs
lever [luhvay] to lift, to raise
se lever to get up
levier de vitesses m [luhv-yay duh veetess] gear lever
lèvre f [levr] lip
lézard m [layzar] lizard
libellez votre chèque à l'ordre de ... please make out your cheque to ...
librairie f [leebrairee] bookshop, bookstore
libre [leebr] free, vacant
libre-service self-service
libre-service affranchissement self-service stamping facility
libre-service bancaire autobank, ATM
lieu m [l-yuh] place
ligne f [leeñ] line
la ligne est encombrée the line is busy
lignes de banlieue suburban lines
lime à ongles f [leem a ONgl] nailfile
limitation de vitesse f [leemeetass-yON duh veetess] speed limit
limite de validité des billets expiry of validity of tickets
lin m [lAN] linen
linge de maison m [lANj duh mezzON] household linen
lingerie f underwear
linge sale m [lANj sal] laundry
lire [leer] to read
liste f [leest] list
lit m [lee] bed
lit de camp [kON] campbed
lit d'enfant [dONfON] cot
literie f [leetuhree] bedding

lit pour deux personnes [duh pairson] double bed
lit pour une personne [oon] single bed
lits superposés mpl [lee soopairpozay] bunk beds
living m living room
livraison f [leevrezzON] delivery
livraison à domicile home deliveries
livraisons interdites de ... à ... no deliveries between ... and ...
livre f [leevr] pound
livre m book
livres et journaux books and newspapers
livre sterling f pound sterling
localité f [lokaleetay] place
location f [lokass-yON] rental; theatre tickets
location à la semaine charge per week
location de ... ... for hire
location de bateaux [bato] boat hire
location de vélos [vaylo] bicycles for hire/rent
location de voitures [vwatoor] car hire/rental
loft m warehouse conversion
logement m [lojmON] accommodation
loger [lojay] to stay
loges des artistes artists' dressing rooms
logiciel m [lojeess-yel] software
loi f [lwa] law
loin [lWAN] far away
plus loin further
loisirs mpl [lwazeer] free time, leisure
Londres [lONdr] London
long, f longue [lON, lON-g] long
longtemps [lONtON] a long time
longue [lON-g] long
longueur f [lONgurr] length
lorsque [lorskuh] when
louer [loo-ay] to rent
à louer to let, for rent, for hire
lourd [loor] heavy; rich; muggy
loyer m [lwy-ay] rent
lui* [lwee] him; to him; to her
lui-même [-mem] himself; speaking
lumière f [loom-yair] light
lundi [lANdee] Monday
lune f [loon] moon
lunettes fpl [loonet] glasses
lunettes de soleil [duh solay] sunglasses
lycée m [leessay] secondary school

M

M, M° (métro) underground
M (Monsieur) Mr
m'* (to) me; myself
ma* my
machine à écrire f [aykreer] typewriter
machine à laver [lavay] washing machine

mâchoire f [mashwahr] jaw
Mademoiselle [mad-mwazel] Miss
magasin m [magazAN] shop, store
magasin d'alimentation grocery store
magasin de chaussures shoe shop
magasin de disques record shop
magasin de vins et spiritueux off-licence, liquor store
magasin diététique health food store
magnétoscope m [man-yaytoskop] video recorder
mai [may] May
maigre [megr] skinny
maigrir [megreer] to lose weight
maillot de bain m [my-o duh bAN] swimming costume
main f [mAN] hand
maintenant [mANtnON] now
mairie f [mairee] town hall
mais [may] but
maison f [mezzON] house
à la maison at home
la maison n'accepte pas les chèques we do not accept cheques
la maison ne fait pas crédit we do not give credit
maison de la culture arts centre
maison des jeunes youth club
maison d'hôtes [doht] guesthouse
mal m pain; trouble; harm
mal badly; wrongly
se faire mal à la main to hurt one's hand
avoir mal au cœur to feel sick
ça fait mal it hurts
malade [malad] ill
maladie f [maladee] disease
mal de gorge m [gorj] sore throat
mal de mer [duh mair] seasickness
mal de tête [tet] headache
mal d'oreilles [doray] earache
mal du pays [payee] homesickness
mâle [mahl] male
malentendu m [malONtONdoo] misunderstanding
malgré [malgray] in spite of
malheureusement [malurr-urzmON] unfortunately
maman f [mamON] mum
Manche f [mONsh] English Channel
manche f sleeve
mandat postal m [mONda poss-tal] postal order
manette du signal d'alarme pull for alarm
manger [mONjay] to eat
manquer [mONkay] to miss
... me manque [muh mONk] I miss ...
manteau m [mONto] coat
manuel de conversation m [mONooel duh konvairsass-yON]

phrase book
maquillage m [makee-ahj] make-up
se **maquiller** [makee-ay] to put one's make-up on
marchand m [marshON] shopkeeper; merchant; dealer
marchand de légumes greengrocer
marchand de vins wine merchant
marchandise: les marchandises dangereuses sont interdites dangerous items are prohibited
marche f [marsh] walking; step; march; running, working
marché m [marshay] market
marche arrière [aree-air] reverse gear
marcher [marshay] to walk; to work, to function
ça marche? OK?
mardi [mardee] Tuesday
marée f [maray] tide
mari m [maree] husband
mariage m [maree-ahj] wedding
marié [maree-ay] married
se **marier (avec)** [suh maree-ay] to get married, to marry
maroquinerie f leather goods
marque déposée registered trademark
marrant [marON] funny
marre: j'en ai marre (de) [jON ay mar] I'm fed up (with)
marron [marON] brown
mars [marss] March
marteau m [marto] hammer
massepain m [massuhpAN] marzipan
matelas m [matuhla] mattress
matin m [matAN] morning
le matin in the morning
mauvais [mo-vay] bad
maux de dents mpl [mo duh dON] toothache
maux d'estomac stomach ache
me* [muh] me; to me; myself
mec m bloke, guy
mécanicien m [maykaneess-yAN] mechanic
mèches fpl [mesh] highlights
médecin m [maydsAN] doctor
médicament m [maydeekamON] medicine
Méditerranée f [maydeetairanay] Mediterranean
méduse f [maydooz] jellyfish
meilleur [mayurr] better
le meilleur the best
meilleur que better than
meilleurs vœux! [vuh] best wishes!
mélanger [maylONjay] to mix
même [mem] even; same
le/la même the same
ménage: faire le ménage [maynahj] to do the housework
mener [muhnay] to lead
menhir m [mayneer] standing stone
mentir [mONteer] to lie

menton m **[mONtON]** chin
menu à ... F set menu costing ... francs
mer f **[mair]** sea
mercerie f haberdasher's, (US) notions store
merci **[mairsee]** thank you; no thank you
merci beaucoup **[bo-koo]** thank you very much
merci de votre visite thanks for your visit
merci, pareillement **[paraymON]** thank you, the same to you
mercredi **[mairkruhdee]** Wednesday
merde! **[maird]** shit!
mère f **[mair]** mother
merveilleux **[mairvay-uh]** wonderful
mes* **[may]** my
messe f **[mess]** mass
messieurs **[mess-yuh]** gentlemen; gents, men's rest room
mesure f **[muhzoor]** measure
à mesure que as
sur mesure to measure
météo f **[maytay-o]** weather forecast
métier m **[maytee-ay]** job
mètre m **[metr]** metre
métro m **[maytro]** underground, subway
mettre **[metr]** to put
se mettre à to begin to
meublé m **[murblay]** furnished accommodation
meubles mpl **[murbl]** furniture
Midi m South of France
midi m midday
mien*: le mien **[luh m-yAN]** mine
mienne*: la mienne **[m-yen]** mine
mien(ne)s*: les mien(ne)s **[m-yAN, m-yen]** mine
mieux **[m-yuh]** better
le mieux (the) best
mignon, mignonne **[meen-yON, meen-yon]** sweet, cute
milieu m **[meel-yuh]** middle
mille m **[meel]** thousand
million f **[meel-yON]** million
mince **[mANss]** thin
minuit m **[meen-wee]** midnight
mirroir m **[meer-wahr]** mirror
mis **[mee]** put
mise en fourrière immédiate illegally parked cars will be removed
mise en marche automatique, placez vos mains sous le volet starts automatically, place your hands under the flap
Mlle (Mademoiselle) Miss
Mme (Madame) Mrs
mobylette f **[mobeelet]** moped
mode f **[mod]** fashion
à la mode fashionable
mode d'emploi directions for use
modèle m **[mo-del]** model; design; style
modes ladies' fashions
moi **[mwa]** me
moi-même **[mwa-mem]** myself

moindre [mwANdr] smaller; less; lesser
le moindre the smallest; the slightest
moins: à moins que [mwAN kuh] unless
au moins at least [o]
moins (de) less
le moins (the) least
mois m [mwa] month
moitié f [mwatee-ay] half
à moitié prix [pree] half-price
molle [mol] soft
mollet m [molay] calf
mon* [mON] my
monde m [mONd] world
tout le monde [too luh] everyone
moniteur m, monitrice f [moneeturr, -treess] instructor
monnaie f [monay] change
monsieur m [muhss-yuh] gentleman, man
Monsieur sir
montagne f [mONtañ] mountain
montant m [mONtON] amount
montant exact exact change
monter [mONtay] to go up; to get in
montre f [mONtr] watch
montrer [mONtray] to show
monument aux morts war memorial
moquette f [moket] carpet
morceau m [morso] piece
mordre to bite
morsure f [morsoor] bite
mort f [mor] death
mort dead
mosquée f [moskay] mosque
mot m [mo] word
moteur m [moturr] engine
moto f motorbike
mou, f molle [moo, mol] soft
mouche f [moosh] fly
mouchoir m [moosh-wahr] handkerchief
mouillé [mooyay] wet
mourir [mooreer] to die
mousse à raser f [razay] shaving foam
moustique m [moosteek] mosquito
mouton m [mootON] sheep
mur m [moor] wall
mûr [moor] ripe
musée m [moozay] museum; art gallery
musée d'art [dar] art gallery
muséum m [moozay-om] natural history museum
musique f [moozeek] music
musulman [moozoolmON] Muslim
myope [mee-op] shortsighted

N

nager [nahjay] to swim
naître [netr] to be born
nana f bird, girl
nappe f [nap] tablecloth
natation f [natass-yON] swimming
nationalité f [nass-yonaleetay] nationality

nature f [natOOr] nature
yaourt nature natural yoghurt
naturel [natOOrel] natural
naturellement [natOOrelmON] naturally, of course
navette f [navet] shuttle service
navette de l'aéroport airport bus
ND (Notre Dame) Our Lady
né born
néanmoins [nay-ONmwAN] nevertheless
ne ... aucun [nuh ... oKAN] no, not any, none
nécessaire [naysessair] necessary
négatif m [naygateef] negative
ne ... guère [gair] hardly
neige f [nej] snow
neiger [nejay] to snow
ne ... jamais [jamay] never
ne ... ni neither ... nor
ne ... nulle part [nOOl par] nowhere, not ... anywhere
ne ... pas* [pa] not
ne pas ... do not ...
ne pas affranchir freepost, do not affix stamp
ne pas avaler do not swallow
ne pas congeler do not freeze
ne pas dépasser ... comprimés par jour do not take more than ... tablets a day
ne pas dépasser la dose prescrite do not exceed the prescribed dose
ne pas déranger do not disturb
ne pas essorer do not spin dry
ne pas laisser à la portée des enfants keep out of the reach of children
ne pas repasser do not iron
ne pas se pencher au dehors do not lean out of the window
ne pas se pencher par la fenêtre do not lean out of the window
ne pas ... sous peine d'amende ... will be fined
ne pas tordre do not wring
ne pas toucher à ... do not touch ...
ne ... personne [pairson] nobody, not anybody
ne ... plus [plOO] no more, no longer
ne ... que [kuh] only
ne quittez pas [nuh keetay pa] hold the line, hold on
ne ... rien [ree-AN] nothing, not anything
ne rien jeter dans les WC do not flush objects down the toilet
ne rien jeter par la fenêtre do not throw anything out of the window
ne tirer la poignée qu'en cas de danger pull handle only in case of emergency
nerveux [nairvuh] nervous

n'est-ce pas? [ness-pa] didn't he/she/it?; isn't it?; isn't that so?
nettoyage à sec dry cleaning; dry clean only
nettoyer [net-wy-ay] to clean
neuf, f neuve [nuhf, nuhv] new
neuf nine
neveu m [nuhvuh] nephew
neuvième [nuhv-yem] ninth
névralgies headaches
névrosé [nayvrozay] neurotic
nez m [nay] nose
ni neither
ni ... ni ... neither ... nor ...
nids-de-poule potholes
nièce f [nee-ess] niece
nocturne late night opening
Noël [no-el] Christmas
noir [nwahr] black
noir et blanc black and white
nom m [nON] name
nom de famille [duh famee] surname, family name
nom de jeune fille [jurn fee] maiden name
nommer: se nommer [suh nomay] to be called
non [nON] no; not
non-fumeurs [-fOOmurr] no smoking
non merci [mairsee] no thank you
nord m [nor] north
au nord de north of
nos* [no] our
note f [not] bill; note
notez le numéro de votre emplacement make a note of the number of your parking space
notre* [notr] our
nôtre*: le/la nôtre [luh/la nohtr] ours
nôtres*: les nôtres ours
n'oubliez pas de composter votre billet do not forget to punch/validate your ticket
n'oubliez pas le guide don't forget to tip the guide
n'oubliez pas votre reçu don't forget your receipt
nourriture f [nooreetOOr] food
nous* [noo] we; (to) us
nous acceptons les cartes de crédit credit cards welcome
nous n'acceptons pas les chèques cheques not accepted
nouveau, f nouvelle [noovo, -vel] new
de nouveau again
nouveau franc new French franc (100 old francs)
Nouvel An m [ON] New Year
nouvelle [noovel] new
nouvelles fpl [noovel] news
novembre [no-vONbr] November
nu [nOO] naked
nuage m [nOO-ahj] cloud
nuageux [nOO-ahjuh] cloudy
nuit f [nwee] night
nul [nOOl] no; lousy
nulle part [nOOl par] nowhere
numéro m [nOOmayro] number
numéro de téléphone phone number

numéro direct direct dialling
numérotez dial
numéro vert freephone
nu-pieds mpl [nOO-p-yay] flip-flops

O

objectif m [objekteef] lens; objective
objets trouvés mpl [objay troovay] lost property office, lost and found
objets volumineux large parcels/packages
oblitérez votre billet punch your ticket
obtenir [obtuhneer] to get
obturateur m [obtOOraturr] shutter
occasion f [okaz-yON] opportunity; occasion; bargain
d'occasion second-hand
occupé [okOOpay] engaged; occupied; busy
s'**occuper de** [sokOOpay] to take care of
octobre [oktobr] October
oculiste m/f eye specialist
odeur f [odurr] smell
œil m [uh-ee] eye
office à ... service at ...
office du tourisme tourist office
offre spéciale special offer
offrir [ofreer] to offer; to give
oiseau m [wazo] bird
ombre f [ONbr] shade
à l'ombre in the shade
ombre à paupières [pohp-yair] eye shadow
on* [ON] one; someone; you; they; people; we
oncle m [ONkl] uncle
ondulé [ONdOOlay] wavy
ongle m [ONgl] nail
ont: ils/elles ont [ON] they have
onze [ONz] eleven
opérer [opayray] to operate
ophtalmologue m/f ophthalmologist
opticien m [opteess-yAN] optician
optimiste optimistic
optique optician's
or m gold
or massif solid gold
orage m [orahj] thunderstorm
orageux [orahjuh] stormy
orchestre m [orkestr] orchestra; stalls
ordinaire [ordeenair] ordinary; equivalent of two-star petrol
ordinateur m [ordeenaturr] computer
ordonnance f [ordonONss] prescription
ordures fpl [ordOOr] litter; refuse; filth
oreille f [oray] ear
oreiller m [oray-yay] pillow
oreillons mpl [orayON] mumps
organiser [organeezay] to organize

orteil **m** [ortay] toe
os **m** [oss] bone
oser [ozay] to dare
ou [oo] or
ou bien [b-yAN] or else
où [oo] where
oublier [ooblee-ay] to forget
ouest **m** [west] west
à l'ouest de west of
oui [wee] yes
outil **m** [ootee] tool
ouvert [oovair] open
ouvert de ... à ... open from ... to ...
ouverture **f** [oovairtOOr] opening
ouverture des guichets hours of opening
ouvre-boîte **m** [oovr-bwat] tin-opener
ouvre-bouteille **m** [-bootay] bottle-opener
ouvreuse **f** [oovrurz] usherette
ouvrier **m** [oovree-ay] (factory) worker
ouvrir [oovreer] to open
ouvrir ici open here

P

pages jaunes **fpl** [pahj jo-n] yellow pages
paire **f** [pair] pair
palais **m** [palay] palace
pâle [pahl] pale
panier **m** [pan-yay] basket
panier (à provisions) shopping basket
panne **f** [pan] breakdown
en panne [ON] out of order; broken down
tomber en panne [tONbay] to break down
panneau de signalisation **m** roadsign
pansement **m** [pONssmON] bandage
pansement adhésif [adayzeef] Elastoplast®, Bandaid®
panser [pONsay] to dress
pantalon **m** [pONtalON] trousers, (US) pants
pantoufles **fpl** [pONtoofl] slippers
papa **m** dad
papeterie **f** stationer's; stationery
papier **m** [pap-yay] paper
papier à lettres writing paper
papier collant [kolON] Sellotape®, Scotch tape®
papier d'aluminium [dalOOmeenee-um] aluminium foil
papier d'emballage [dONbalahj] wrapping paper
papier hygiénique [eejee-ayneek] toilet paper
papiers papers; litter
papiers, s'il vous plaît your identity papers, please
papillon **m** [papee-yON] butterfly
Pâques [pak] Easter
paquet **m** [pakay] package, packet
par by; through
parachute ascensionnel **m**

[assONsee-onel] parascending
parachutisme **m** parachuting
parages: dans les parages [dON lay parahj] in the vicinity
paraître [paretre] to seem; to come out, to be published
parapluie **m** [paraplwee] umbrella
parc **m** park
parce que [parss-kuh] because
parcmètre **m** parking meter
parcotrain **m** parking for train users
pardessus **m** [par-duhsoo] overcoat
par-dessus over
par-dessous [-duhsoo] under
pardon [par-dON] excuse me, pardon (me); thank you
pare-brise **m** [par-breez] windscreen
pare-chocs **m** [-shok] bumper
parents **mpl** [parON] parents; relatives
paresseux [paressuh] lazy
parfait [parfay] perfect
parfois [parfwa] sometimes
parfum **m** [parfAN] perfume
parfumerie **f** perfume and cosmetics shop
parking **m** [parkeeng] car park, parking lot
parking à étages [aytahj] multi-storey car park, parking garage
parking courte durée short-term car park
parking longue durée long-term car park
parking non gardé unsupervised parking
parking payant paying car park
parking privé private car park
parking public public car park
parking réservé aux clients de l'hôtel parking for hotel guests only
parking souterrain underground car park
parking surveillé car park with attendant
parler [parlay] to speak
parler ici talk here
parmi among
pars: je/tu pars [par] I/you leave, I/you go away
part **f** [par] piece; share
à part except
de la part de from; on behalf of
de la part de qui? [duh kee] who shall I say is calling?
partager [partahjay] to share
parterre **m** stalls
partir [parteer] to leave
partout [partoo] everywhere
pas* [pa] not
pas de ... no ...
pas de remboursement we cannot give cash refunds
pas encore not yet
passage à niveau **m** [passahj a neevo] level crossing, (US) railroad crossing
passage à niveau gardé/non gardé manned/unmanned

level crossing
passage clouté pedestrian crossing
passage interdit no entry
passage piétons pedestrian crossing
passage protégé priority road
passager m [passahjay] passenger
passage souterrain underpass
passeport m [pass-por] passport
passer [passay] to pass
qu'est-ce qui se passe? [keskee suh pass] what's happening?
passer par to go through
passerelle f gangway
passe-temps m [pass-tON] pastime
passionnant [pass-yonON] exciting
passionné de [pass-yonay] very keen on
pastilles pour la gorge fpl [pastee poor la gorj] throat pastilles
patientez svp please wait
patinage m [pateenahj] skating
patiner [pateenay] to skate
patinoire f [pateenwahr] ice rink
patins à glace mpl [patAN a glass] ice skates
patron m [pa-trON] boss; owner
pauvre [pohvr] poor
payer [pay-ay] to pay
payer comptant to pay cash
payez à la caisse pay at the cash desk
payez à la sortie pay on your way out
payez à l'ordre de ... payable to ...
payez ici pay here
pays m [payee] country
paysage m [payee-zahj] scenery
Pays de Galles m [payee duh gal] Wales
PCV m [pay-say-vay] collect call, reverse charge call
péage m [payahj] toll
peau f [po] skin
pêche f [pesh] fishing; peach
pêche interdite no fishing
pêcher [peshay] to fish
pêche sous-marine underwater fishing
peigne m [peñ] comb
se **peigner** [suh pen-yay] to comb one's hair
peindre [pANdr] paint
peine: à peine [pen] hardly
ce n'est pas la peine it's not worth it; it's not necessary
peinture f [pANtoor] painting
peinture fraîche wet paint
pelle f [pel] spade
pellicule f film
pelouse f [puhlooz] lawn
pénalité pour abus penalty for misuse
pendant [pONdON] during
pendant que while
penser [pONsay] to think
pension f [pONs-yON]

guesthouse
pension complète [kONplet] full board
pension de famille guesthouse
pente f [pONt] slope
perdre [pairdr] to lose
se perdre to get lost
père m [pair] father
périphérique m [payreefayreek] ring road
permanente f [pairmanONt] perm
permettre [pairmetr] to allow
permis [pairmee] allowed
permis de conduire m [duh kONdweer] driving licence, driver's license
perruque f [pairOOk] wig
personne f [pairson] person
personne nobody
personne ne sait ... nobody knows ...
personnes handicapées disabled
peser [puhzay] to weigh
pétanque f [paytONk] French bowling game
petit [puhtee] small
petit ami m [tamee] boyfriend
petit déjeuner m [dayjuhnay] breakfast
petite amie f [tamee] girlfriend
petite cuillère f teaspoon
petite-fille f [puhteet-fee] granddaughter
petit-fils m [puhtee-feess] grandson
petits-enfants mpl [puhtee-zONfON] grandchildren
peu: peu de ... [puh] few ...
un peu (de) a bit (of)
peur f [purr] fear
de peur que for fear that
j'ai peur (de) I'm afraid (of)
peut-être [puht-etr] maybe
peut: il/elle peut [puh] he/she/it can
il peut y avoir ... there may be ...
peuvent: ils/elles peuvent [puhv] they can
peux: je/tu peux [puh] I/you can
phallocrate m [falokrat] male chauvinist pig
phare m [far] headlight; lighthouse
phare antibrouillard [ONtee-broo-yar] fog lamp
pharmacie f [farmassee] chemist's, pharmacy
pharmacie de garde duty chemist/pharmacy, late-night chemist
pharmacie de service duty chemist
photographe m photographer; camera shop
photographie f [foto-grafee] photograph
photographier [foto-grafyay] to photograph
photomètre m [foto-metr] light meter
pièce f [p-yess] coin; room; part
la pièce each, apiece

pièce de théâtre [duh tay-atr] play
pièces de rechange [ruhshONj] spare parts
pièces détachées [daytashay] parts
pièces rejetées reject coins
pied m [p-yay] foot
à pied on foot
pierre f stone
piéton m [p-yaytON] pedestrian
piétons passez en deux temps pedestrians cross in two stages
pile f [peel] battery; pile
pilote m [peelot] pilot
pilule f [peelool] pill
pince f [pANss] pliers; clip
pince à épiler [aypeelay] tweezers
pince à linge [lANj] clothes peg
pince à ongles [ONgl] nail clippers
pinceau m [pANso] paint brush
piquant [peekON] hot, spicy
piquer [peekay] to sting
piqûre f [peekoor] injection; bite
piqûre d'insecte [dANsekt] insect bite
pire [peer] worse
le pire worst
piscine f [peesseen] swimming pool
pissoir m public urinal
piste balisée f [baleezay] marked ski path
piste cyclable [seeklabl] cycle path
piste de ski ski track, piste
piste pour débutants [dayboOtON] nursery slope
place f [plass] seat; square
place principale [prANseepal] main square
placer [plassay] to place
place réservée aux ... this seat is intended for ...
place(s) assise(s) seat(s)
places debout standing passengers
places libres spaces free (in car park)
plafond m [plafON] ceiling
plage f [plahj] beach
plaindre: se plaindre [suh plANdr] to complain
plaire [plair] to please
plaisanterie f [plezzONtree] joke
plaît: s'il vous plaît [seel voo play] please
plan m [plON] map
planche de surf f [plONsh] surfboard
planche à voile [vwal] sailboard
plancher m [plONshay] floor
plan de métro underground map
plan de ville map of the town
plan du quartier map of the district
plan du réseau network map
planning familial m [pla-neeng] family planning
plante f [plONt] plant
plaque minéralogique f

[meenayralojeek] number plate
plat m [pla] dish
plat flat
plateau m tray
plateaux-repas light meals served on trains
plâtre m plaster; plaster cast
plats à emporter take-away meals
plein [plAN] full
faire le plein to fill up
pleurer [plurray] to cry
pleut: il pleut [pluh] it's raining
pleuvoir [pluhvwahr] to rain
plombage m [plONbahj] filling
plombier m plumber
plongée f [plONjay] diving
plongée interdite no diving
plongée sous-marine skin-diving
plonger [plONjay] to dive
pluie f [plwee] rain
plupart: la plupart de [plOOpar duh] most of
plus [plOO] more
plus jamais never again
plus de ... more; no more ...
plus ... que ...-er than
le plus [plOOss] (the) most
plusieurs [plOOz-yurr] several
plutôt [plOOto] rather
pluvieux [plOOv-yuh] rainy
PMU betting on horses
pneu m [p-nuh] tyre
pneu crevé [kruhvay] flat tyre
pneu de rechange [duh ruhshONj] spare tyre
poche f [posh] pocket
poche en plastique plastic bag
poêle f [pwal] frying pan
poids m [pwa] weight
poids lourds [pwa loor] heavy vehicles
poids maximum maximum weight
poids net net weight
poignée f [pwan-yay] handle
poignet m [pwan-yay] wrist
point de rencontre m [pwAN duh rONkONtr] meeting point
point de vue [vOO] viewpoint
point noir accident blackspot; blackhead
point panoramique viewpoint
point phone pay-phone
pointure f [pwANtOOr] shoe size
poissonnerie f fishmonger
poitrine f [pwatreen] chest; breast
poli [polee] polite
police f police
police de l'aéroport airport police
police de la route traffic police
police du port harbour police
police secours emergency police
politique f politics
politique political
pollué [polOO-ay] polluted
pommade f [pomahd] ointment
pompiers mpl [pONp-yay] fire brigade
poney m pony
pont m [pON] bridge; deck

pont à péage [payahj] toll bridge
port de pêche m [por duh pesh] fishing port
porte f [port] door; gate
porte-bébé m [-baybay] carry-cot
portefeuille m [portfuh-ee] wallet
porte-jarretelles fpl suspenders
porte-monnaie m [port-monay] purse
porter [portay] to carry
bien se porter to be well
portes automatiques automatic gates
portier m [port-yay] porter
portière f [port-yair] door
portillon automatique m automatic gate
posologie directions for use, dosage
posséder [possayday] to own; to possess
poste f [posst] post office
poste de police m police station
poster [postay] to post
poste restante poste restante, (US) general delivery
pot m [po] jug
pot d'échappement [dayshapmON] exhaust
poterie f [potree] pottery
poubelle f [poobel] dustbin
poudre f [poodr] powder
pouls m pulse
poumons mpl [poomON] lungs
poupée f [poopay] doll
pour [poor] for
pourboire m [poorbwahr] tip
pourboire interdit please do not tip
pour cent [sON] per cent
pour entrer ..., to enter ...
pour ouvrir appuyer push to open
pour que [kuh] in order that, so that
pourquoi [poorkwa] why
pourrai: je pourrai [pooray] I will be able
pourra: il/elle pourra [poora] he/she/it will be able
pourras: tu pourras [poora] you will be able
pourrez: vous pourrez [pooray] you will be able
pourri [pooree] rotten
pourrons: nous pourrons [poorON] we will be able
pourront: ils/elles pourront [poorON] they will be able
pourtant [poortON] however
pour tous renseignements, s'adresser à ... for enquiries, please see ...
pourvu que [poorvoo kuh] provided that
pousser [poossay] to push
poussette f pushchair
poussez [poossay] push
pouvoir m [poovwahr] power
pouvoir to be able to
pratique practical
précautions d'emploi instructions for use

préfecture f [prayfektoor] regional administrative headquarters
préfecture de police police headquarters
préféré [prayfayray] favourite
préférence f [prayfayrONss] preference
préférer [prayfayray] to prefer
premier m [pruhm-yay] first floor; (US) second floor
premier first
première f first class; première
premier étage first floor, (US) second floor
premiers secours mpl [pruhm-yay suhkoor] first aid
premiers soins [SWAN] first aid
prendre [prONdr] to take; to catch
à prendre à jeun to be taken on an empty stomach
à prendre après les repas to be taken after meals
à prendre au coucher to be taken at bedtime
à prendre avant le coucher to be taken before going to bed
à prendre avant les repas to be taken before meals
à prendre ... fois par jour to be taken ... times a day
prendre ... comprimés à la fois take ... pills at a time
prendre ... comprimés ... fois par jour take ... pills ... times a day
prenez: vous prenez [pruhnay] you take
prenez un caddy take a trolley/cart
prenez un chariot take a trolley/cart
prenez un jeton à la caisse buy a token at the cash desk
prenez un panier take a basket
prenez un ticket take a ticket
prénom m [praynON] Christian name, first name
prenons: nous prenons [pruhnON] we take
préparer [prayparay] to prepare, to get ready
préparez votre monnaie have your change ready
presbyte [prezbeet] long-sighted
prescrire [preskreer] to prescribe
près de [pray duh] near
présenter [prayzONtay] to introduce; to present
préservatif m [prayzairvateef] condom
presque [presk] almost
pressing m dry-cleaner's
pression f [press-yON] pressure; draught beer
pression de l'air air pressure
pression des pneus tyre pressure
prêt [pray] ready
prêt-à-porter ready-to-wear clothes

prêter [pretay] to lend
prêtre m [pretr] priest
prier [pree-ay] to ask; to pray
je vous en prie [juh voo zON pree] don't mention it, you're welcome
prière f [pree-air] prayer
prière de ... please ...
prière de frapper avant d'entrer please knock before entering
prière de ne pas déranger please do not disturb
prière de ne pas faire de bruit après 22 heures please do not make any noise after 10 p.m.
prière de ne pas fumer please do not smoke
prière de ne pas toucher please do not touch
prière de refermer la porte please close the door
prière de s'essuyer les pieds avant d'entrer please wipe your feet
prière de tenir les chiens en laisse please keep dogs on a lead
primeurs fruit shop, greengrocer's
principal [prANseepal] main
printemps m [prANtON] spring
prioritaire [pree-oreetair] priority; priority-rate; having right of way
priorité f [pree-oreetay] right of way; priority
priorité à droite right of way for traffic coming from the right
pris [pree] taken
prise f [preez] plug; socket
prise en charge minimum charge
prise multiple [mOOlteepl] adaptor
privé [preevay] private
prix m [pree] price; fee; prize
prix cassés reduced prices
prix coûtant at cost price
prix des places ticket prices
prix par jour price per day
prix par personne price per person
prix par semaine price per week
prix réduit reduced price
prix sacrifiés prices slashed
probablement [prob-abluhmON] probably
prochain [proshAN] next
à la prochaine [proshen] see you soon
prochaine levée next collection
prochaine séance à ... heures next performance at ...
produits de beauté cosmetics
produits d'entretien household cleaning materials
produits naturels health food
produit toxique poison
professeur m [professurr] teacher; lecturer; professor
profond [profON] deep
profondeur f [profONdurr] depth

promenade f walk
promenades à cheval horse riding
promener: aller se promener [alay suh promnay] to go for a walk
promettre [prometr] to promise
promotion: en promotion on special offer
prononcer [pronONsay] to pronounce
propre [propr] clean; own
propriétaire m/f [propee-aytair] owner
propriété privée private property
propriété privée défense d'entrer private property, keep out; no trespassing
prospectus m brochure
protège-couches mpl [protej-koosh] nappy-liners
protéger [protejay] to protect
provenance: en provenance de (arriving) from
prudence f [prOOdONss] caution
prudent [prOOdON] careful
P & T (Postes et Télécommunications) post office (with telephone)
PTT (Postes, Télégraphes, Téléphones) [pay-tay-tay] post office (with telephone)
pu: il a pu [pOO] he was able to
public m [pOObleek] audience; public
puce f [pOOss] flea
puis [pwee] then
puisque [pweess-kuh] since
pull(over) m sweater
pure laine vierge pure new wool
puzzle m [pOOsl] jigsaw
PV (procès verbal) m [pay-vay] parking ticket

Q

quai m [kay] platform; track; quay
quand [kON] when
quand même [mem] anyway; all the same
quant à [kONta] as for
quarante [karONt] forty
quart m [kar] quarter
quartier m [kart-yay] district
quatorze [katorz] fourteen
quatre [katr] four
quatre-vingt-dix [katr-vAN-deess] ninety
quatre-vingts [katr-vAN] eighty
quatrième [katree-em] fourth
que [kuh] that; what; than; who(m); which
que ...? what ...?
que désirez-vous? what would you like?
quel [kel] which
quelque chose [kelkuh shohz] something
quelque part [par] somewhere
quelque(s) [kelkuh] some
quelques-uns [kelkuh-zAN]

some, a few
quelqu'un [kelKAN] somebody
qu'est-ce que ...? [keskuh] what ...?
qu'est-ce que vous avez dit? what did you say?
qu'est-ce qu'il y a? [keskeel ya] what's the matter?
qu'est-ce qui ...? [keskee] what ...?
queue f [kuh] tail; queue
faire la queue to queue
qui [kee] who
quincaillerie f [KAN-ky-ree] ironmonger, hardware store
quinzaine f [KANzen] fortnight; about fifteen
quinze [KANZ] fifteen
quitter [kitay] to leave
ne quittez pas [nuh kitay pa] hold the line
quoi? [kwa] what?
quoique [kwa-kuh] although

R

rabais m [rabay] discount, reduction
raccourci m [rakoorsee] shortcut
raccrochez: ne raccrochez pas [nuh rakroshay pa] hold the line
raccrochez svp replace the receiver
radiateur m [rad-yaturr] heater; radiator
radio(graphie) f X-ray
raide [red] steep; straight
raison f [rezzON] reason
avoir raison [avwahr] to be right
raisonnable [rezzonabl] sensible; reasonable
ralentir [ralONteer] to slow down
ralentisseurs speed bumps; rumble strip
ralentissez slow down
rallonge f [ralONj] extension lead
rame f [ram] train (on underground)
randonnée f [rONdonay] rambling; hike; trekking; ride; trip; hill-walking
ranger [rONjay] to tidy; to put away
rapide [rapeed] fast
rapide m inter-city train
rappel m reminder, reminder sign
rappeler [rapuhlay] to call back
se rappeler to remember, to recall
raquette de tennis f tennis racket
rarement [raruhmON] seldom
se **raser** [suh razay] to shave
rasoir m [razwahr] razor
rasoir électrique electric shaver
rater [ratay] to miss
RATP (Régie autonome des transports parisiens) Paris public transport company

ravi de faire votre connaissance [ravee duh fair votr konessONss] how do you do, nice to meet you
ravissant [raveessON] lovely
rayon m [rayON] spoke; department
rayon jouets toy department
rayons X mpl [rayON eex] X-ray
récépissé m [raysaypeessay] receipt
recette f [ruhset] recipe
recevoir [ruhsuhvwahr] to receive; to have guests
recharge f [ruhsharj] refill
réchaud à gaz m [rayshoh] camping gas stove
réclamations fpl [rayklamass-yON] complaints; faults service
recommander [ruhkomONday] to recommend
envoyer une lettre en recommandé to send a letter by recorded delivery
reconnaissant [ruhkonessON] grateful
reconnaître [ruhkonetr] to recognize
reçu m [ruhsoo] receipt
réductions familles nombreuses special rates for large families
regarder [ruhgarday] to look (at); to watch
régime m [rayjeem] diet
être au régime to be on a diet
règlement m [reglmON] regulation
règles fpl [regl] period
rein m [rAN] kidney
reine f [ren] queen
reins mpl [rAN] back
relâche closed
relais routier m [ruhlay root-yay] transport café (often quality restaurant)
relevez lift up
remarquer [ruhmarkay] to notice
remboursement m [rONboorsmON] refund
rembourser [rONboorsay] to refund
remercier [ruhmairs-yay] to thank
remettez mes amitiés à ... [ruhmetay may zameet-yay] give my regards to ...
remise f [ruhmeez] reduction
remonte-pente m [ruhmONt-pONt] ski lift; ski tow
remorque f [ruhmork] trailer
remorquer [ruhmorkay] to tow
remplir [rONpleer] to fill in, to fill
rencontrer [rONkONtray] to meet
rendez-vous m appointment
prendre rendez-vous to make an appointment
rendre [rONdr] to give back, to return; to make
se rendre à to go to
renouveler [ruhnoovuhlay] to renew
renseignements mpl [rONsen-yuhmON] information;

directory enquiries
renseignements internationaux international directory enquiries
renseigner [rONsen-yay] to inform
se **renseigner** to find out; to enquire
rentrer [rONtray] to return
rentrer à la maison to go home
renverser [rONvairsay] to knock over
réparations fpl [rayparass-yON] repairs
réparer [rayparay] to repair
repas m [ruhpa] meal
repasser [ruhpassay] to iron; to come back
répéter [raypaytay] to repeat
répondre [raypONdr] to answer
réponse f [raypONss] answer
repos m [ruhpo] rest
reposer: se reposer [suh ruhpozay] to take a rest
représentant m [ruhprayzONtON] agent
représentation f [ruhprayzONtass-yON] representation; performance
reprise f [ruhpreez] revival; renewal; resumption
RER (Réseau express régional) m [air-uh-air] fast, limited-stop metro line in Paris
résa f [rayza] reservation ticket on TGV
réservation obligatoire booking essential
réservé [rayzairvay] reserved
réservé au personnel staff only
réservé aux clients patrons only
réservé aux clients de l'hôtel hotel patrons only
réservé aux membres de l'équipage reserved for the crew, crew only
réserve de chasse hunting preserve
réserver [rayzairvay] to book, to reserve
réservoir m [rayzairvwahr] tank
respectez le silence de ces lieux please respect the sanctity of this place
respectez les pelouses please do not walk on the grass
respirer [respeeray] to breathe
responsable [respONsabl] responsible
resquilleur m [reskeeyurr] fare dodger
ressembler à [ruhsONblay] to look like
ressort m [ruhsor] spring
restaurant de poisson fish restaurant
restauration à votre place meal served at your seat (1st class only)
reste m [rest] rest
rester [restay] to stay
resto m restaurant
restoroute m roadside café
retard m [ruhtar] delay
en retard late

retardé [ruhtarday] delayed
retirer [ruhteeeray] to withdraw
retirez votre argent take your money
retirez votre carte remove your card
retirez votre reçu (d'opération) take your receipt
retour m [ruhtoor] return
de retour dans une heure back in an hour
retourner [ruhtoornay] to return
retrait de colis et lettres recommandées collection of parcels and recorded delivery letters
retrait des bagages m [ruhtray day bagahj] baggage claim
retrait d'espèces cash withdrawal
retraité(e) m/f [ruhtretay] old-age pensioner
retraits withdrawals
rétroviseur m [raytroveezurr] rearview mirror
réunion f [ray-oon-yON] meeting
réussir [rayoosseer] to succeed
rêve m [rev] dream
réveil m [rayvay] alarm clock; waking up
réveillé [rayvay-yay] awake
réveiller [rayvay-yay] to wake
se réveiller to wake up
revenir [ruhvuhneer] to come back
revêtement temporaire temporary road surface
revue f magazine
rez-de-chaussée m [rayd-shoh-say] ground floor, (US) first floor
RF (République française) French Republic
rhume m [room] cold
rhume des foins [day fwAN] hay fever
riche [reesh] rich
rideau m [reedo] curtain
rien [ree-AN] nothing
de rien you're welcome
rien à déclarer nothing to declare
rire [reer] to laugh
risque d'avalanche danger of avalanche
rivage m [reevahj] shore
rive f [reev] bank
riverains autorisés no entry except for access, residents only
rivière f river
RN (route nationale) **f** [air-en] national highway
robe f [rob] dress
robe de chambre [duh shONbr] dressing gown
robinet m [robeenay] tap
rocher m [roshay] rock
roi m [rwa] king
Roi-Soleil [solay] Louis XIV (The Sun King)
roman m [romON] novel
roman Romanesque
rond [rON] round
rond-point m [-pwAN] roundabout, (US) traffic

circle
ronfler [rONflay] to snore
rose f [roz] rose
rose pink
rôtisserie f [roteesree] steak-house
roue f [roo] wheel
roue de secours [duh suhkoor] spare wheel
rouge [rooj] red
rouge à lèvres m [rooj a levr] lipstick
rougeole f [roojol] measles
roulez au pas drive at walking pace
roulez sur une file single lane traffic
rousse [rooss] red-haired
route f [root] road; route
route barrée road closed; road blocked
route départementale secondary road
route du vin route taking in vineyards, wine route
route nationale [nass-yonal] national highway, main road
routier m [root-yay] truck; truck-driver; roadside café
roux, f rousse [roo, rooss] red-haired
Royaume-Uni m [rwy-ohm oonee] United Kingdom
RU (Royaume Uni) UK
rubéole f [roobayol] German measles
rue f [roo] street
rue commerçante [komairsONt] shopping street
rue piétonne [p-yayton] pedestrian precinct
rue piétonnière [p-yayton-yair] pedestrian precinct
ruisseau m [rweesso] stream

S

SA (société anonyme) [ess-ah] Ltd, Inc
sa* his; her; its
sable m [sabl] sand
sables mouvants quicksand
sac m bag
sac à dos [doh] rucksack
sac à main [mAN] handbag, (US) purse
sac de couchage [duh kooshahj] sleeping bag
sac en plastique [ON plasteek] plastic bag
saignement m [sen-yuhmON] bleeding
saigner [sen-yay] to bleed
sais: je/tu sais [say] I/you know
je ne sais pas I don't know
saison f [sezzON] season
en haute saison in the high season
sait: il/elle sait [say] he/she knows
salaud [salo] bastard
sale [sal] dirty
salé [salay] salty; savoury
salle à manger f [sal a mONjay] dining room

salle climatisée [kleemateezay] dining room with air conditioning
salle d'attente [datONt] waiting room
salle de bain [duh bAN] bathroom
salle de cinéma [duh seenayma] cinema
salon m [salON] lounge
salon de coiffure [duh kwafoor] hairdressing salon
salon d'essayage [dessayahj] fitting room
salon de thé [duh tay] tearoom
salon privé [preevay] private lounge
salut! [saloo] hi!; cheerio!
samedi [samdee] Saturday
SAMU (Service d'Aide Medicale d'Urgence) **m** [samoo] emergency medical service
sang m [sON] blood
sanisette f [saneezet] automated public toilet on the street
sanitaires mpl [saneetair] toilets and showers
sans [sON] without
sans agent de conservation contains no preservatives
sans alcool non-alcoholic
sans doute [doot] undoubtedly
sans issue no through road, dead end
sans plomb lead-free
santé! [sontay] cheers!; bless you!
santé f health
en bonne santé healthy, in good health
bon pour la santé healthy
SARL (société à responsabilité limitée) Ltd, Inc
satellite m [-eet] section of airport terminal; satellite
sauf [sohf] except; safe
sauf indication contraire du médecin unless otherwise stated by your doctor
sauf le ... except on ...
sauf riverains access only
saurai: je saurai [soray] I will know
saura: il/elle saura [sora] he/she/it will know
sauras: tu sauras [sora] you will know
saurez: vous saurez [soray] you will know
saurons: nous saurons [sorON] we will know
sauront: ils sauront [sorON] they will know
sauter [sotay] to jump
sauvage [sovahj] wild
savoir [savwahr] to know
savon m [savON] soap
scandaleux [skONdaluh] shocking
se* [suh] him; to him; himself; her; to her; herself; each other
séance f [say-ONss] showing
seau m [so] bucket
sec, f sèche [sek, sesh] dry

sèche-cheveux **m** [sesh-shuhvuh] hair dryer
sécher [sayshay] to dry
second **m** [suhgON] second floor, (US) third floor
seconde **f** [suhgONd] second; second class
secours **m** [suhkoor] help
au secours! [oh] help!
secours de montagne [duh mONtañ] mountain rescue
Secours routier français [root-yay] French motoring organization
secrétaire **m/f** [suhkraytair] secretary
sécurité: en sécurité [ON saykOOreetay] safe
séduisant [saydweezON] attractive
sein **m** [sAN] breast
au sein de within
seize [sez] sixteen
seizième: le seizième [sez-yem] the 16th arrondissement, up-market area of Paris
séjour **m** [sayjoor] stay
self **m** self-service restaurant
selle **f** [sel] saddle
selon [suhlON] according to
sels de bain **mpl** [sel duh bAN] bath salts
semaine **f** [suhmen] week
par semaine per week
semblable [sONblabl] similar
sembler [sONblay] to seem
semelle **f** [suhmel] sole
semi-remorque **m** [suhmee-ruhmork] articulated lorry
sens **m** [sONss] direction
sens giratoire [jeeratwahr] roundabout; (US) traffic circle
sensible [sONseebl] sensitive
sens interdit one-way street; no entry
sens unique one-way street
sentier **m** [sONt-yay] path
sentier balisé marked footpath
sentiment **m** [sONteemON] feeling
sentir [sONteer] to feel; to smell
séparé [sayparay] separate
séparément [sayparaymON] separately
sept [set] seven
septembre [septONbr] September
septième [set-yem] seventh
serai: je serai [suhray] I will be
sera: il/elle sera [suhra] he/she/it will be
serais: je/tu serais [suhray] I/you would be
seras: tu seras [suhra] you will be
serez: vous serez [suhray] you will be
sérieux [sayree-uh] serious
seriez: vous seriez [suhree-ay] you would be
serions: nous serions [suhree-ON] we would be
serons: nous serons [suhrON] we will be

seront: ils/elles seront [suhrON] they will be
serpent m [sairpON] snake
serrez à droite keep to the right
serrure f [sair-rOOr] lock
serveur m [sairvurr] waiter
serveuse f [sairvurz] waitress
servez-vous please take one
service m [sairveess] service; service charge; ward; department
service! not at all! (Switzerland)
service après vente after-sales service
service de retouches alteration/tailoring service
service des urgences casualty department
service d'urgence emergency ward, emergencies
service non-stop 24-hour service
serviette f [sairvee-et] towel; briefcase; serviette, napkin
serviette (de table) serviette, napkin
serviette de toilette [twalet] towel
serviette hygiénique [eejee-ayneek] sanitary towel/napkin
servir [sairveer] to serve
se servir to help oneself
se servir de to use
ses* [say] his; her; its
seul [surl] alone; single; only
seulement [surlmON] only
sexe m [sex] sex
shamp(o)oing m [shONpwAN] shampoo
shamp(o)oing - mise en plis [meez ON plee] shampoo and set
si if; so; yes
SIDA m [seeda] AIDS
siècle m [see-ekl] century
siège m [see-ej] seat
sien*: le sien [luh s-yAN] his; hers; its
sienne*: la sienne [s-yen] his; hers; its
sien(ne)s*: les sien(ne)s [s-yAN, s-yen] his; hers; its
signal d'alarme m alarm; emergency lever
signer [seen-yay] to sign
signifier [seen-yeefee-ay] to mean
silence m [seelONss] silence
silencieux [seelONssee-uh] silent
s'il te plaît [seel tuh play] please; excuse me
s'il vous plaît [seel voo play] please; excuse me
simple [sANpl] simple; mere
sinon [seenON] otherwise
sirop pour la toux m [too] cough medicine
site historique m [seet eestoreek] place of historical interest
six [seess] six
sixième [seez-yem] sixth
ski m ski; skiing
faire du ski to go skiing
ski de descente [duh dessONt] downhill skiing

ski de fond [fON] cross-country skiing
skier [skee-ay] to ski
ski nautique waterski
slip m [sleep] pants, underpants
slip de bain [duh bAN] swimming trunks
snack m snack bar
SNCB (Société Nationale des Chemins de Fer Belges) **f** [ess-en-say-bay] Belgian railways/railroad
SNCF (Société Nationale des Chemins de Fer Français) **f** [ess-en-say-ef] French railways/railroad
société f [sos-yay-tay] company; society
sœur f [surr] sister
soi [swa] oneself
soie f [swa] silk
soif: j'ai soif [jay swaf] I'm thirsty
soigner [swan-yay] to treat, to nurse, to tend
soir m [swahr] evening
le soir in the evening
ce soir tonight
soirée f [swahray] evening; evening performance
soirée privée private party
sois [swa] be
soit ... soit ... [swa] either ... or ...
soixante [swassONt] sixty
soixante-dix [-deess] seventy
sol m ground
soldé [solday] reduced
solde: en solde [ON sold] reduced
solder [solday] to sell at a reduced price
soldes fpl [sold] sale
soldes d'été [daytay] summer sale
soleil m [solay] sun
au soleil in the sun
sombre [sONbr] dark
sommeil: j'ai sommeil [jay somay] I'm sleepy
sommes: nous sommes [som] we are
sommet m [somay] summit
somnifère m [somneefair] sleeping pill
son* [sON] his; her; its
son m sound
sonnette f bell
sonnette d'alarme alarm bell
sonnette de nuit night bell
sont: ils/elles sont [sON] they are
sorte f [sort] sort
de sorte que so that
sortie f [sortee] exit, way out
sortie de camions vehicle exit
sortie de secours emergency exit
sortie piétons exit for pedestrians
sortir [sorteer] to go out; to take out
SOS Femmes [ess-o-ess fam] Women's Aid Centre
SOS Médecin [mayd-sAN] 24-hour emergency medical

service found in large towns
souci m [soossee] worry
se faire du souci (pour) to worry (about)
soucoupe f [sookoop] saucer
soudain [soodAN] suddenly
souffrant [soofrON] unwell
souffrir [soofreer] to be in pain; to suffer
souffrir de to suffer from
souhait: à vos souhaits [soo-ay] bless you
souhaiter [soo-ettay] to wish (for)
souliers mpl [sool-yay] shoes
sourcil m [soorseel] eyebrow
sourd [soor] deaf
sourire [sooreer] to smile
souris f [sooree] mouse
sous [soo] under
sous réserve de toute modification subject to modifications
sous-sol m basement
sous-titré [-teetray] subtitled
sous-titres mpl [-teetr] subtitles
sous-vêtements mpl [-vetmON] underwear
soutien-gorge m [soot-yAN-gorj] bra
souvenir: se souvenir de [suh soovuhneer duh] to remember
souvent [soovON] often
soyez [swy-yay] be
soyez le bienvenu [luh b-yAN-vuhnoo] welcome
sparadrap m [sparadra] plaster, Bandaid®
spécialement [spays-yalmON] especially
spectacle m [spektakl] show
spéléologie f pot-holing
sports d'hiver mpl [spor deevair] winter sports
stade m [stad] stadium
stage m [stahj] training course
standardiste m/f [stONdardeest] operator
starter m choke
station de métro f [stass-yON duh maytro] underground/subway station
station de taxis taxi rank
stationnement à durée limitée restricted parking
stationnement alterné parking on alternate sides of the street on 1st-15th and 16th-31st of the month
stationnement en épis interdit no angle parking
stationnement gênant no parking please
stationnement interdit no parking
stationnement limité à 30 minutes parking restricted to 30 minutes
stationnement payant pay to park here
stationnement réglementé limited parking
stationnement toléré 2 minutes parking for 2

minutes only
stationner [stass-yonay] to park
station-service f [stass-yON-sairveess] petrol/gas station
station thermale [tairmahl] spa
stérilet m [stayreelay] IUD, coil
strapontin m [strapontAN] fold-down seat
studio m flatlet
stylo m [steelo] pen
stylo à bille [bee] biro®
stylo-feutre [furtr] felt-tip pen
su [sOO] known
substance dangereuse dangerous substance
sucette f [sOOsset] lollipop
sucré [sOOkray] sweet
sud m [sOOd] south
au sud de south of
suffire [sOOfeer] to be sufficient
ça suffit [sa sOOfee] that's enough
suis: je suis [swee] I am
Suisse f [sweess] Switzerland
suisse Swiss
Suisse romande [romONd] French-speaking Switzerland
suivant [sweevON] next
suivre [sweevr] to follow
faire suivre to forward
sujet: au sujet de [o sOOjay duh] about
super m [sOOpair] 4 star petrol; (US) premium (gas)
super! great!
supermarché m [sOOpairmarshay] supermarket
supplément m [sOOplaymON] extra charge, supplement
supporter [sOOportay] to tolerate, to stand; to support
supposer [sOOpozay] to suppose
sur [sOOr] on
sûr [sOOr] sure; safe; reliable
surgelé [sOOrjelay] frozen
surgelés mpl frozen food
surnom m [sOOrnON] nickname
surprenant [sOOrpruhnON] surprising
surtout [sOOrtoo] above all; especially
surveillant m [sOOrvayON] supervisor; guard
surveillant de plage [duh plahj] lifeguard
survêtement de sport m [sOOrvetmON duh spor] tracksuit
SVP (s'il vous plaît) please
sympa [sANpa] nice
sympathique [sANpateek] nice
syndicat d'initiative m [sANdeeka deeneess-yateev] tourist information centre

T

t'* (to) you; yourself
ta* your
tabac m [taba] tobacco; tobacconist and newsagent (also sells stamps)
tabac-journaux m newsagent, tobacco store and news

vendor (also sells stamps); newspaper kiosk
tableau m [tablo] painting
tableau de bord [duh bor] dashboard
tache f [tash] stain
taille f [tī] size; waist
tailleur m [tī-urr] tailor; lady's suit
taisez-vous [tezzay-voo] shut up
tais-toi [tay-twa] shut up
talc m talcum powder
talon m [talON] heel
talon-minute heel bar
tandis que [tONdee kuh] whereas; while
tant (de) [tON] so much; so many
tant mieux [m-yuh] so much the better
tant pis [pee] too bad
tant que as long as
tante f [tONt] aunt
tapis m [tapee] rug
tapis roulant [roolON] moving walkway; baggage carousel
tard [tar] late
tarif m [tareef] price
tarif des consommations price list
tarif normal first-class mail
tarif réduit reduced fare; second-class mail
tarifs postaux postage rates
tarifs postaux intérieurs inland postage rates
tarifs postaux pour l'étranger overseas postage rates
tasse f [tass] cup
taureau m [toro] bull
taux m [toh] rate
taux à l'achat buying rate
taux à la vente selling rate
taux de change [duh shONj] exchange rate
taxis - tête de station taxi rank, queue here
TCF (Touring club de France) **m** [tay-say-ef] French automobile association
te* [tuh] (to) you; yourself
TEE (Trans-Europe-Express) **m** [tay-uh-uh] first class trans-European express
teint m [tAN] complexion
teint dyed
teinte f [tANt] colour, shade
teinturerie f [tANtoor-uhree] dry cleaner's
teinturier m [tANtooree-ay] dry cleaner's
télé f [taylay] TV
télécarte f [taylay-kart] phonecard
télécartes en vente ici phonecards sold here
télécopie f fax
téléférique m [taylayfayreek] cable car
téléphone à carte m cardphone
téléphone interurbain long-distance telephone
téléphoner (à) [taylayfonay] to phone
télésiège m [taylaysee-ej] chairlift, ski lift

téléski **m** ski tow
Télétel® free computerized service available in post offices instead of the phonebook
téléviseur **m** [taylayveezurr] television set
tellement [telmON] so
tellement de so much; so many
tel(s) such
témoin **m** [taymwAN] witness
tempête **f** [tONpet] storm
tempête de neige [duh nej] snowstorm
temple **m** [tONpl] Protestant church
temps **m** [tON] time; weather
de temps en temps from time to time
tenez votre droite keep to the right
tenir [tuhneer] to hold; to keep
tennis **fpl** [tenneess] trainers
tente **f** [tONt] tent
terminer [tairmeenay] to finish
terrain **m** [terrAN] pitch, field, ground
terrain de camping [duh kONpeeng] campsite
terrain pour caravanes [poor karavan] caravan site
terre **f** [tair] earth
tes* [tay] your
tête **f** [tet] head
tête de station taxi rank, queue here
TGV (Train à grande vitesse) **m** [tay-jay-vay] high-speed train
théière **f** [tay-air] teapot
tiède [t-yed] lukewarm
tien*: le tien [luh t-yAN] yours
tienne*: la tienne [t-yen] yours
à la tienne! your health!
tiennent: ils/elles tiennent [t-yen] they hold
tien(ne)s*: les tien(ne)s [t-yAN, t-yen] yours
tiens: je/tu tiens [t-yAN] I/you hold
tient: il/elle tient [t-yAN] he/she/it holds
timbre **m** [tANbr] stamp
timbres de collection collectors' stamps
tir **m** [teer] shooting
tire-bouchon **m** [teer-booshON] corkscrew
tirer [teeray] to pull; to shoot
tirez [teeray] pull
tissu **m** [teessOO] material
tissus fabrics
titre de transport ticket
toi* [twa] you
toilette: faire sa toilette [twalet] to have a wash
toilettes **fpl** [twalet] toilets; (US) rest room
les toilettes sont dans la cour the toilet is in the back yard
toit **m** [twa] roof
tomber [tONbay] to fall
tomber en panne [ON pan] to break down
tomber en panne d'essence to run out of petrol

tomber malade to fall ill
ton* [tON] your
tonalité f [tohnaleetay] dialling tone
tonnage limité weight limit
tonnerre m [tonair] thunder
torchon à vaisselle m [torshON a vess-el] tea towel
tort: avoir tort [avwahr tor] to be wrong
tôt [toh] early
toucher [tooshay] to touch
toujours [toojoor] always; still
tour m tour; turn
tour f tower
tour de hanches m [duh ONsh] hip measurement
tour de poitrine [pwatreen] bust/chest measurement
tour de taille [tī] waist measurement
tour en voiture [vwatOOr] drive
tourner [toornay] to turn
tournevis m [toornuhvee] screwdriver
tous [too] all; every
 tous les deux both of them
 tous les jours every day
 tous les jours sauf ... every day except ...
 tous les matins every morning
tousser [toossay] to cough
tout [too] everything; all; every
 pas du tout not at all
 en tout altogether
 à tout à l'heure! [a toota lurr] see you later!
tout à fait [too ta fay] entirely; altogether
tout compris [kONpree] all inclusive
tout de suite [toot sweet] immediately
tout droit [drwa] straight ahead
toute [toot] all; every
 toute la journée all day
toutefois [tootfwa] however
toute personne prise en flagrant délit de vol sera poursuivie all shoplifters will be prosecuted
toutes [toot] all; every
toutes directions all directions
toutes opérations all transactions
toutes taxes comprises inclusive of taxes
tout le monde [too luh mONd] everyone
toux f [too] cough
traduction f [tradOOx-yON] translation
traduire [tradweer] to translate
train m [trAN] train
 un train peut en cacher un autre there may be another train hidden behind this one
 être en train de faire quelque chose to be doing something
train à supplément train for which you must pay a supplement

train auto-couchettes motorail
train direct direct train
train en partance pour ... train leaving for ...
train omnibus slow train
train rapide express train
trains au départ departures
train supplémentaire extra train
traitement m [tretmON] (course of) treatment
traitement de texte word processing; word processor
traiteur m [treturr] delicatessen
tranche f [trONsh] slice
tranquille [trONkeel] quiet
transactions avec l'étranger overseas business
transpirer [trONspeeray] to sweat
travail m [travī] work
travailler [travī-ay] to work
travaux mpl [travo] roadworks; building work
traversée f [travairsay] crossing
traverser [travairsay] to cross, to go through
treize [trez] thirteen
trembler [trONblay] to tremble
trente [trONt] thirty
très [tray] very
très bien, merci [b-yAN] very well, thank you
tribunal m [treebOOnal] court
tricot m [treeko] knitting; jumper
tricoter [treekotay] to knit
tricots knitwear
triste [treest] sad
trois [trwa] three
troisième [trwaz-yem] third
tromper [trONpay] to deceive
se tromper to be wrong
se tromper de numéro to dial the wrong number
trop [tro] too; too much
trop de too much; too many
trottoir m [trotwahr] pavement
trou m [troo] hole
trouver [troovay] to find
truc m [trOOk] thing
TTC (toutes taxes comprises) inclusive of tax
tu* [tOO] you
tuer [tOO-ay] to kill
tunnel de lavage m [tOOnel duh lavahj] car-wash tunnel
tutoyer [tOOtwy-ay] to use the familiar 'tu' form
tuyau m [twee-yo] pipe
TVA (taxe sur la valeur ajoutée) f [tay-vay-ah] VAT
TV par câble f [tay-vay par kahbl] cable TV

U

UE f [OO-uh] EU, European Union
ulcère m [OOlsair] ulcer
un* [AN] a; one
une* [OOn] a; one
unité f [OOneetay] unit
urgence f [OOrjONss] emergency

urinoir m [OOreenwahr] public urinal
usage: l'usage des WC est interdit pendant l'arrêt du train en gare do not use the toilet while the train is in a station
usage externe for external use
usine f [OOzeen] factory
ustensiles de cuisine cooking utensils
utile [OOteel] useful
utilisateur m [OOteeleezaturr] user
utiliser [OOteeleezay] to use
utiliser avant ... use before ...
utilisez un stylo à bille et appuyez fortement use a ball-point pen and write firmly

V

va: il/elle va he/she/it goes
comment ça va? [komON sa] how are you?
il va bien [eel va b-yAN] he's well
il va mal he's not well
le bleu me va bien blue suits me
vacances fpl [vakONss] holiday, vacation
vacances annuelles annual holiday
vaccin m [vaxAN] vaccination
vache f [vash] cow
vachement [vashmON] bloody, damn(ed)
vagin m [vajAN] vagina
vague f [vag] wave
vague de chaleur [duh shalurr] heatwave
vais: je vais [vay] I go
vaisselle f [vess-el] crockery
faire la vaisselle to do the washing up
valable [val-abl] valid
valable jusqu'au ... valid until ...
validez [valeeday] validate
valise f [valeez] suitcase
vallée f [valay] valley
valoir [valwahr] to be worth
varappe f [varap] rock climbing
variable [varee-abl] changeable
varicelle f [vareessel] chickenpox
vase m [vahz] vase
vas: tu vas [va] you go
vas-y [va-zee] go on
vaut: il vaut [vo] it is worth
véhicule m [vay-eekOOl] vehicle
vélo m [vaylo] bike
faire du vélo to cycle
vélomoteur m [-moturr] moped
vendanges fpl [vONdONj] wine harvest
vendangeur: on demande des vendangeurs grape pickers wanted
vendeur m, vendeuse f [vONdurr, -urz] shop assistant; salesman; saleswoman
vendre [vONdr] to sell

à vendre for sale
vendredi [vONdruhdee] Friday
vendu uniquement sur ordonnance sold on prescription only
venir [vuhneer] to come
venir de faire quelque chose to have just done something
faire venir to send for
vent m [vON] wind
vente f [vONt] sale; selling rate
en vente ici available here
ventes hors taxes à bord duty free sales aboard
vent fort strong wind
ventilateur m [vONteelaturr] fan
ventre m [vONtr] stomach
verglas m [vairgla] black ice
vérifier [vayreef-yay] to check
vérifiez votre monnaie check your change
vernis à ongles m [vairnee a ONgl] nail polish
verrai: je verrai [vairray] I will see
verra: il/elle verra [vairra] he/she/it will see
verras: tu verras [vairra] you will see
verre m [vair] glass
verre à eau [o] tumbler
verre à vin [VAN] wineglass
verrez: vous verrez [vairray] you will see
verrons: nous verrons [vairrON] we will see
verront: ils/elles verront [vairrON] they will see
verrou m [vairroo] bolt
verrouiller [vairoo-yay] to bolt; to lock
vers m [vair] verse
vers towards; about
versement m [vairss-mON] payment, deposit
verser [vairsay] to pay; to pour
version originale f [vairss-yON oreejeenal] in the original language
vert [vair] green
vessie f [vessee] bladder
veste f [vest] jacket
vestiaire m [vestee-air] cloakroom; (US) checkroom; changing room
vêtements mpl [vetmON] clothes
vêtements dames ladies' fashions
vêtements enfants children's wear
vêtements femmes ladies' wear
vêtements hommes menswear
vêtements messieurs menswear
vétérinaire m [vaytayreenair] vet
veuf m [vurf] widower
veuillez ... [vuh-ee-yay] please ...
veuillez établir votre chèque à l'ordre de ... please make cheques payable to ...
veuillez éteindre votre moteur please switch off engine

veuillez fermer la porte please close the door
veuillez libérer votre chambre avant midi please vacate your room by 12 noon
veuillez patienter please wait
veuillez patienter, nous traitons votre demande please wait, your request is being processed
veulent: ils/elles veulent [vurl] they want
veut: il/elle veut [vuh] he/she/it wants
cela veut dire ... that means ...
veuve f [vurv] widow
veux: je/tu veux [vuh] I/you want
vexer [vexay] to offend
vidange f [veedONj] oil change
vide [veed] empty
vide-ordures m [-ordoor] garbage chute
vie f [vee] life
vieille [v-yay] old
vieille ville f [veel] old town
viendrai: je viendrai [v-yANdray] I will come
viendra: il/elle viendra [v-yANdra] he/she/it will come
viendras: tu viendras [v-yANdra] you will come
viendrez: vous viendrez [v-yANdray] you will come
viendrons: nous viendrons [v-yANdrON] we will come
viendront: ils/elles viendront [v-yANdrON] they will come
viennent: ils/elles viennent [v-yen] they come
viens: je/tu viens [v-yAN] I/you come
vient: il/elle vient [v-yAN] he/she/it comes
vieux, f vieille [v-yuh, v-yay] old
vignette f [veen-yet] road tax disc; postage label
vignettes montant au choix select postage labels to required value
vignoble m [veen-yobl] vineyard
vilebrequin m [veelbruhkAN] crankshaft
ville f [veel] town
en ville in town; to town
ville jumelée avec ... twin town ...
vingt [vAN] twenty
vins et spiritueux wine merchant
viol m [veeol] rape
violet [veeolay] purple
violon m [veeolON] violin
virage m [veerahj] bend
virage dangereux dangerous bend
virages sur ... km bends for ... km
virement m [veermON] transfer
vis f [vee] screw
visage m [veezahj] face
viseur m [veezurr] viewfinder
visite guidée f [veezeet geeday] guided tour
visiter [veezeetay] to visit

visitez ... visit ...
vite [veet] quick; quickly
vitesse f speed; gear
vitesse limitée à ... speed limit ...
vitre f [veetr] window
vitrine f [veetreen] shop window
vivant [veevON] alive
vivre [veevr] to live
VO (version originale) [vay-o] in the original language
vœux: meilleurs vœux [may-yurr vuh] best wishes
voici [vwa-see] here is; here are; here you are
voie f [vwa] platform; track; lane
par voie orale orally
voie ferrée railway
voie pour véhicules lents crawler lane
voilà [vwala] here is; here are; there you are
le voilà there he is
voile f [vwal] sail; sailing
voilier m [vwal-yay] sailing boat
voir [vwahr] to see
voisin m, voisine f [vwazAN, -zeen] neighbour
voiture f [vwatoor] car; coach; carriage
en voiture by car
voiture de queue rear car
voiture de tête front car
voix f [vwa] voice
vol m flight; theft
volant m [volON] steering wheel
vol à voile [vwal] gliding
vol direct direct flight
voler [volay] to steal; to fly
volets mpl [volay] shutters
voleur m [volurr] thief
volley m [volay] volleyball
vols intérieurs mpl [vol zANtayree-urr] domestic flights
vols internationaux [zANtairnass-yono] international flights
vomir [vomeer] to be sick, to vomit
vont: ils/elles vont [vON] they go
vos* [vo] your
votre* [votr] your
vôtre*: le/la vôtre [luh/la vohtr] yours
à la vôtre! cheers!
vôtres*: les vôtres [lay vohtr] yours
voudraient: il/elles voudraient [voodray] they would like
voudrais: je/tu voudrais [voodray] I/you would like
voudrait: il/elle voudrait [voodray] he/she/it would like
voudriez: vous voudriez [voodree-ay] you would like
voudrions: nous voudrions [voodree-ON] we would like
voulez: que voulez-vous? [kuh voolay-voo] what do you want?
voulez-vous ...? do you want ...?
voulez-vous un reçu? do you want a receipt?

vouloir [voolwahr] to want
vouloir dire [deer] to mean
voulu [voolOO] wanted
vous* [voo] you; (to) you
vous désirez? can I help you?
vous êtes ici you are here
vouvoyer [voovwy-ay] to use the polite 'vous' form
voyage m [vwy-ahj] trip, journey
voyage d'affaires [dafair] business trip
voyage de noces [duh noss] honeymoon
voyage organisé [organeezay] package tour
voyager [vwy-ahjay] to travel
voyageur m [vwy-ahjurr] traveller
voyagiste m [vwy-ahjeest] tour operator
vrai [vray] true; real
à vrai dire actually
vraiment [vraymON] really
vu [vOO] seen
vue f [vOO] view

W

wagon m [vagON] carriage
wagon-lit [-lee] sleeper, sleeping car
wagon-restaurant [-restorON] dining car
WC mpl [vay-say] toilet, rest room

Y

y [ee] there; it
y a-t-il ...? [yateel] is there ...?; are there ...?
yeux mpl [yuh] eyes

Z

zéro [zayro] zero
zone bleue f [zon bluh] restricted parking area
zone piétonne [p-yayton] pedestrian precinct
zone piétonnière [p-yaytonair] pedestrian precinct

Menu Reader

Food

abats [aba] offal
abricot [abreeko] apricot
agneau [an-yo] lamb
aiguillette de bœuf [ay-gwee-yet duh burf] slices of rump steak
ail [ī] garlic
ailloli [ī-olee] garlic mayonnaise
à la broche [ala brosh] roasted on a spit
à l'ail [alī] with garlic
à la jardinière [ala jardeen-yair] with assorted vegetables
à l'ancienne [alONs-yen] traditional style
à la normande [ala normOND] in cream sauce
à la provençale [ala provONsahl] cooked in olive oil with tomatoes, garlic and herbs
alose [aloze] shad (fish)
amande [amOND] almond
ananas [anana] pineapple
anchois [ONshwa] anchovies
andouillette [ONdoo-yet] small, spicy tripe sausage
anguille [ONgwee] eel
araignée de mer [aren-yay duh mair] spider crab
arête [aret] fishbone
artichaut [artee-sho] artichoke
asperge(s) [aspairj] asparagus
aspic de volaille [vol-ī] chicken in aspic
assaisonnement [assezonuhmON] seasoning; dressing
assiette anglaise [ass-yet ONglez] selection of cold meats
aubergine aubergine, eggplant
au choix ... [o shwa] choice of ...
aux câpres [o kapr] in caper sauce
avocat [avoka] avocado

baba au rhum [o rum] rum baba
baguette stick of bread, French stick
banane [banan] banana
bananes flambées [banan flONbay] bananas flambéd in brandy
barbue [barbOO] brill (fish)
bâtard [batar] a half-size French stick (250g)
bavaroise [bavarwaz] light mousse
bavette à l'échalote [bavet a layshalot] grilled beef with shallots
béarnaise [bay-arnez] with béarnaise sauce (sauce made from eggs and butter)
beaufort [bofor] hard cheese from Savoie
bécasse [baykass] woodcock
béchamel [bayshamel] white sauce, béchamel sauce
beignet [ben-yay] fritter, doughnut
beignet aux pommes [o pom] apple fritter

betterave [betrahv] beetroot; (US) red beet
beurre [burr] butter
beurre d'anchois [dONshwa] anchovy paste
beurre d'estragon [destragON] tarragon butter
beurre noir [nwahr] dark melted butter
bien cuit [b-yan kwee] well done (meat)
bifteck [beeftek] steak
bifteck de cheval [duh shuhval] horsemeat steak
biscuit de Savoie [beess-kwee duh savwa] sponge cake
bisque d'écrevisses [beesk daykruhveess] freshwater crayfish soup
bisque de homard [duh omar] lobster bisque
bisque de langoustines [lONgoosteen] saltwater crayfish soup
blanquette de veau [blONket duh vo] veal stew
bleu [bluh] very rare; rare; blue
bleu d'Auvergne [dovairn] blue cheese from Auvergne
bœuf [burf] beef
bœuf à la ficelle [feesel] beef cooked in stock
bœuf bourguignon [boor-geen-yON] beef cooked in red wine
bœuf en daube [ON dohb] beef casserole
bœuf miroton [meerotON] boiled beef with onions
bœuf mode [mod] beef stew with carrots
boisson [bwassON] drink
bolet [bolay] boletus (mushroom)
bouchée à la reine [booshay ala ren] vol au vent
boudin [boodAN] black pudding
boudin blanc [blON] white pudding
boudin noir [nwahr] black pudding
bouillabaisse [booyabess] spicy fish soup from the Midi
bouilli [boo-yee] boiled
bouillon [booyON] stock
bouillon de légumes [duh laygoom] vegetable stock
bouillon de poule [pool] chicken stock
boulette [boolet] meatball
bouquet rose [bookay roz] prawns
boutargue [bootarg] smoked fish roe
braisé [brezay] braised
brandade de morue [brONdad duh moroo] cod and potatoes, mashed
brioche [bree-osh] round bun
brochet [broshay] pike
brochette [broshet] kebab
brugnon [broon-yON] nectarine

cabillaud [kabee-yo] cod
cacahuètes [kaka-wet] peanuts
caille [kī] quail

cake fruit cake
cal(a)mar squid
canapé [kanapay] small open sandwich, canapé
canard [kanar] duck
canard à l'orange [lorONj] duck in orange sauce
canard aux cerises [o suhreez] duck with cherries
canard aux navets [o navay] duck with turnips
canard laqué [lakay] Chinese roast duck, Peking duck
canard rôti [rotee] roast duck
caneton [kantON] duckling
cantal [kONtal] hard cheese from Auvergne
câpres [kapr] capers
carbonnade [karbonad] stew made with beef, onions and beer
cardon [kardON] cardoon, vegetable similar to celery
cari [karee] curry
carotte [karot] carrot
carottes râpées [rapay] grated carrots (with vinaigrette)
carottes Vichy carrots in butter and parsley
carpe [karp] carp
carré d'agneau [karray dan-yo] rack of lamb
carrelet [karlay] plaice
carte [kart] menu
carvi [karvee] caraway
casse-croûte [kass-kroot] sandwich; snack
cassis [kasseess] blackcurrant
cassoulet [kassoolay] casserole with pork, sausages and beans
céleri (en branches) [selree (ON brONsh)] celery
céleri rave [rahv] celeriac
céleri rémoulade [raymoolad] celeriac in mayonnaise and mustard dressing
cèpe [sep] cep (mushroom)
cerise [suhreez] cherry
cerises à l'eau de vie [lo duh vee] cherries in brandy
cervelas [sairvuhla] saveloy (highly seasoned sausage made from brains)
cervelle [sairvel] brains
chabichou [shabeeshoo] goats' and cows' milk cheese
champignon [shONpeen-yON] mushroom
champignons de Paris [duh paree] white button mushrooms
champignons à la grecque [grek] mushrooms in olive oil, tomatoes and herbs
chanterelle chanterelle (mushroom)
charlotte dessert consisting of layers of fruit, cream and biscuits
chasselas [shassla] white grape
châtaigne [shateñ] sweet chestnut
chausson aux pommes [shohsON o pom] apple turnover
cheval [shuhval] horse

chèvre [shevr] goats' milk cheese
chevreuil [shevruh-ee] venison
chicorée [sheekoray] endive, chicory
chicorée frisée [freezay] curly lettuce
chiffonnade d'oseille [sheefonad dozay] sorrel cooked in butter
chips [sheeps] crisps, (US) potato chips
chocolatine [shokolateen] chocolate puff pastry
chou [shoo] cabbage
chou à la crème cream puff
choucroute [shookroot] sauerkraut with sausages and smoked ham
chou-fleur [shooflurr] cauliflower
chou-fleur au gratin [o gratAN] cauliflower cheese
chou rouge [shoo rooj] red cabbage
choux de Bruxelles [duh brOO-sel] Brussels sprouts
ciboulette [seeboolet] chives
cigarette [seegaret] kind of finger biscuit (eg to serve with ice cream)
citron [seetrON] lemon
citron vert [vair] lime
civet de lièvre [seevay duh lee-evr] jugged hare
clafoutis [klafootee] batter pudding with fruit
cochon de lait [koshON duh lay] sucking pig
cocktail de crevettes [kruhvet] prawn cocktail
cœur [kurr] heart
cœur d'artichaut [darteesho] artichoke heart
coing [kWAN] quince
colin [kolAN] hake
compote [kONpot] stewed fruit
compris [kONpree] included
comté [kONtay] hard cheese from the Jura area
concombre [kONkONbr] cucumber
confit de canard [kONfit duh kanar] duck preserve
confit d'oie [kONfee dwa] goose preserve
confiture [kONfeetoor] jam
confiture d'orange [dorONj] marmalade
congre [kONgr] conger eel
consommé [kONsommay] clear soup made from meat or chicken
consultez aussi l'ardoise other suggestions on the slate
consultez notre carte des desserts have a look at our dessert menu
coq au vin [kok o VAN] chicken in red wine
coque [kok] cockle
coquelet [koklay] young cockerel, poult
coquilles Saint-Jacques [kokee SAN jak] scallops
côte de porc [koht duh por] pork chop

côtelette [kotlet] chop
côtelette de porc [duh por] pork chop
cotriade bretonne [kotree-ad bruhton] fish soup from Brittany
coulis [koolee] creamy sauce or soup
coulis de framboises [duh frONbwahz] raspberry sauce
coulis de langoustines [lONgoosteen] saltwater crayfish sauce
coulommiers [koolom-yay] rich medium-soft cheese
coupe [koop] ice cream dessert
coupe Danemark [danmark] vanilla ice cream with hot chocolate sauce
coupe des îles [day zeel] vanilla ice cream with syrup, fruit and whipped cream
courgette courgette, zucchini
court-bouillon [koor-booyON] stock for poaching fish or meat
couscous [kooskooss] semolina (usually served with meat, vegetables and hot spicy sauce)
couscous royal [rwy-al] couscous with meat
couvert [koovair] cover charge
crabe [krab] crab
crème [krem] cream; creamy sauce or dessert
crème à la vanille [vanee] vanilla custard
crème anglaise [ONglez] custard
crème brûlée à la cassonade [brOOlay ala kassonad] custard covered with brown sugar and 'grilled'
crème Chantilly [shONtee-yee] whipped cream
crème d'asperges [daspairj] cream of asparagus soup
crème de bolets [duh bolay] cream of mushroom soup
crème de marrons [marON] chestnut purée
crème de volaille [vol-ī] cream of chicken soup
crème d'huîtres [weetr] cream of oyster soup
crème fouettée [foo-etay] whipped cream
crème pâtissière [pateessee-air] confectioner's custard
crème renversée [rONvairsay] custard dessert in a mould
crème vichyssoise [veeshee-swaz] cold potato and leek soup
crêpe [krep] pancake
crêpe à la béchamel [bayshamel] pancake with béchamel sauce
crêpe à la chantilly [shONtee-yee] pancake with whipped cream
crêpe à la crème de marrons [krem de marON] pancake with chestnut purée
crêpe à l'œuf [al-uhf] pancake

with a fried egg
crêpe au chocolat [o shokola] pancake with chocolate sauce
crêpe au fromage [fromahj] cheese pancake
crêpe au jambon [jONbON] ham pancake
crêpe au sucre [sOOkr] pancake with sugar
crêpe au thon [tON] tuna pancake
crêpe de froment [duh fromON] wholemeal flour pancake
crêpes Suzette pancakes flambéd with orange sauce
crépinette [kraypeenet] sausage patty wrapped in fat
cresson [kressON] cress
crevette [kruhvet] prawn
crevette grise [greez] shrimp
crevette rose [roz] prawn
croque-madame [krok madam] toasted cheese sandwich with ham and eggs
croque-monsieur [krok muhss-yuh] toasted cheese sandwich with ham
crottin de Chavignol [krotAN duh shaveen-yol] small goats' cheese
crottin de chèvre chaud [shevr sho] small goats' cheese served hot
croûte au fromage [kroot o fromahj] toasted cheese
croûte forestière [forest-yair] mushrooms on toast
crudités [krOOdeetay] selection of salads or chopped raw vegetables
crustacés [krOOstassay] shellfish
cuit cooked
cuisses de grenouille [kweess duh gruhnoo-yuh] frogs' legs
cuissot de chevreuil [kweeso duh shevruh-ee] haunch of venison

darne de saumon grillée [darn duh somON gree-yay] grilled salmon steak
dartois [dartwa] pastry with jam
datte [dat] date
daurade [dorad] gilthead (fish)
dinde [dAND] turkey

échalote [ayshalot] shallot
écrevisse [aykruhveess] freshwater crayfish
écrevisses à la nage [nahj] freshwater crayfish in wine and vegetable sauce
émincé de veau [aymANsay duh vo] finely cut veal in cream sauce
emporter: à emporter [ONportay] to take away; (US) to go
endive [ONdeev] chicory, endive
endives au jambon [o jONbON] chicory with ham baked in the oven
endives braisées [brezay] braised chicory

entrecôte [ONtr-koht] rib steak
entrecôte au poivre [o pwahvr] steak fried with black peppercorns
entrecôte maître d'hôtel [metr dotel] steak with butter and parsley
entrée [ONtray] first course
entremets [ONtr-may] dessert
épaule d'agneau farcie [aypol dan-yo farsee] stuffed shoulder of lamb
éperlan [aypairlON] smelt (fish)
épice [aypeess] spice
épinards [aypeenar] spinach
épinards à la crème spinach with cream
épinards en branches [ON brONsh] leaf spinach
escalope à la crème escalope in cream sauce
escalope de dinde à la crème et aux champignons [duh dAND] turkey cutlet with cream and mushrooms
escalope de veau milanaise [duh vo meelanez] veal escalope with tomato sauce
escalope de veau normande [normONd] veal escalope in cream sauce
escalope panée [panay] breaded veal escalope
escargots [eskargo] snails
escargots de Bourgogne à la douzaine dozen Burgundy snails
espadon [espadON] swordfish
estouffade de bœuf [estoofad duh burf] beef casserole
estragon [estragON] tarragon

faisan [fezzON] pheasant
fait maison [fay mezzON] homemade
farci [farsee] stuffed
farine [fareen] flour
faux filet sauce béarnaise [fo feelay] fillet steak with béarnaise sauce
fenouil [fenoo-yuh] fennel
fèves [fev] broad beans
ficelle [feessel] French stick thinner than a baguette
figue [feeg] fig
figue de barbarie prickly pear
filet [feelay] fillet
filet de bœuf Rossini [duh burf] fillet of beef with foie gras
filet de canard au poivre vert [duh kanar o pwahvr vair] duck breast with green pepper sauce
filet de perche [pairsh] perch fillet
financière [feenONss-yair] rich sauce (served with sweetbread, dumplings etc)
fines herbes [feen zairb] herbs
flageolets [flajolay] flageolets, small green beans
flambé [flONbay] flambé
flan [flON] custard tart; crème caramel; egg custard
flétan [flaytON] halibut
foie [fwa] liver
foie de veau [duh vo] veal liver

foie gras [gra] duck or goose liver preserve
foies de volaille [vol-ī] chicken livers
fondant au chocolat [fONdON o shokola] chocolate fondant; kind of brownie
fonds d'artichaut [fON darteesho] artichoke hearts
fondue [fONdoo] Swiss dish of cheese melted in white wine
fondue bourguignonne [boor-geen-yon] meat fondue (cooked in oil)
fondue savoyarde [savwy-ard] cheese fondue
forêt noire [foray nwahr] Black Forest gateau
fraise [frez] strawberry
fraise des bois [day bwa] wild strawberry
framboise [frONbwahz] raspberry
frangipane [frONjeepan] almond pastry
frisée [freezay] curly lettuce
frisée aux lardons [o lardON] curly lettuce with bacon
frit [free] deep fried
frites [freet] chips, French fries
fromage [fromahj] cheese
fromage blanc [blON] cream cheese
fromage de chèvre [duh shevr] goats' cheese
fruité [frweetay] fruity
fruits [frwee] fruit
fruits de mer [duh mair] seafood
fumé [foomay] smoked

galantine [galONteen] cold meat in aspic
galette [galet] round flat cake; buckwheat pancake
garni [garnee] with French fries or rice and/or vegetables
gâteau au fromage [o fromahj] cheesecake
gaufre [gohfr] wafer; waffle
gaufrette [gohfret] wafer
gelée [juhlay] jelly
en gelée [ON] in aspic
génisse [jayneess] heifer
génoise [jaynwahz] sponge cake
gésier [jayzee-ay] gizzard
gibelotte de lapin [jeeblot duh lapAN] rabbit stewed in white wine
gibier [jeeb-yay] game
gigot d'agneau [jeego dan-yo] leg of lamb
gigue de chevreuil [jeeg duh shuhvruh-ee] haunch of venison
girolle [jee-rol] chanterelle (mushroom)
glace [glass] ice cream; ice
goujon [goojON] gudgeon (fish)
grand veneur [grON vuhnurr] sauce for game
gras-double [gra-doobl] tripe
gratin [gratAN] baked cheese dish

au gratin [o] baked in a milk, cream and cheese sauce
gratin dauphinois [dofeen-wa] potato gratin with grated cheese
gratin de carottes [duh karot] carrots au gratin
gratin de langoustines [lONgoosteen] saltwater crayfish au gratin
gratin de queues d'écrevisses [kuh daykruhveess] freshwater crayfish au gratin
gratinée [grateenay] onion soup with cheese topping
grenade [gruhnad] pomegranate
grillade [gree-yad] grilled meat
grillé [gree-yay] grilled
grive [greev] thrush
grondin [grONdAN] gurnard (fish)
groseille blanche [grossay blONsh] white currant
groseille rouge [rooj] red currant
gruyère [grwee-yair] hard Swiss cheese

hachis parmentier [ashee parmONtee-ay] shepherd's pie
hareng mariné [arON mareenay] marinated herring
haricot de mouton [areeko duh mootON] mutton stew with beans
haricots [areeko] green beans; beans
haricots blancs [blON] haricot beans
haricots verts [vair] green beans
herbes [airb] herbs
herbes de Provence [duh provONss] herbs from Provence
homard [omar] lobster
homard à l'américaine [lamaireeken] lobster with tomato and white wine sauce
huile de soja [weel duh soja] soya oil
huile de tournesol [toornuhsol] sunflower oil
huile d'olive [doleev] olive oil
huître [weetr] oyster

îles flottantes [eel flotONt] floating islands (poached whisked egg whites on top of custard)

jambon [jONbON] ham
jambon au madère [o madair] ham in Madeira wine
jambon de Bayonne [duh ba-yon] smoked and cured ham
jardinière (de légumes) [jardeen-yair (duh laygoom)] with mixed vegetables
jarret de veau [jarray duh vo] shin of veal
julienne (de légumes) [joolee-en (duh laygoom)] soup with chopped vegetables

julienne type of white fish

kugelhof [kOOgelhohf] cake from Alsace

laitue [lettOO] lettuce
langouste [lONgoost] crayfish
langoustine [lONgoosteen] scampi
langue de bœuf [lON-g duh burf] ox tongue
langue de chat [sha] kind of finger biscuit (served with ice cream etc)
lapereau [lapero] young rabbit
lapin [lapAN] rabbit
lapin à la Lorraine rabbit in mushroom and cream sauce
lapin à la moutarde [mootard] rabbit in mustard sauce
lapin chasseur [shassurr] rabbit in white wine and herbs
lapin de garenne [garren] wild rabbit
lard [lar] bacon
lardons [lardON] small cubes of bacon
laurier [loree-ay] bay leaf
léger [layjay] light
légumes [laygOOm] vegetables
lentilles [lONteel] lentils
lièvre [lee-evr] hare
limande [leemONd] dab, lemon sole
livarot [leevaro] strong, soft cheese from the north of France
longe [lONj] loin
lotte [lot] burbot
loup au fenouil [loo o fuhnoo-yuh] bass with fennel

macaron [makarON] macaroon
macaroni au gratin [o gratAN] macaroni cheese
macédoine de légumes [massaydwan duh laygOOm] mixed vegetables with mayonnaise
mâche [mash] lamb's lettuce
magret de canard [magray duh kanar] duck breast
mangue [mON-g] mango
maquereau au vin blanc [makro o VAN blON] mackerel in white wine sauce
marcassin [marcassAN] young wild boar
marchand de vin [marshON duh van] in red wine sauce
mariné [mareenay] marinated
marrons [marrON] chestnuts
menthe [mONt] mint
menu [muhnOO] set menu
menu du jour [dOO joor] today's menu
menu gastronomique [gastronomeek] gourmet menu
merlan au vin blanc [mairlON o VAN blON] whiting in white wine
mérou [mayroo] grouper
miel [mee-el] honey
millefeuille [meel-fuh-ee] custard slice

mont-blanc [MON-blON] chestnut sweet topped with whipped cream
morilles [moree] morels (mushroom)
morue [moroo] cod
mouclade [mooklad] mussels in creamy sauce with saffron, turmeric and white wine
moules [mool] mussels
moules à la poulette [poolet] mussels in rich white wine sauce
moules marinière [mareen-yair] mussels in white wine
mousse au chocolat [o shokola] chocolate mousse
mousse au jambon [jONbON] light ham pâté
mousse de foie [duh fwa] light liver pâté
moutarde [mootard] mustard
mouton [mootON] mutton
mulet [moolay] mullet
munster [mANstair] strong cheese from eastern France
mûre [moor] blackberry
muscade [mooskad] nutmeg
myrtille [meertee] bilberry

nature [natoor] plain
navarin [navarAN] mutton stew with vegetables
navet [navay] turnip
nèfle [nefl] medlar
noisettes [nwazet] hazelnuts
noisette d'agneau [dan-yo] small, round lamb steak
noix [nwa] walnuts; nuts
nouilles [noo-yuh] noodles

œuf [urf] egg
œuf à la coque [kok] soft-boiled egg
œuf cocotte à la tomate [kokot ala tomat] egg cooked with tomato in the oven
œuf dur [door] hard-boiled egg
œuf en gelée [ON juhlay] egg in aspic
œuf mayonnaise egg mayonnaise
œuf mollet [molay] soft-boiled egg
œuf poché [poshay] poached egg
œufs à la neige [uh ala nej] floating islands (poached whisked egg whites on top of custard)
œufs au lait [o lay] egg custard
œufs au vin [VAN] eggs poached in red wine
œufs brouillés [broo-yay] scrambled eggs
œufs en meurette [ON murret] poached eggs in wine sauce
œuf sur le plat [urf soor luh pla] fried egg
oie [wa] goose
oignon [onyON] onion
olive [oleev] olive
omelette au fromage [fromahj] cheese omelette
omelette au jambon [jONbON]

ham omelette
omelette au naturel [natOOrel] plain omelette
omelette aux champignons [o shONpeen-yON] mushroom omelette
omelette aux fines herbes [feen zairb] omelette with herbs
omelette nature [natOOr] plain omelette
omelette paysanne [pay-eezan] omelette with potatoes and bacon
opéra [opayra] plain chocolate and coffee gateau
orange givrée [geevray] orange sorbet served in a scooped-out orange
oseille [ohzay] sorrel
oursin [oorsAN] sea urchin

pain [pAN] bread; loaf
pain au chocolat [o shokola] type of pastry with chocolate filling
pain au lait [lay] kind of sweet bun
pain aux noix [nwa] walnut bread
pain aux raisins [o rezzAN] kind of brioche with custard and sultanas
pain bagnat [ban-ya] tuna salad sandwich in wholemeal bread roll (from the French Riviera)
pain blanc [blON] white bread
pain complet [kONplay] wholemeal bread
pain de campagne [kONpañ] farmhouse bread/loaf
pain de mie [mee] sliced white bread
pain de seigle [segl] rye bread
pain de son [sON] bran bread
pain viennois [vee-enwa] Vienna loaf
palette de porc [palet duh por] pork shoulder
palourde [paloord] clam
pamplemousse [pONpl-mooss] grapefruit
panaché ... [panashay] mixed ...
panade [panad] bread soup
pané [panay] breaded
papillote: en papillote [ON papee-yot] baked in foil or paper
parfait glacé [parfay glassay] frozen sweet
pastèque [pastek] water melon
pâte d'amandes [paht damONd] marzipan
pâté de canard [duh kanar] duck pâté
pâté de foie de volaille [fwa duh volī] chicken liver pâté
pâte feuilletée [paht fuh-ee-etay] puff pastry
pâtes [paht] pasta
pâtisserie [pateesree] cake; cake shop
pâtisserie maison [mezzON] home made gateau
paupiettes de veau [pohp-yet

duh vo] rolled-up stuffed slices of veal
pavé de rumsteak [pavay duh] thick piece of steak
pêche [pesh] peach
pêche Melba peach melba
perdreau [pairdro] young partridge
perdrix [pairdree] partridge
persil [pairsee] parsley
petit beurre [puhtee burr] petit beurre biscuit
petite friture [puhteet freetoor] whitebait
petit gâteau biscuit
petit pain [pAN] roll
petits pois [puhtee pwa] peas
petits fours [foor] decorated small cakes and biscuits
petit suisse [sweess] light cream cheese
pieds de cochon/porc [p-yay duh koshON/por] pigs' trotters
pigeon [peejON] pigeon
pigeonneau [peejono] young pigeon
pignatelle [peen-yatel] small cheese fritter
pilaf rice dish with meat, pilaf
pilaf de mouton [duh mootON] rice dish with mutton
pintade [pANtad] guinea fowl
pipérade [peepayrad] Basque dish with egg and tomatoes
pissaladière [peessaladee-yair] Provençal dish similar to pizza
pissenlit [peess-ON-lee] dandelion
pistache [peestash] pistachio
pizza quatre saisons [katr sezzON] four seasons pizza
plat de résistance [pla duh rayseestONss] main course
plat du jour [pla doo joor] dish of the day
plateau de fromages [plato duh fromahj] cheese board
plateau de fruits de mer [duh frwee duh mair] seafood platter
plat principal [pla prANseepal] main course
pochouse [poshooz] fish casserole with white wine
point: à point [pwAN] medium
poire [pwahr] pear
poireau [pwahro] leek
poire belle-Hélène [bel aylen] pear in chocolate sauce
pois chiches [pwa sheesh] chickpeas
poisson [pwassON] fish
poivre [pwahvr] pepper (seasoning)
poivron [pwahvrON] pepper (vegetable)
poivron farci [farsee] stuffed pepper
pomme [pom] apple
pomme au four [o foor] jacket potato
pomme bonne femme [bon fam] baked apple
pomme de terre [duh tair] potato

pommes alumettes [pom alOOmet] French fries
pommes dauphine [dofeen] potato fritters
pommes de terre à l'anglaise [pom duh tair a lONglez] boiled potatoes
pommes (de terre) en robe de chambre [ON rob duh shONbr] jacket potatoes
pommes (de terre) en robe des champs [ON rob day shON] jacket potatoes
pommes (de terre) sautées [sotay] fried potatoes
pommes frites [freet] chips, French fries
pommes paille [pī] finely cut chips, French fries
pommes vapeur [vapurr] boiled potatoes
porc [por] pork
potage [potahj] soup
potage bilibi [beeleebee] fish and oyster soup
potage Crécy [kraysee] carrot and rice soup
potage cressonnière [kressonee-yair] watercress soup
potage parmentier [parmONt-yay] leek and potato soup
potage printanier [prANtan-yay] fine vegetable soup
potage Saint-Germain [SAN jairmAN] split pea soup
potage velouté [vuhlootay] creamy soup
pot-au-feu [potofuh] beef and vegetable stew
potée [potay] vegetable and meat hotpot
potiron [poteerON] pumpkin
poularde [poolard] fattened chicken
poule [pool] chicken
poule au pot [o po] chicken and vegetable stew
poule au riz [o ree] chicken with rice
poulet [poolay] chicken
poulet à l'estragon [lestragON] chicken in tarragon sauce
poulet basquaise [baskez] chicken with ham, tomatoes and peppers
poulet chasseur [shassurr] chicken with mushrooms and white wine
poulet créole [kray-ol] chicken in white sauce served with rice
poulet grillé [gree-yay] grilled chicken
poulet rôti [ro-tee] roast chicken
poulpe [poolp] octopus
praire [prair] clam
provençale [provONsal] with tomatoes, garlic and herbs
prune [prOOn] plum
pruneau [prOOno] prune
pudding plum pudding
purée [pOOray] mashed potatoes
purée de marrons [duh marrON] chestnut purée
purée de pommes de terre

[pom duh tair] mashed potatoes

quatre-quarts [katr-kar] similar to Madeira cake
quenelle [kuhnel] dumpling, generally made with chicken or pike
queue de bœuf [kuh duh burf] oxtail
quiche lorraine quiche with bacon

râble de chevreuil [rabl duh shuhvruh-ee] saddle of venison
râble de lièvre [duh lee-evr] saddle of hare
raclette [raklet] Swiss dish of melted cheese with boiled potatoes and cold meat
radis [radee] radish
ragoût [ragoo] stew
raie [ray] skate
raie au beurre noir [o burr nwahr] skate fried in butter
raifort [rayfor] horseradish
raisin [rezzAN] grape(s)
râpé [rapay] grated
rascasse [raskass] scorpion fish
ratatouille [ratatoo-yuh] dish of stewed peppers, courgettes/zucchinis, aubergines/eggplants and tomatoes
ravigote [raveegot] dressing with herbs and shallots
reblochon [ruhbloshON] strong cheese from Savoie
reine-claude [ren-klohd] greengage
religieuse au chocolat/au café [ruhleejurz o shokola/o kafay] cream puff with chocolate or coffee icing/frosting
rémoulade [ray-moolad] mayonnaise dressing with mustard and herbs
rigotte [reegot] small goat cheese from the Lyons area
rillettes [ree-yet] potted pork and goose meat
rillettes de saumon frais et fumé [duh somON fray ay foomay] fresh and smoked salmon paté
ris de veau [ree duh vo] veal sweetbread
rissole [reessol] meat pie
riz [ree] rice
riz à l'impératrice [lANpayratrees] sweet rice dish
riz pilaf spicy rice with meat or seafood
rognon [rON-yON] kidney
rognons au madère [rON-yON zo madair] kidneys in Madeira wine
romarin [romarAN] rosemary
roquefort [rokfor] blue ewes' milk cheese from the south of France
rosette de Lyon [rozet duh lee-ON] dry salami-type sausage
rôti de porc [rotee duh por] roast pork

rouget [roo-jay] mullet
rouille [roo-yuh] spicy sauce to go with bouillabaisse

sabayon [saba-yON] dessert made from egg yolks and Marsala wine
sablé [sablay] shortbread
saignant [sen-yON] rare
saint-honoré [sANt-onoray] cake with cream and choux pastry decoration
saint-marcellin [sAN-marsuh-lAN] goats' cheese
salade [sa-lad] salad; lettuce
salade aux noix [o nwa] green salad with walnuts
salade composée [kompozay] mixed salad
salade de gésiers [jayzee-ay] green salad with gizzards
salade de tomates [tomat] tomato salad
salade niçoise [neess-wahz] salad with olives, tomatoes, anchovies and hard boiled eggs
salade russe [rooss] diced vegetables in mayonnaise
salade verte [vairt] green salad
salmis [salmee] game stew
salsifis [salseefee] oyster plant, salsify
sandwich au fromage [sONdweech o fromahj] cheese sandwich
sandwich au jambon [jONbON] ham sandwich
sandwich au saucisson [soseesON] salami sandwich
sandwich aux rillettes [ree-yet] pâté sandwich
sandwich crudités salad sandwich
sandwich thon/mayonnaise [tON] tuna/mayonnaise sandwich
sanglier [sON-glee-yay] wild boar
sauce aurore [o-ror] white sauce with tomato purée
sauce aux câpres [o kapr] white sauce with capers
sauce béarnaise [bay-ar-nez] sauce made from egg yolks, lemon juice or vinegar, butter and herbs
sauce béchamel [bayshamel] white sauce
sauce blanche [blONsh] white sauce
sauce grand veneur [grON vuhnurr] sauce for game
sauce gribiche [greebeesh] dressing with hard boiled eggs, capers and herbs
sauce hollandaise [olONdez] rich sauce made with eggs, butter and vinegar, served with fish
sauce madère [madair] Madeira sauce
sauce matelote [matlot] wine sauce
sauce Mornay [mornay] béchamel sauce with cheese
sauce mousseline [moossleen]

hollandaise sauce with cream
sauce poulette [poolet] sauce with mushrooms, egg yolks and wine
sauce ravigote [raveegot] dressing with shallots and herbs
sauce rémoulade [ray-moolad] dressing made from mayonnaise, mustard and herbs
sauce suprême [sooprem] creamy sauce
sauce tartare mayonnaise with herbs, gherkins and capers
sauce veloutée [vuhlootay] white sauce with egg yolks and cream
sauce vinot [veeno] wine sauce
saucisse [sosseess] sausage
saucisse de Francfort [duh frONkfor] frankfurter
saucisse de Strasbourg [strazboorg] beef sausage
saucisson [sosseessON] salami
saumon [somON] salmon
saumon à l'oseille [lozay] salmon with sorrel
saumon fumé [somON fOOmay] smoked salmon
sauté de dindonneau [dANdonno] sauté of turkey poult
savarin [savarAN] crown-shaped rum baba
seiche [sesh] cuttlefish
sel salt
selle d'agneau [sel dan-yo] saddle of lamb
selon arrivage depending on availability
service (non) compris service (not) included
sole bonne femme [bon fam] sole in white wine and mushrooms
sole meunière [muhn-yair] sole dipped in flour and fried in butter
soufflé au chocolat [o shokola] chocolate soufflé
soufflé au fromage [fromahj] cheese soufflé
soufflé au jambon [jONbON] ham soufflé
soupe [soop] thick soup
soupe à l'ail [lI] garlic soup
soupe à la tomate [tomat] tomato soup
soupe à l'oignon [lonyON] onion soup
soupe à l'oseille [lozay] sorrel soup
soupe au pistou [o peestoo] thick vegetable soup with basil
soupe aux choux [shoo] cabbage soup
soupe aux moules [o mool] mussel soup
soupe aux poireaux et pommes de terre [pwaro ay pom duh tair] leek and potato soup
soupe de légumes [laygOOm]

vegetable soup
soupe de poisson [pwassON] fish soup
steak au poivre [o pwahvr] pepper steak
steak frites [freet] steak and chips/French fries
steak haché [ashay] minced meat
steak sauce au poivre [o pwahvr] steak with pepper sauce
steak sauce au roquefort [rokfor] steak with roquefort cheese sauce
steak tartare raw minced beef with a raw egg
sucre [sOOkr] sugar
suprême de volaille [sOOprem duh volī] chicken in cream sauce
surgelés [sOOrjuhlay] frozen food
surprise du chef [sOOrpreez dOO shef] chef's surprise (gateau)

tajine [tajeen] North African stew of mutton or chicken, vegetables and prunes cooked in an earthenware dish
tanche [tONsh] tench (fish)
tartare tartar(e); raw
tarte [tart] tart; pie
tarte au citron meringuée [o seetrON muhrANgay] lemon meringue pie
tarte aux fraises [o frez] strawberry tart/pie
tarte aux myrtilles [meertee] bilberry tart
tarte aux poireaux [pwahro] leek flan
tarte aux pommes [pom] apple tart/pie
tarte frangipane [frONjeepan] almond cream tart/pie
tartelette [tartuh-let] small tart/pie
tarte Tatin [tatAN] baked apple dish
tartine [tarteen] buttered slice of bread
tendrons de veau [tONdrON duh vo] veal breast
terrine [terreen] rougher type of pâté
terrine du chef [dOO shef] pâté maison, chef's special pâté
tête de veau [tet duh vo] calf's head
thon [tON] tuna fish
thon Mirabeau [meerabo] tuna cooked in eggs and milk
thym [tAN] thyme
tomate [tomat] tomato
tomme de Savoie [tom duh savwa] white cheese from Savoie
tourte [toort] pie
tourteau [toorto] kind of crab
tous nos plats sont garnis all our dishes are served with vegetables
tripes [treep] tripe
tripes à la mode de Caen [duh kON] tripe in spicy vegetable sauce

truffe [troof] truffle
truite au bleu [trweet o bluh] poached trout
truite meunière [muhn-yair] trout coated in flour and fried in butter

vacherin [vashrAN] strong, soft cheese from the Jura area
vacherin glacé [glassay] ice cream meringue
veau [vo] veal
velouté d'asperges [vuhlootay daspairj] cream of asparagus soup
velouté de tomates [tomat] cream of tomato soup
velouté de volaille [volī] cream of chicken soup
velouté d'huîtres [dweetr] cream of oyster soup
vermicelle [vairmeesel] very fine pasta used in soups
viande [vee-ONd] meat
viande hachée [ashay] minced meat
vichyssoise [veesheeswahz] cold vegetable soup
vinaigre [veenegr] vinegar
volaille [volī] poultry

yaourt [ya-oort] yogurt

Menu Reader

Drink

alcool [alkool] alcohol
AOC (Appellation d'Origine Contrôlée) guarantee of the quality of a wine

Banyuls® [banyoolss] a sweet apéritif wine
bière [bee-air] beer
bière (à la) pression [press-yON] draught beer
bière (blonde) lager
bière brune [brOOn] bitter; dark beer
bière rousse [rooss] relatively sweet, fairly dark beer
blanc [blON] white wine; white
blanc de blancs [duh blON] white wine from white grapes
blanquette de Limoux [blONket duh leemoo] sparkling white wine from Languedoc
boisson [bwassON] drink
Bourgogne [boor-goñ] wine from the Burgundy area
Brouilly [broo-yee] red wine from the Beaujolais area
brut [brOOt] very dry

café [kafay] espresso, very strong black coffee
café au lait [o lay] white coffee
café crème [krem] white coffee
café glacé [glassay] iced coffee
café soluble [solOObl] instant coffee
café viennois [vee-enwa] coffee with whipped cream
calvados apple brandy from Normandy
camomille [kamomee] camomile tea
capiteux [kapeetuh] heady
carte des vins [kart day VAN] wine list
Chablis [shablee] dry white wine from Burgundy
chambré [shONbray] at room temperature
champagne [shONpañ] champagne
champagnisé [shONpan-yeezay] sparkling
chartreuse [shartrurz] herb liqueur
Château-Margaux [shato margo] red wine from the Bordeaux area
Châteauneuf-du-Pape [shatonurf dOO pap] red wine from the Rhône valley
chocolat chaud [shokola sho] hot chocolate
chocolat glacé [glassay] iced chocolate drink
cidre [seedr] cider
cidre bouché [booshay] cider in bottle with a cork
cidre doux [doo] sweet cider
51® (cinquante-et-un) [sankONtay-AN] a brand of pastis
citron pressé [seetrON pressay] fresh lemon juice

cognac [kONyak] brandy
crème [krem] white coffee
crème de cassis [duh kasseess] blackcurrant liqueur
cru [krOO] vintage
cru classé high quality wine

décaféiné [daykafay-eenay] decaffeinated
délimité de qualité supérieure superior quality wine
demi [duhmee] small draught beer; quarter of a litre of beer
demi-sec [duhmee-sek] medium dry
diabolo menthe/fraise etc [d-yabolo mONt/frez] mint/strawberry etc cordial with lemonade
digestif [deejesteef] liqueur

eau [o] water
eau de vie [duh vee] spirit made from fruit
eau minérale [meenayral] mineral water
eau minérale gazeuse [gazurz] sparkling mineral water

Fendant [fONdON] Swiss dry white wine
fine [feen] fine brandy, liqueur brandy
Fleurie [flurree] red wine from Beaujolais
frappé [frapay] well chilled, on ice

gazeux [gazurz] fizzy
Gewurztraminer [guh-wOOrztrameenair] dry white wine from Alsace
gin-tonic gin and tonic
Gini® a kind of bitter lemon
glaçon [glassON] ice cube
grand crème [grON krem] large white coffee
grand cru [krOO] fine vintage
Graves [grahv] red wine from the Bordeaux area

infusion [anfOOz-yON] herb tea

jus [jOO] juice
jus de pommes [duh pom] apple juice
jus d'orange [dorONj] orange juice

kir white wine with blackcurrant liqueur
kir royal champagne with blackcurrant liqueur
kirsch cherry brandy

lait [lay] milk
lait fraise/grenadine [frez/gruhnadeen] milk with strawberry/grenadine cordial
limonade [leemonad] lemonade

Mâcon [makON] wine from Burgundy
marc [mar] clear spirit distilled from grapes
Médoc [maydok] red wine

from the Bordeaux area
menthe à l'eau [mONt a lo] mint cordial
méthode champenoise made in the same way as champagne
Meursault [murrso] wine from Burgundy
millésime [meelay-zeem] vintage
mousseux [moossuh] sparkling
Muscadet [mooskaday] dry white wine from the Nantes area
muscat [mooska] sweet white wine

Noilly-Prat® [nwa-yee pra] an apéritif wine similar to Dry Martini
Nuits-Saint-Georges [nwee sAN jorj] red wine from Burgundy

orange pressée [orONj pressay] fresh orange juice

panaché [panashay] shandy
Passe-Tout-Grain [pass too grAN] red wine from Burgundy
pastis [pasteess] aniseed-flavoured alcoholic drink
Pernod® [pairno] a brand of pastis
pétillant [paytee-ON] sparkling
porto port
Pouilly-Fuissé [poo-yee-fweessay] dry white wine from Burgundy
premier cru [pruhm-yay croo] vintage wine
pression [press-yON] draught beer, draught

rhum [rom] rum
Ricard® [reekar] a brand of pastis
Rivesaltes® [reevsalt] a sweet apéritif wine
rosé [rozzay] rosé wine
rouge [rooj] red

Saint-Amour [sANtamoor] red wine from Beaujolais
Saint-Emilion [sAN-taymeelee-yON] red wine from the Bordeaux area
Sauternes [sotairn] fruity white wine from the Bordeaux area
Schweppes® tonic water
scotch scotch whisky
sec [sek] dry; neat
servir frais serve cool
sirop [seero] cordial

thé [tay] tea
thé à la menthe [mONt] mint tea
thé au lait [o lay] tea with milk
thé citron [seetrON] lemon tea
thé nature [natoor] tea without milk
tilleul [tee-yurl] lime-flower tea

VDQS (Vin Délimité de Qualité

Supérieure) a category of wine between vin de table and AOC
verveine [vairven] verbena tea
vin [vAN] wine
vin blanc [blON] white wine
vin de pays [duh payee] regional wine
vin de table [duh tahbl] table wine
vin rosé [rozzay] rosé wine
vin rouge [rooj] red wine

Yvorne [eevorn] Swiss dry white wine